I0900980

IMAGES
of America

KENNEBUNK MAIN STREET

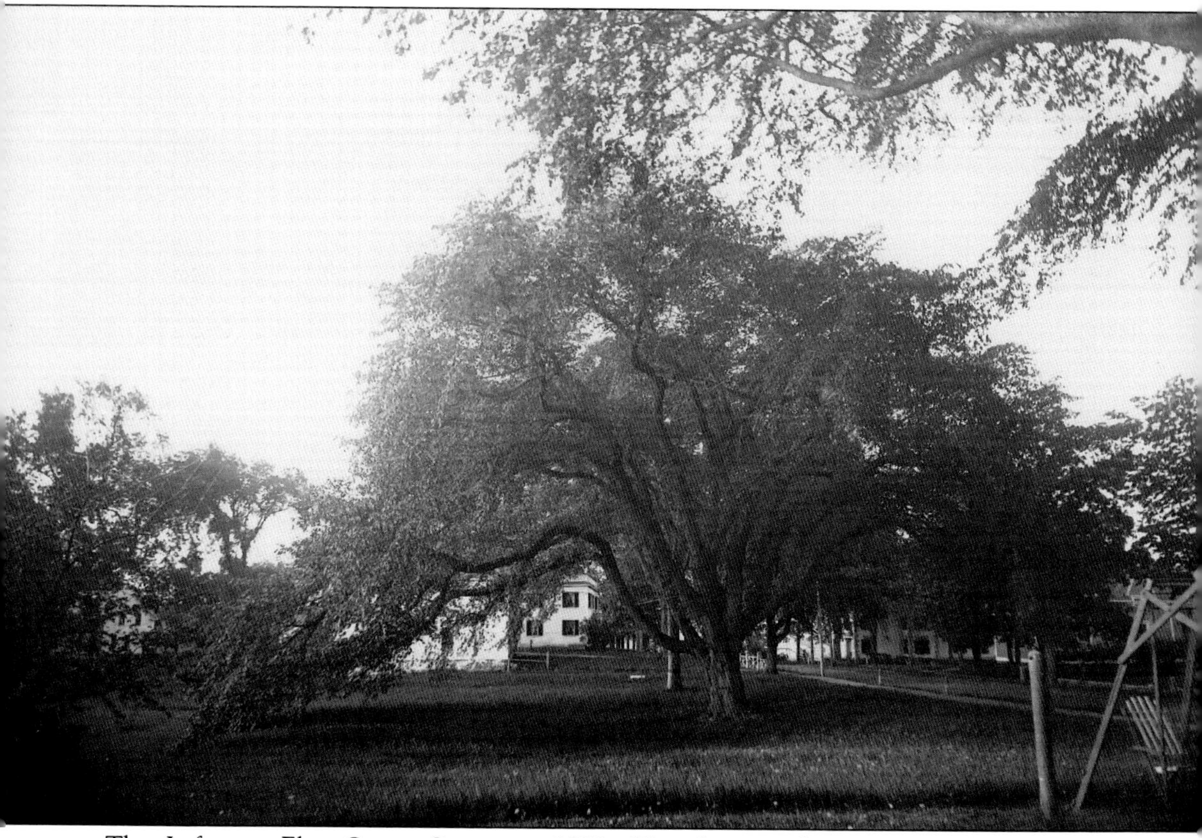

The Lafayette Elm, Storer Street, *c.* 1890. This famous elm was named in honor of General Lafayette's visit to Kennebunk in 1825, and it first appeared on the town seal and on town reports in 1918. It was once the second largest elm tree in the state, but it succumbed to Dutch Elm disease and was cut down in 1971. The Brick Store Museum has preserved pieces of the tree.

IMAGES
of America

KENNEBUNK MAIN STREET

Steven Burr

ARCADIA
PUBLISHING

ISBN 978-0-7385-8846-9

Published by Arcadia Publishing
Charleston, South Carolina

Printed in the United States of America

Library of Congress Catalog Card Number: Applied For

For all general information contact Arcadia Publishing at:
Telephone 843-853-2070
Fax 843-853-0044
E-mail sales@arcadiapublishing.com
For customer service and orders:
Toll-Free 1-888-313-2665

Visit us on the Internet at www.arcadiapublishing.com

Dedicated to Chris
for his strength, courage, and humor . . .
And to Greg
for helping me to rediscover my love of history,
and for his ongoing support and encouragement.
It's an honor and a privilege to be his "sidekick."

And for those with AIDS,
their families, friends,
and caregivers.

Contents

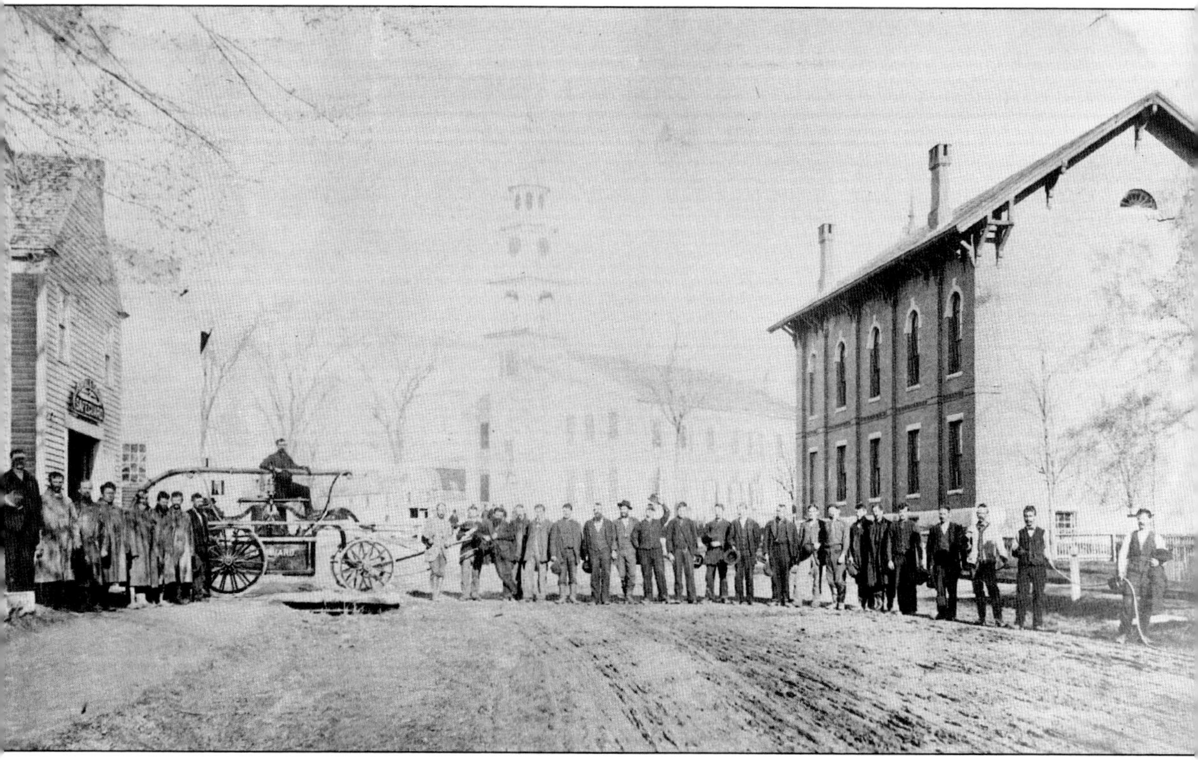

Firemen gather outside the Safeguard Fire House, April 30, 1881. That morning the first Ross Block had burned to the ground, and the firemen are posing for a photograph before putting away their equipment. The men were proud of the new pumper, with its 500 feet of hose, purchased in 1880.

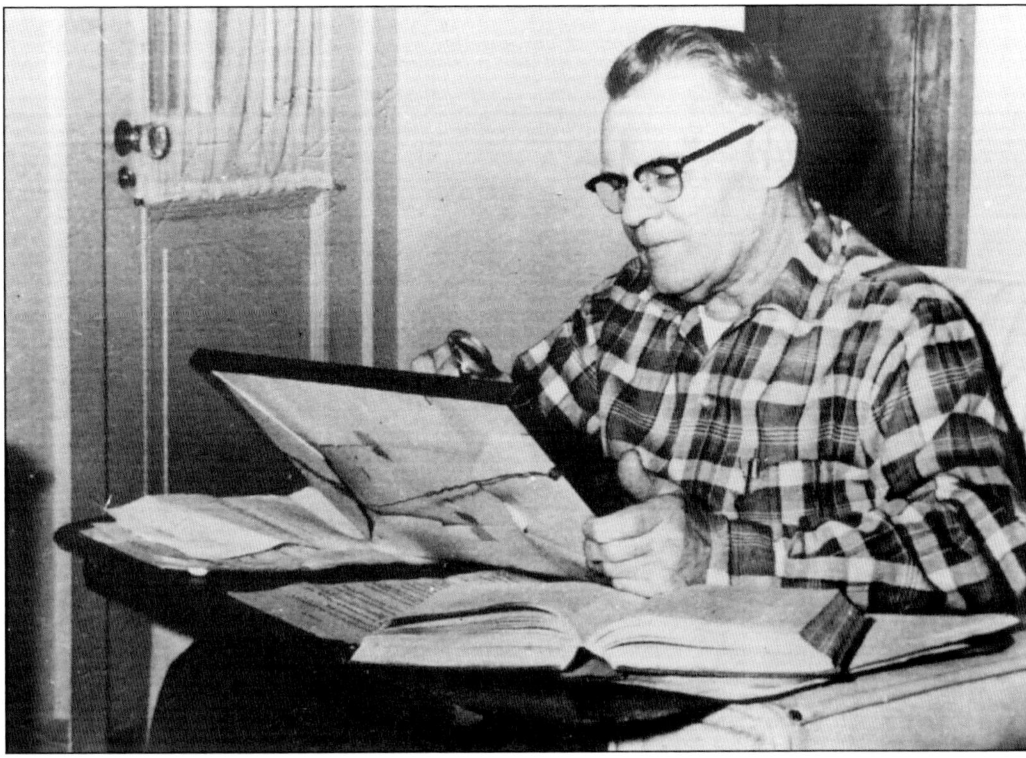

Introduction

In 1960 Kenneth Joy, a Kennebunk resident and historian, began a new column for the *York County Coast Star* called "Out of The Past." Combining antique photographs from his own collection with his personal recollections of growing up in Kennebunk, Joy brought to life historic events and the people from Kennebunk's past. Born in South Berwick, Maine, in 1908, Joy became the link between Kennebunk's past and present. He personally witnessed Kennebunk's change from small village to large town, and was fortunate to have known the men and women who had grown up and lived in this small village. Through him, their stories and memories were recorded for future generations to enjoy. Joy himself was quoted in an article as saying "The old things can pull a town together, give them spirit . . ."

Joy's family moved to Kennebunk when he was three years old. His father operated a bakery on Main Street for several years. Growing up, Joy was fascinated with the stories of Kennebunk's people and the early settlers. He visited forgotten graveyards and the sites of old homes, researched their history, and recorded their locations. Kennebunk residents knew him well and knew of his interest in local history. They began giving him old photographs and telling him their stories. He collected old maps, books, newspapers, diaries, and deeds. Eventually, he put together a complete history of Kennebunk from the time of its first settlement in 1643.

In World War II, Joy served with the 12th Infantry Regiment of the 4th Army Division, and was wounded twice. When he returned to Kennebunk, he went to work for the Kesslen Shoe

Company, where he became a foreman. In his spare time he pursued his interest in history and gave lectures to schools, churches, and clubs. On July 10, 1967, the town of Kennebunk appointed him the first official town historian.It was under his guidance and supervision that Kennebunk celebrated its sesquicentennial in 1970.

When Ken Joy passed away in 1981, Kennebunk lost a good friend and an important and valuable resource. He left his remarkable collection of photographs to the Kennebunk Library, but, sadly, all of his notes and ephemera have disappeared. Nason College, Sanford, had published the first and only book based on Joy's weekly column, back in 1967. It was a huge success, but contained only fifty photographs. Those of us who love old photographs and reading about history have had to be satisfied for all these years with those few images.

Over the past two years I have been cataloging and storing Ken Joy's collection of antique photographs, and have come to realize that many Kennebunkers—both long-time residents and newcomers—have never seen the collection. Wishing to make Joy's collection available to the people of Kennebunk and also to celebrate the opening of the remodeled, historic Kennebunk Free Library, I approached the library's Board of Directors and offered to research and compile this book. The royalties from the sale of every copy of the book will be donated to the library for the preservation of both the Joy Collection and other important material in the library's archives.

The Kennebunk Free Library was founded in 1881 and was originally located in Cobby's store on Garden Street. It soon outgrew the available space. Andrew Walker, a retired businessman, offered his store for the library's use. The new location, called Walker Hall, is now part of the Brick Store Museum complex. The library reopened in its present location on October 24, 1888. By 1905 it was clear that a new building was needed. The idea of a building designed specifically to house a village library was not a new one. Andrew Carnegie was the principal force behind the concept that every small town should have one.. He was also the principle benefactor for many towns.

In 1906, the library directors began looking for their own "Carnegie" to give the town a new library. That's when George Parsons—a York County, Maine, boy who had prospered—stepped forward. Working with Reverend John Parsons, he had already given to the town of Alfred a library in memory of his brother Edwin. The cost of constructing the Kennebunk Library was borne solely by George Parsons. The library was built on the site of the Osborn House, which had been moved. The corner stone, containing coins and papers of interest, was laid on September 13, 1906, and the new library was dedicated on August 2, 1907, during the celebrations for old Home Week.

This library served the needs of the community for eighty-eight years before it became clear that space was again becoming a problem. Beginning in the late 1970s, solutions were discussed, floor plans developed and discarded, and funding explored. Aside from funding, the major problem was the small size of the library lot. The Board of Directors was committed both to keeping the library at its downtown site, and to ensuring that the original building would be preserved. Ultimately, a plan was developed that met both needs. The Webhannett Women's Club, which had formerly stood behind the library, was relocated to West Kennebunk. Architectural designs were approved, and fundraising began. Money raised privately was combined with a bond issue to pay for the addition. Ground was broken in the summer of 1994, and by the time you read this the newly expanded library will be open for business.

For 113 years, the Kennebunk Free Library Association has served the town of Kennebunk. Staff and volunteers have kept the lights on and the shelves full. The Board of Directors has kept the bills paid and the building standing. Together, they ensure that the library will continue to meet the needs of the community.

This is a chance to recognize and celebrate the important contribution that the staff and directors of the library—past and present—have made to this community. It's also just in time to celebrate Kennebunk's 175th anniversary of incorporation. I hope you enjoy the photographs as much as I have enjoyed selecting them and working on this project. I'm sure that Ken Joy would approve.

Steven Burr
Vice President
The Preservation Foundation
August 1, 1995
Kennebunk

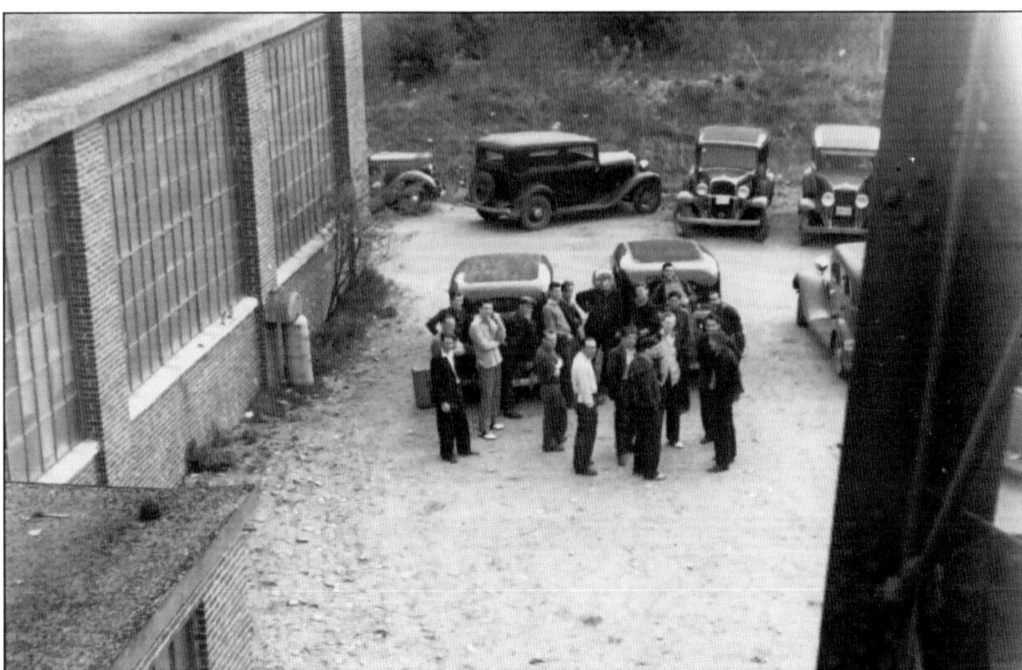

Kesslen Shoe workers gather at the West Kennebunk plant during the 1940 strike. Ken Joy is in the center with his arms folded.

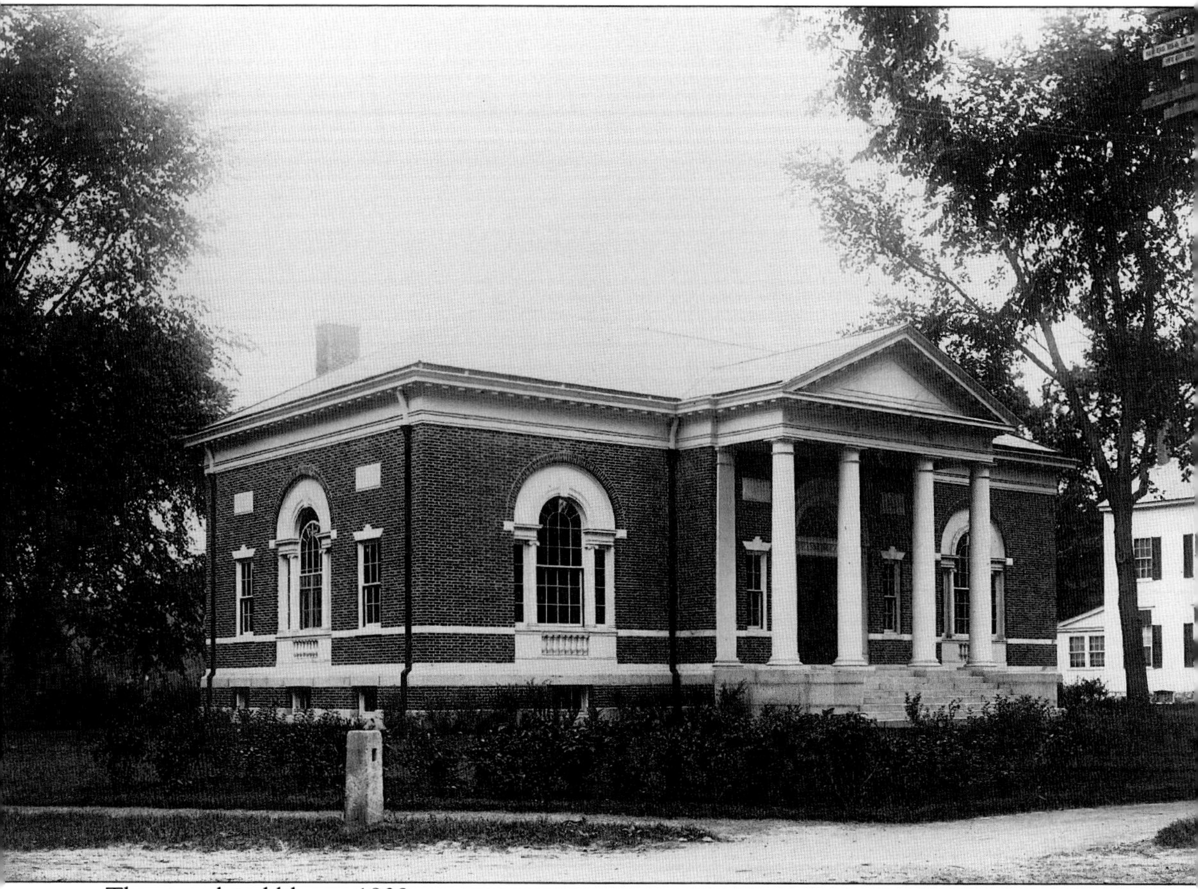

The completed library, 1908.

One

Fletcher Street to Post Office Square

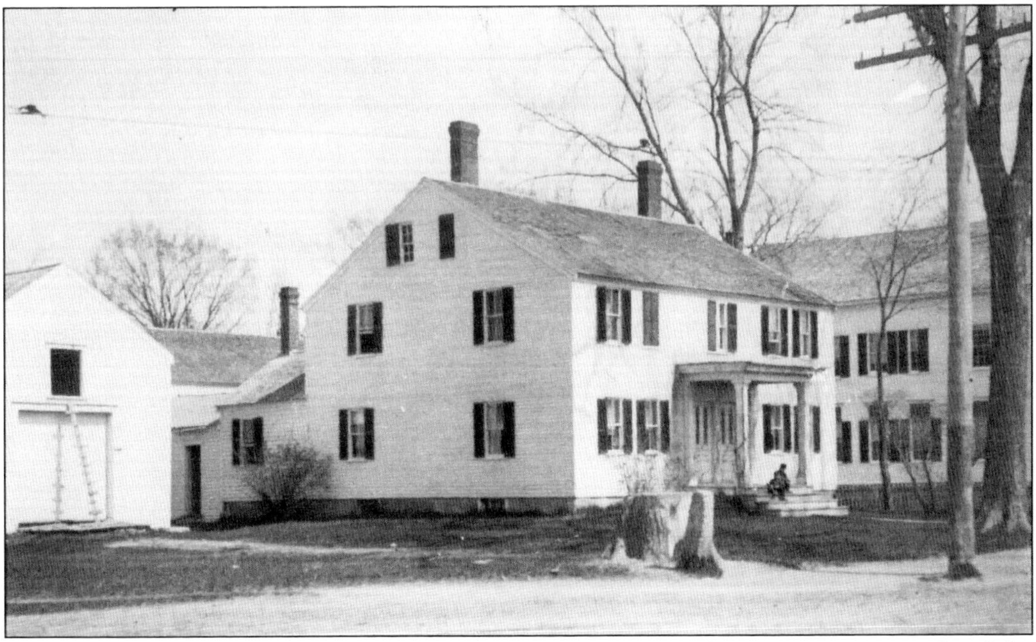

The Osborn House, *c.* 1900. The house was framed in April 1792. It was completed for James Osborn, a local merchant, whose son, James Osborn Jr., was the town postmaster. The post office was located here until he retired. This photograph shows the home after its conversion into a two-family dwelling. In 1906, it was moved to Grove Street, so that the library could be built on the site. In 1963 it was razed for a parking lot.

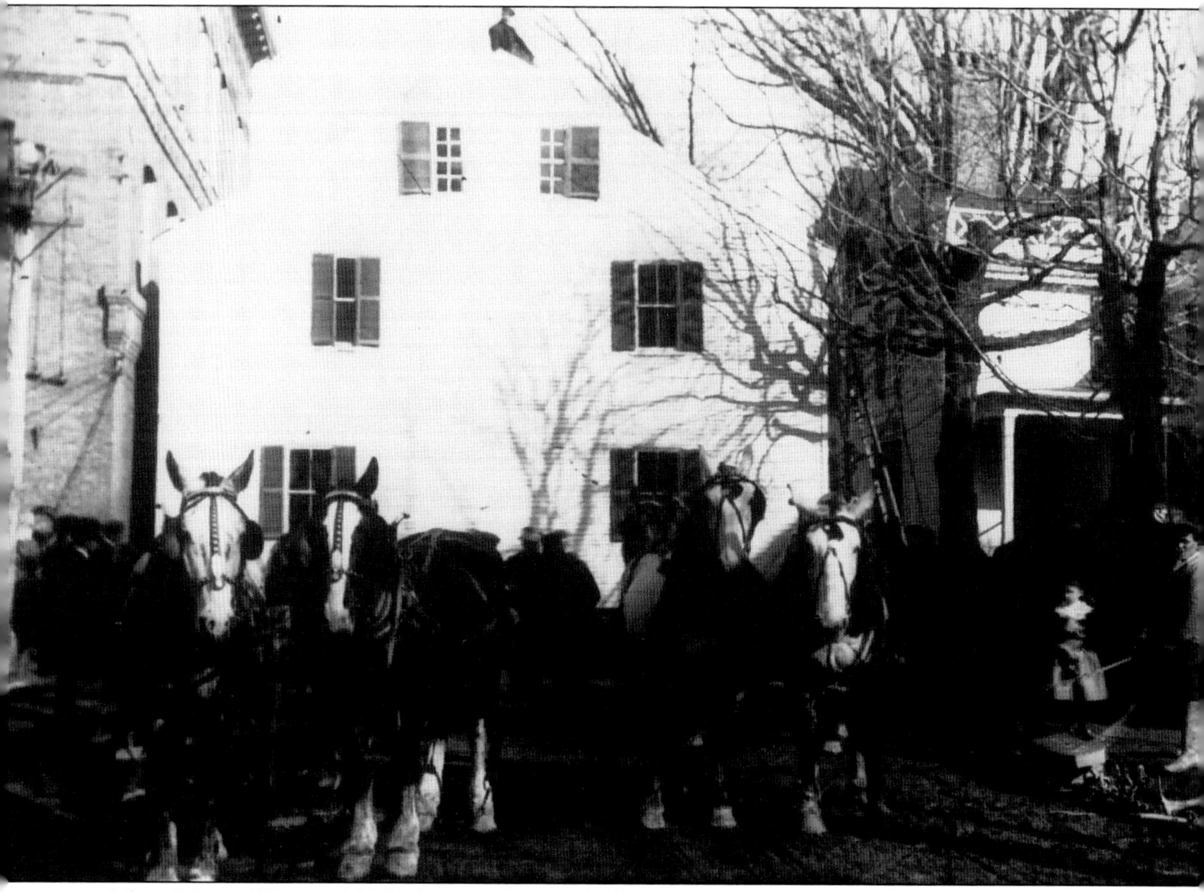

The Osborn House, 1906. Captain Henry Fuller Curtis moved many Main Street buildings, including the Osborn House. House moving was not uncommon; few buildings were razed if they could be re-used elsewhere. "Hink" Maling from Kennebunkport was Curtis' principal assistant at the turn of the century. To move a house, he would bring his crew and his old sorrel horse, along with a windlass and greased planks. The windlass was placed in front of the building and the horse was the hitched to the top of the windlass. The horse then circled the windlass—often all day—winding the rope around the drums and pulling the building off its foundation and onto skids or rollers. Then a team of horses or oxen would pull the building to its new site.

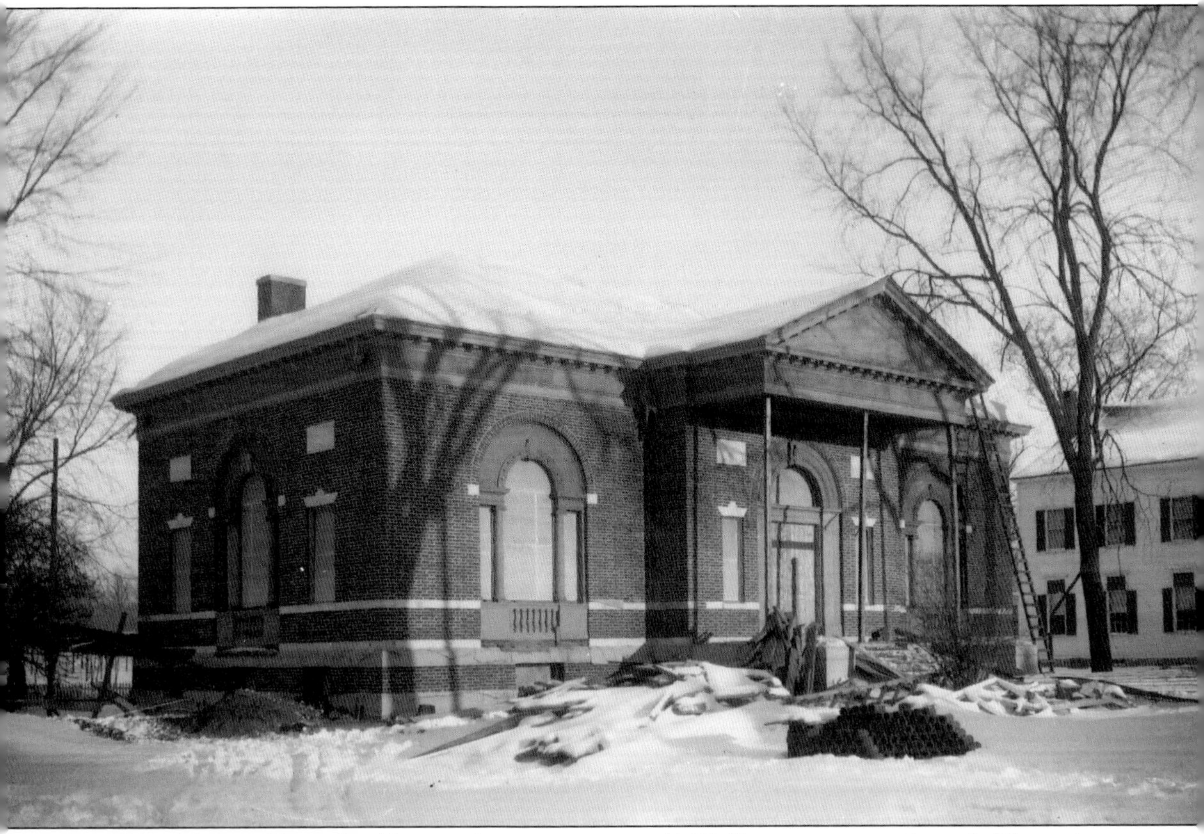

Kennebunk's new library building under construction, 1907. For many years the only library in town was located at the First Parish Church. By 1881 the need for a town library was apparent, and on the evening of December 19, 1881, the ladies of the Woman's Christian Temperance Union met to decide what to do. Only a handful of people turned out for the meeting. Instead of waiting until there was more support for a library, the group decided to proceed and hope that support would follow. A study committee of men and women were appointed, and at the next meeting it was decided that a library was indeed needed. Committee members raised funds by soliciting donations from former Kennebunk residents with strong ties to the area. The library opened on April 29, 1882, in the Cobby store. Within a year, 169 people had subscribed to the library, which had over 1,000 books. Although the institution was called the Kennebunk Free Library, patrons paid an annual fee to borrow books. The library became free in 1898 when those attending the annual town meeting voted to give the library $200, on the condition that local residents were not charged for its use.

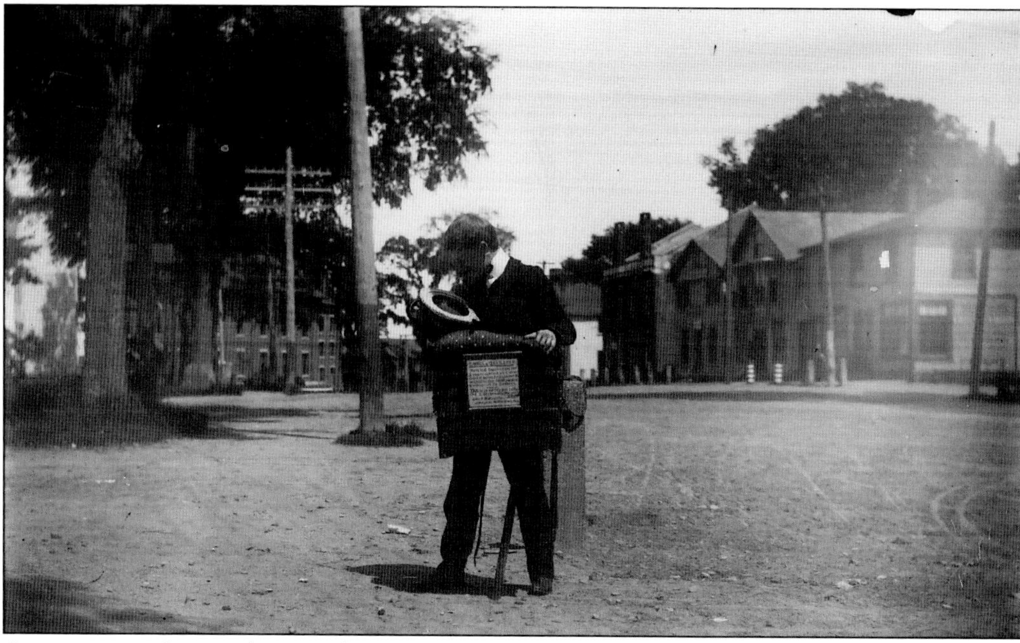

An organ grinder standing on the corner of Main and Fletcher Street, c. 1890. His sign reads: "Ladies and Gentleman, I have had rheumatism for two years and can't work on account of having two ribs broken by a electric car. I didn't receive anything from the company. This is to certify that I attended [unreadable] last year."

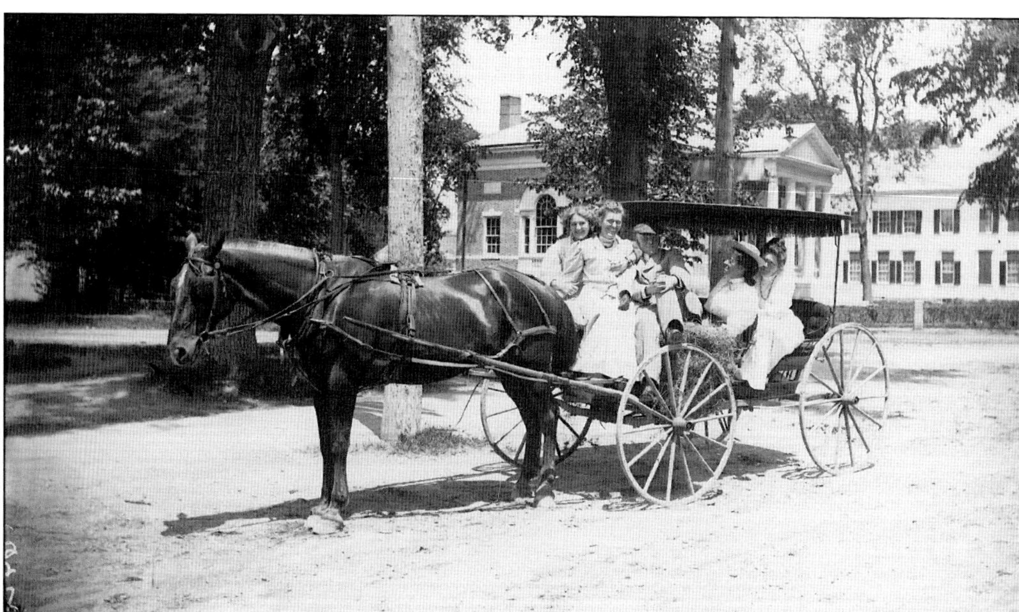

Out for a ride in their surry, these people stopped for a photograph, c. 1915.

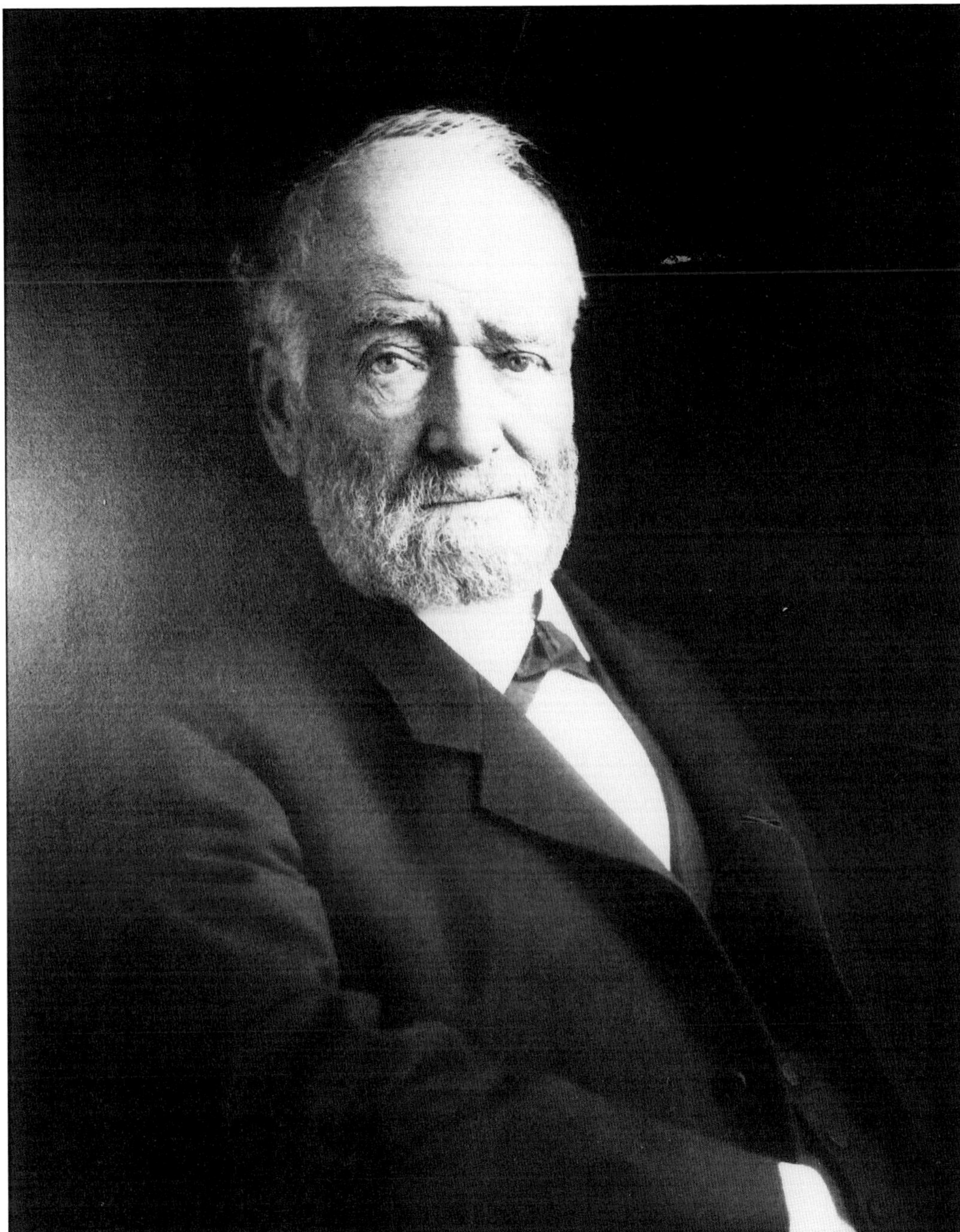

George Parsons, the Kennebunk Free Library Association's principal benefactor. Born in Alfred, Maine, he moved to Georgia as a young man. Parsons entered into the cotton brokerage business with his brother Edwin. He made a fortune through business interests which included railroading, mining, and real estate. In 1869 Parsons returned to Maine and purchased the house that still stands behind the present library. He also owned a four-story brownstone in New York City on Madison Avenue. Parsons died in December 1907, not long after the dedication of the new library.

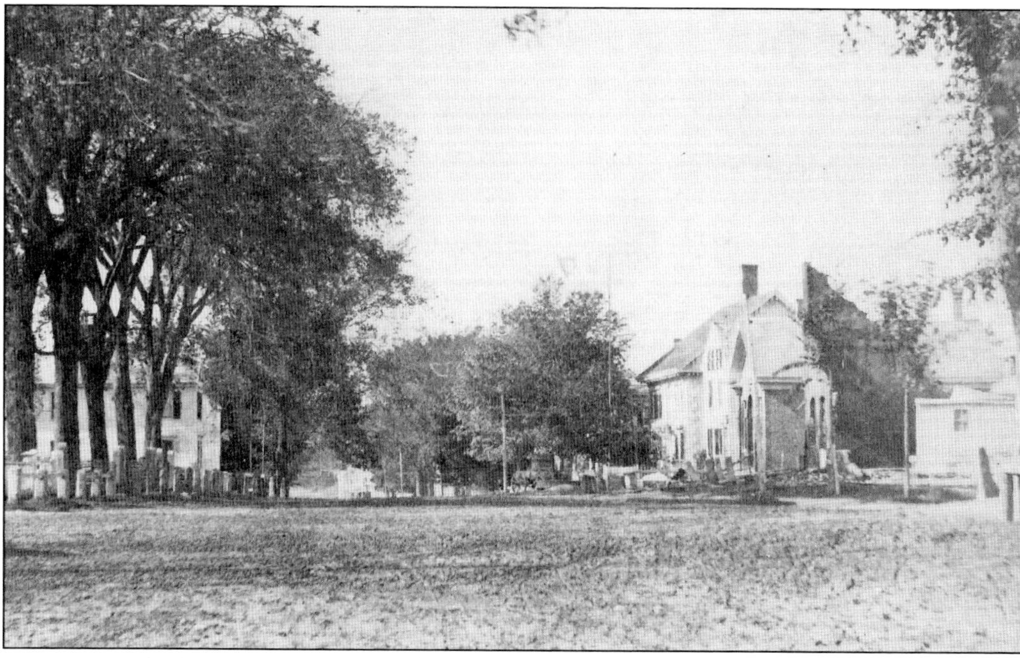

Main Street looking south, c. 1875. This photograph shows the new Ocean National Bank building, constructed in 1870. The ruins of the Old Brick (see p. 18), which burned in 1869, stand beside it.

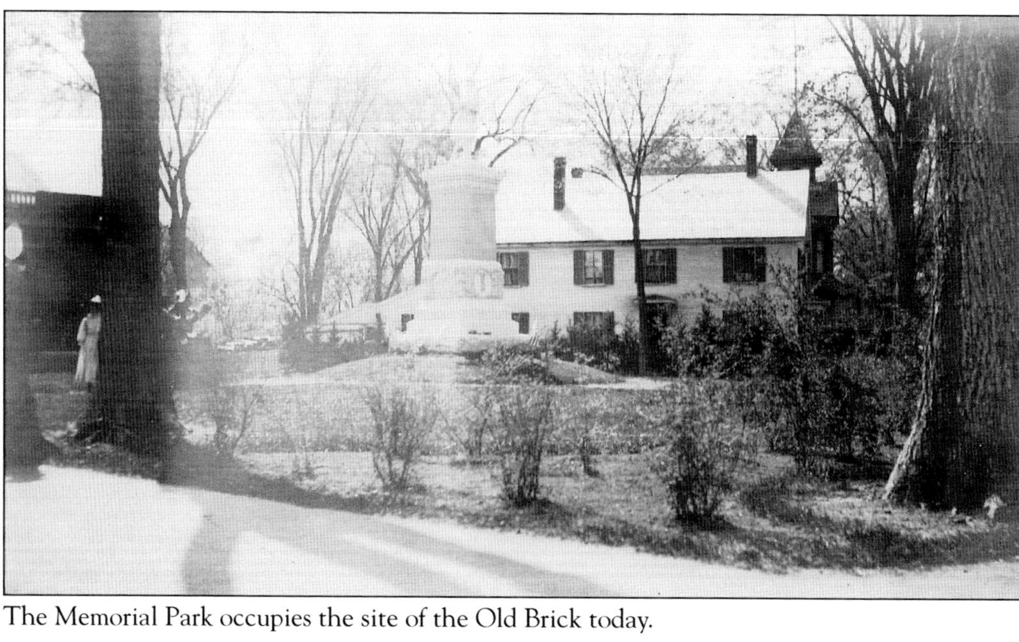

The Memorial Park occupies the site of the Old Brick today.

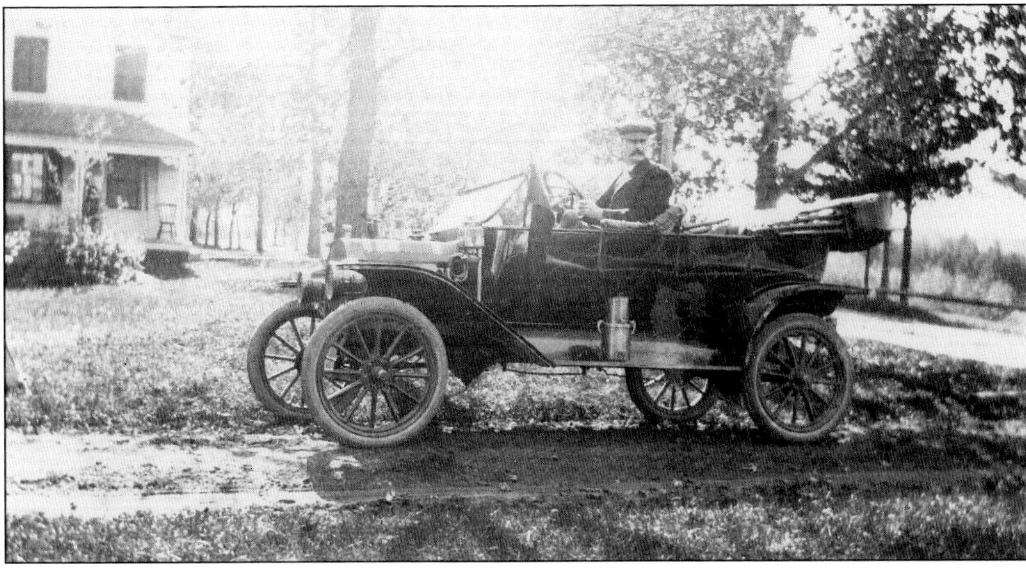

Prescott Littlefield, c. 1910. Littlefield was a very popular merchant in town. His partner in his first business was Eugene A. Fairfield. Later Littlefield owned a grocery on Depot Street before going into business with his brother-in-law Will Webber. Littlefield was 6 feet tall, wore a full black mustache, and had a loud, booming voice. He was a talented singer and a gifted prankster. He would often show up at the Bourne Mansion early in the morning and in a loud voice yell "Come, come, Bert, it is time to get up." Perhaps Bert was his horse or someone then living in the Bourne Mansion. In any case, he managed not only to wake up the household but also the neighbors as well.

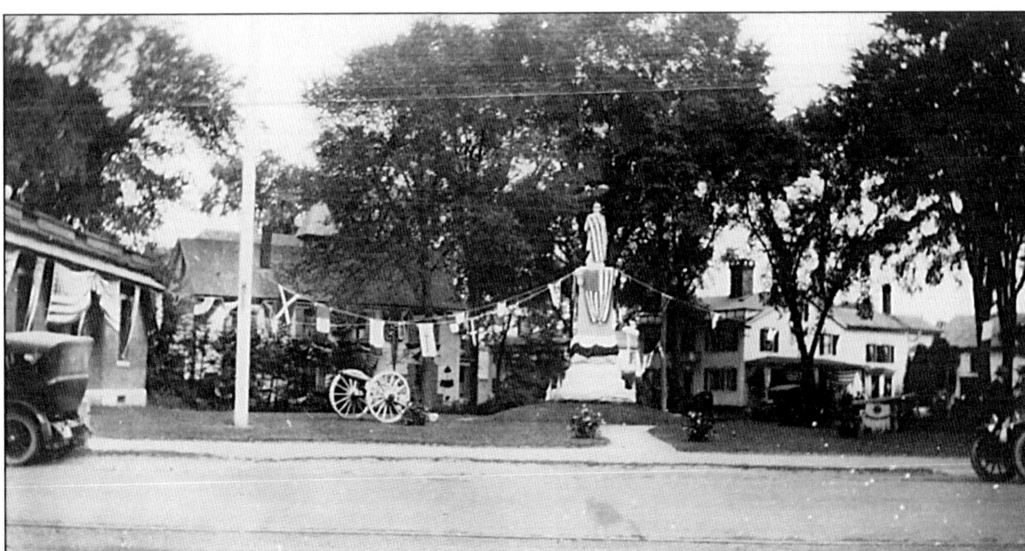

The Memorial Park at its dedication in 1908. Henry Parsons bought both buildings in 1907 and had the lots cleared. He then gave the land to the town to be used for a memorial park.

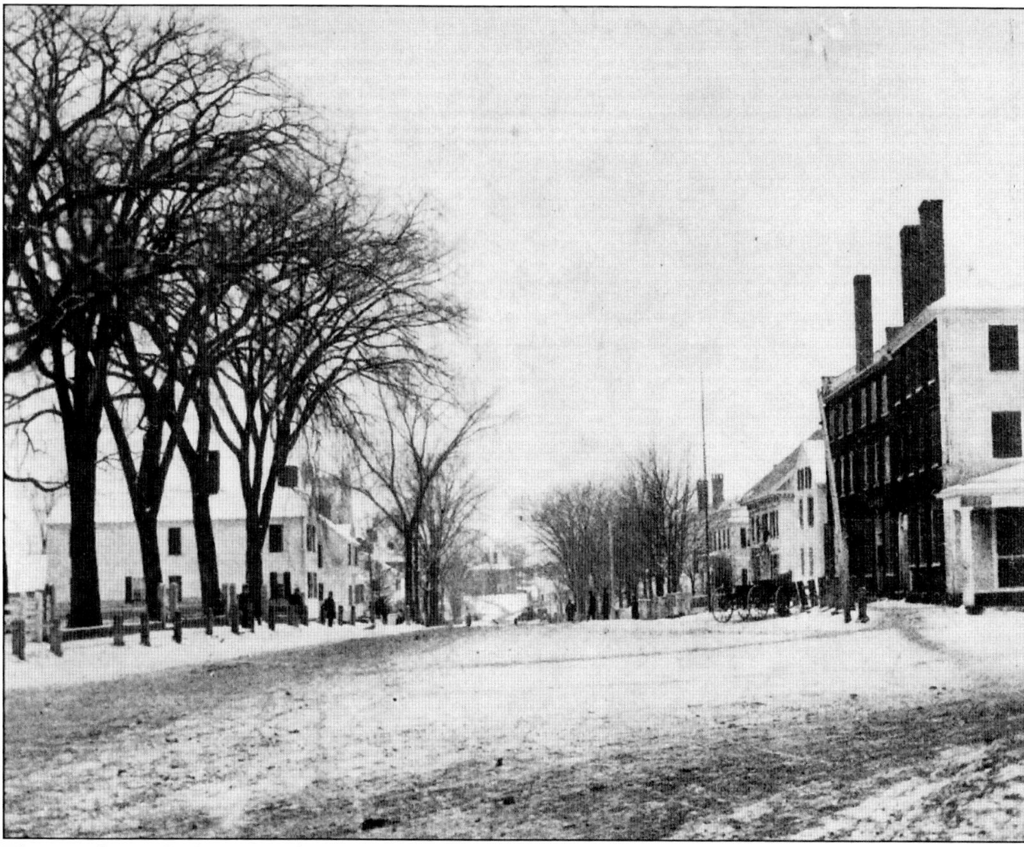

This is the only known photograph of Kennebunk's first brick commercial building, taken c. 1865. The Old Brick, as it was eventually called, was built in 1806 on the corner of Main and Fletcher Streets, where the Memorial Park is now located. It was the center of local business for many years. On the first floor were located a general store, several businesses, and (for a while) the post office. On the second floor, Edward E. Bourne had his law office. On August 3, 1824, a fire seriously damaged the building, which was soon rebuilt. The building was then known as the Phoenix Building for many years. In 1826, Daniel Wise Jr. built a wooden addition with a brick front on the eastern end, which he used as a store. Jonathan Stone of Kennebunkport fitted the store out as a hotel, which he named The Mousam House. In November 1869, the building was completely destroyed by fire.

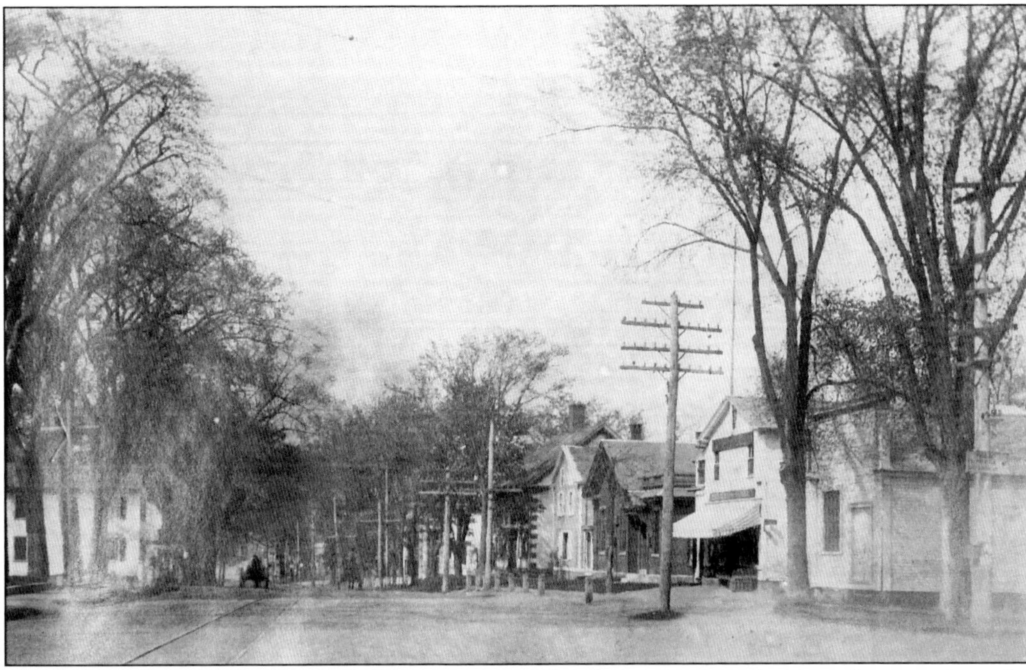

The corner of Fletcher and Main Streets, 1906. At the time this photograph was taken, the building pictured second from the right housed the Littlefield and Webber Grocery store. Previously, this was the Osborn Store and it had been moved to this site from its original location beside the Osborn House. The first building on the right was Charlie Stevens' watch repair shop, which had originally stood next to the old town hall, across from the First Parish Church.

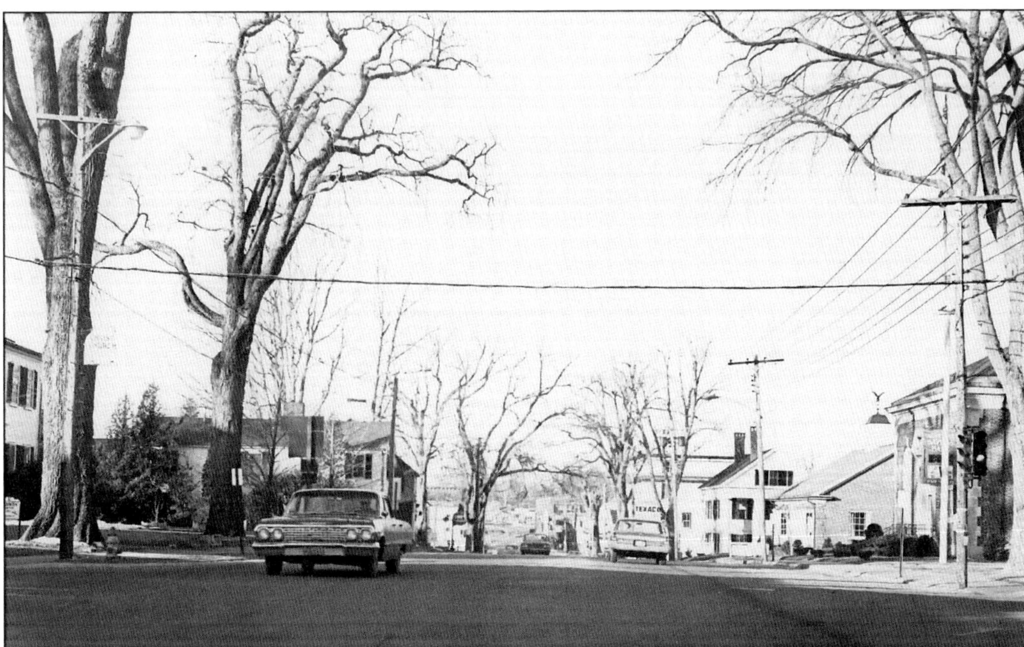

The same corner in 1970, just before the wires were laid underground.

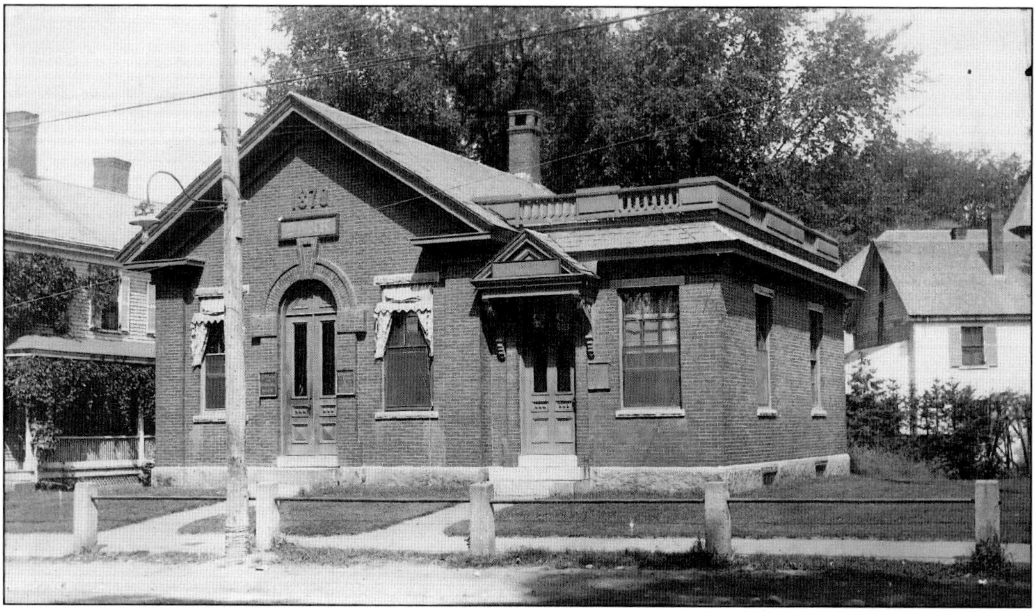

The Ocean National Bank, *c.* 1915. The Ocean National Bank was formed in 1854, and was originally located on the second floor of the Old Brick. When that building burned, a new bank was constructed near the ruins.

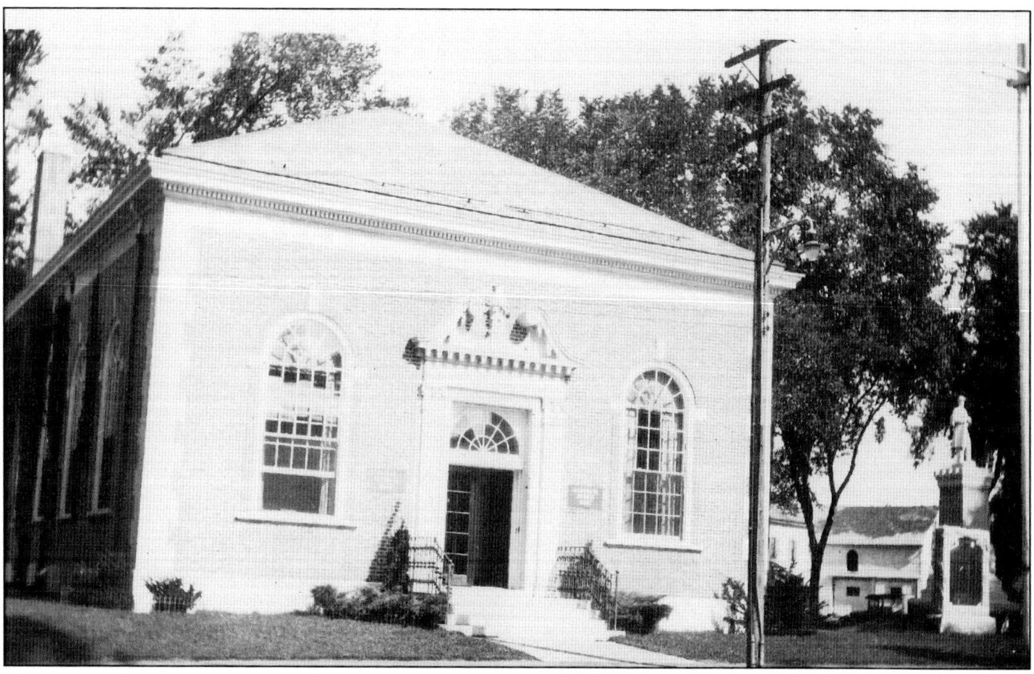

The Kennebunk Savings Bank was organized in 1871 and shared space with the Ocean National Bank within the Ocean National Bank building, which was later expanded to accommodate both banks. The building was razed in 1929, when the present Kennebunk Savings Bank (pictured here) was built.

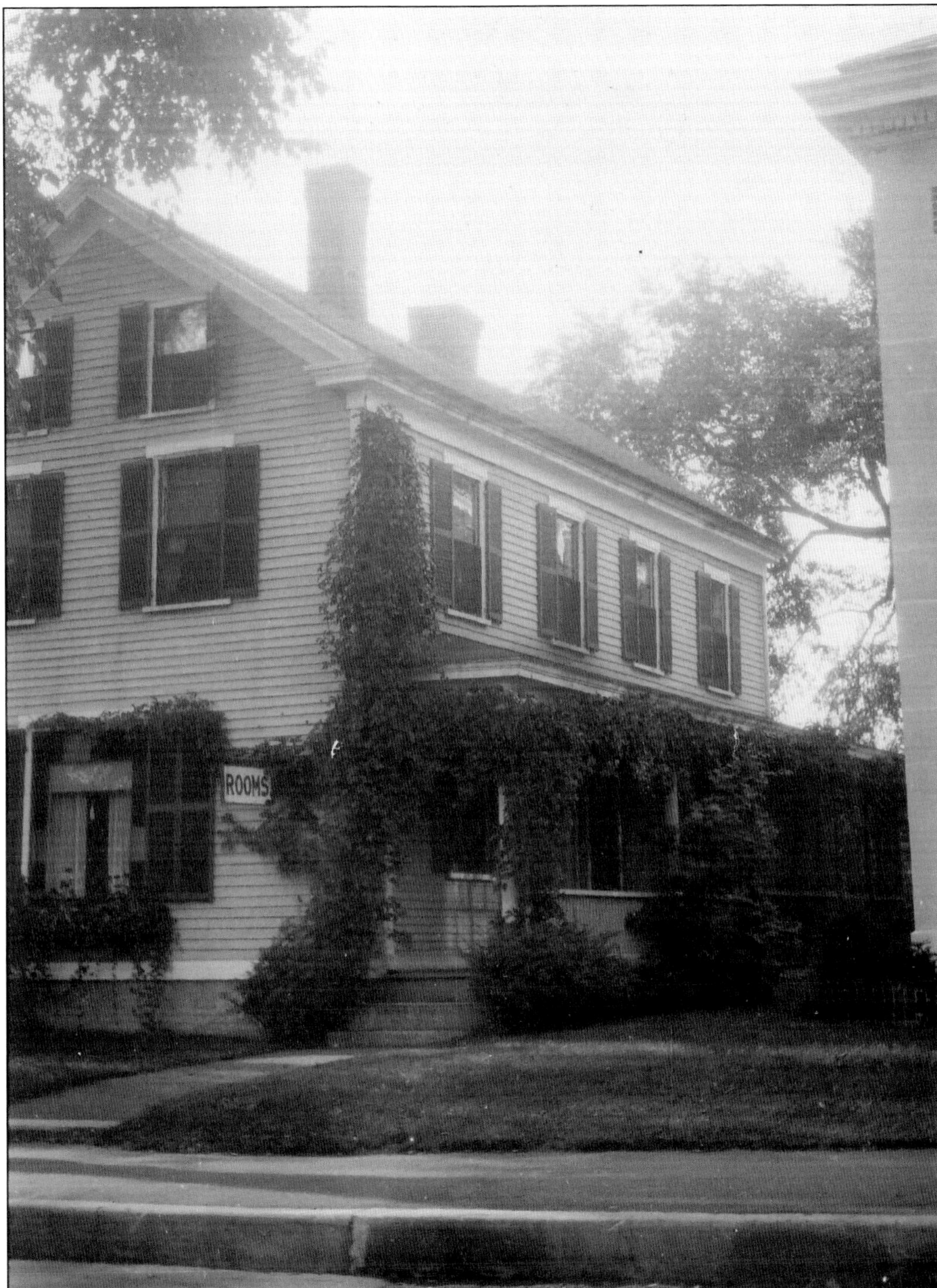

The Oliver Bartlett House, *c.* 1935. In 1807, Daniel Hodson and Jamin Savage built a three-story cabinet makers' shop on this site. That building burned in 1824, and Oliver Bartlett then constructed this building, which he used as his home and bakery. Francis Dow purchased the home in 1957 and had it razed. This is the current site of the Ocean National Bank building.

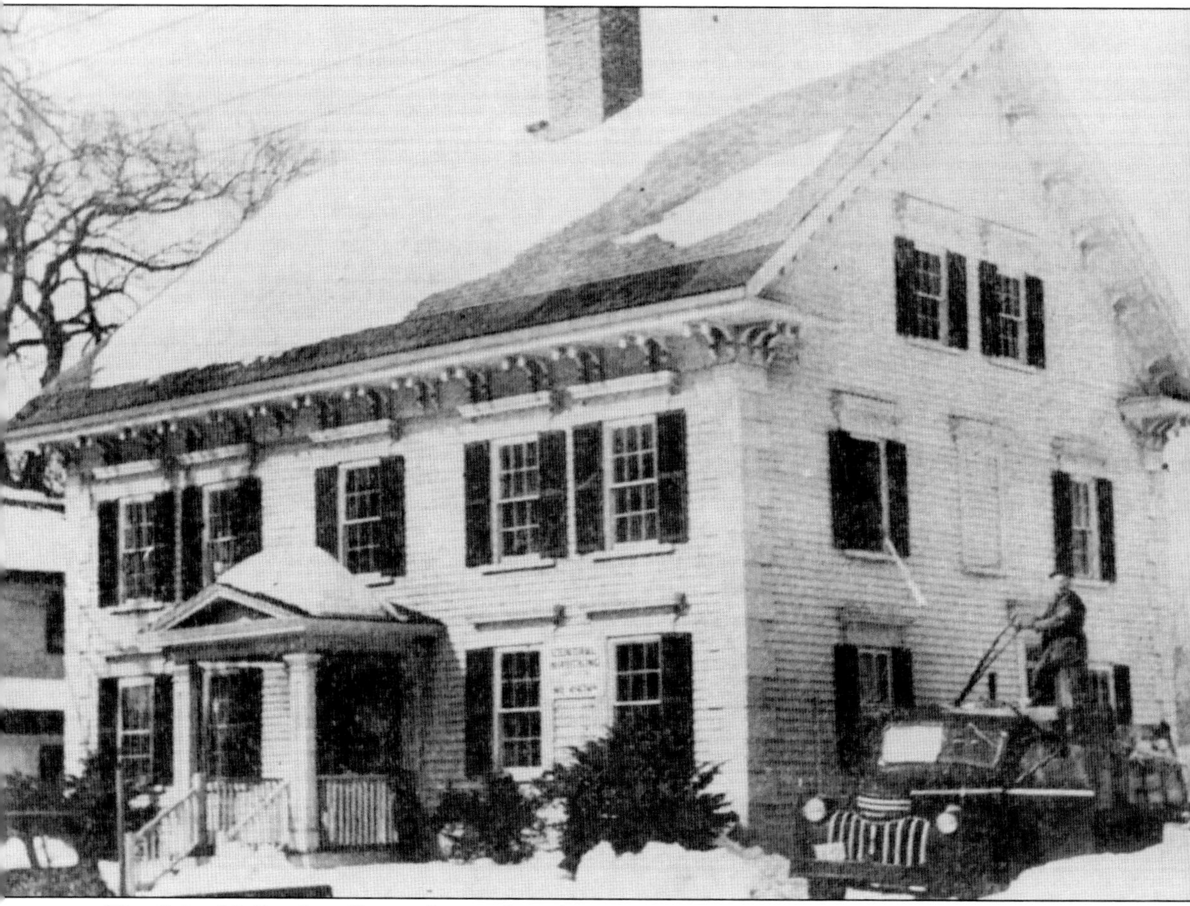

The John H. Bartlett House during demolition in 1963. In the early hours of August 3, 1824, a destructive fire began in the barn of Mr. Bartlett's first home on this site. It destroyed not only his home but the Walker House to the west and the cabinet maker's shop to the east. Dr. Elbridge purchased and greatly improved the 1825 house after Bartlett's death.

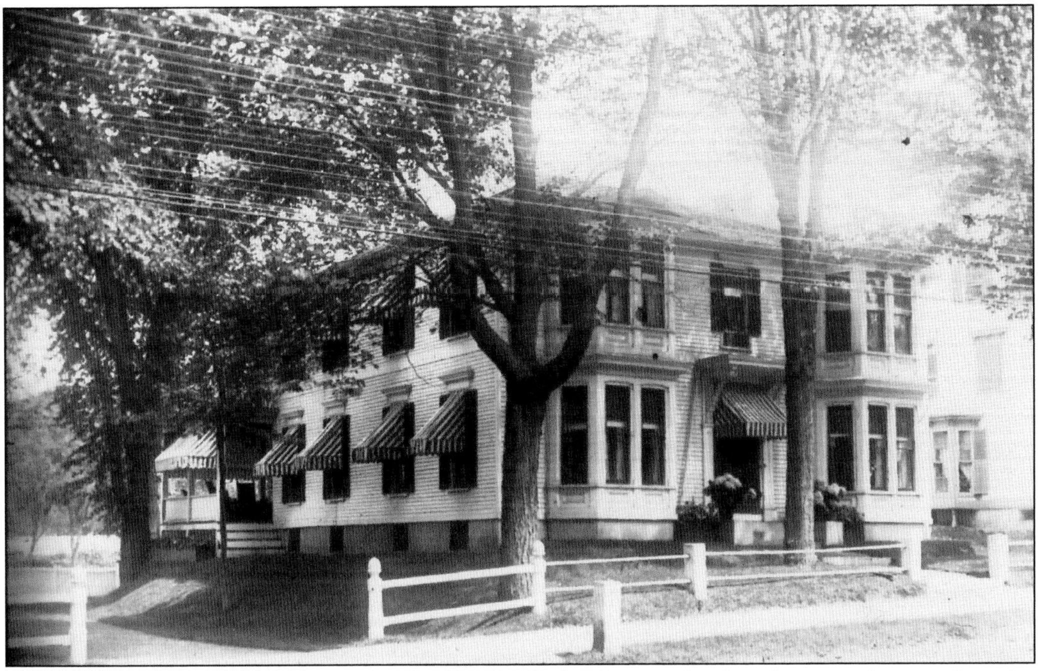

The Palmer Walker House, *c.* 1900. Walker built this home after his first was destroyed in the 1824 fire. After his death in 1878 the house was occupied by Colonel Charles R. Littlefield, who added the bay windows and made other improvements to the building. This house was razed in 1963 to make way for the bank building.

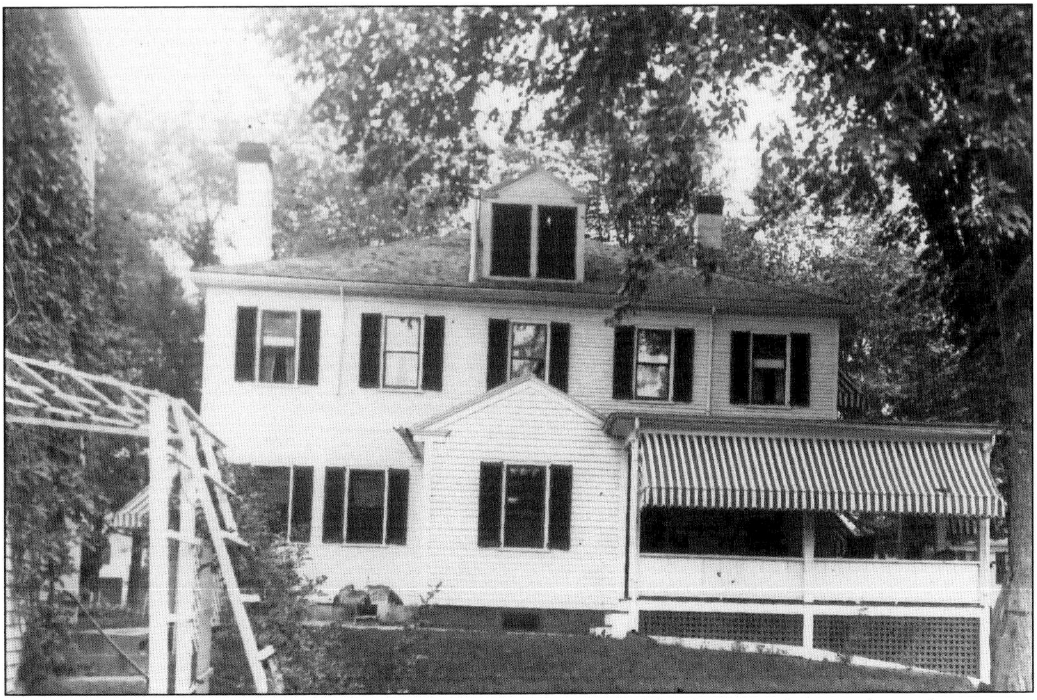

The rear yard of the Walker House. How cool and enjoyable that porch must have been on a hot summer day!

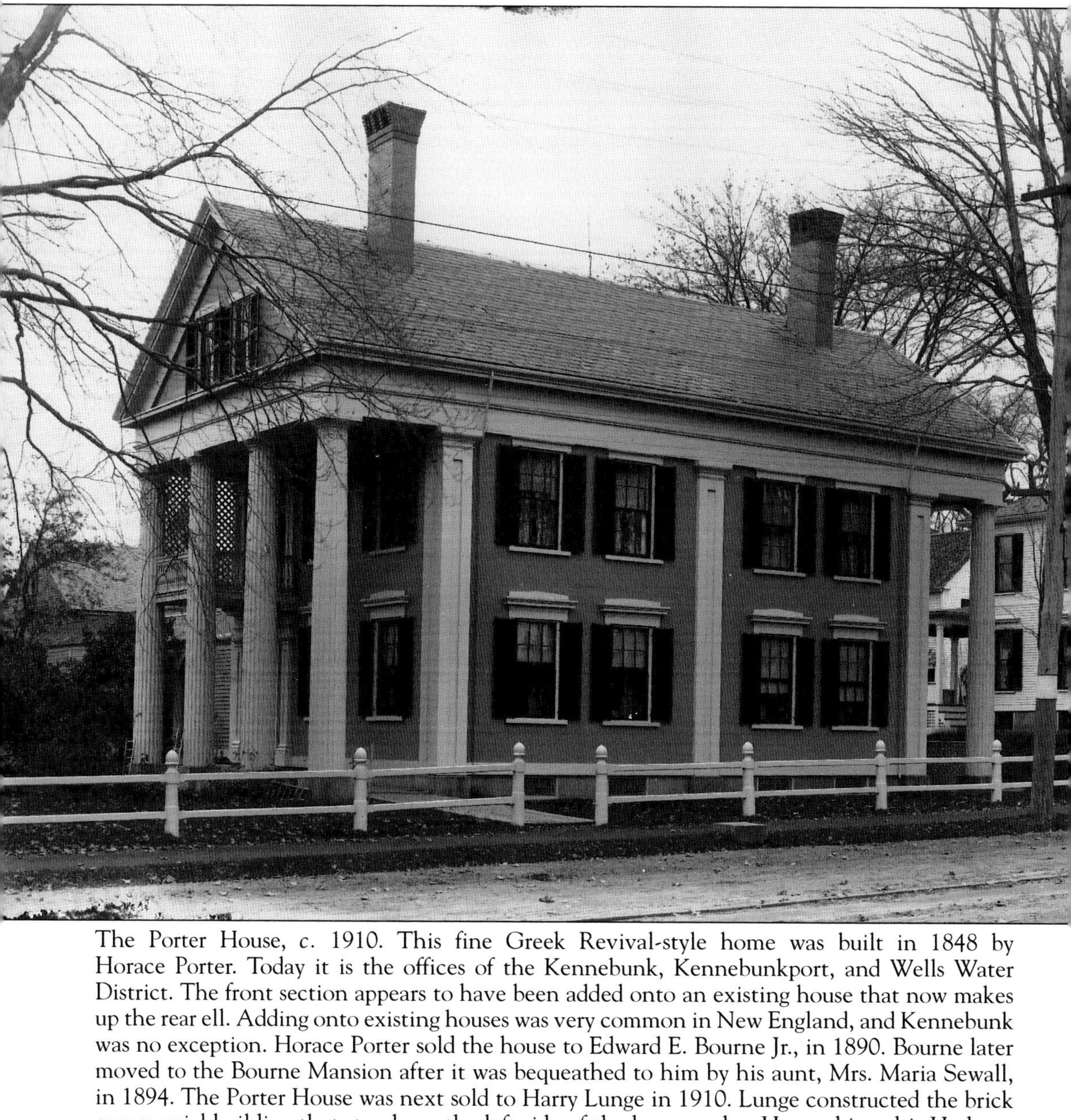

The Porter House, *c.* 1910. This fine Greek Revival-style home was built in 1848 by Horace Porter. Today it is the offices of the Kennebunk, Kennebunkport, and Wells Water District. The front section appears to have been added onto an existing house that now makes up the rear ell. Adding onto existing houses was very common in New England, and Kennebunk was no exception. Horace Porter sold the house to Edward E. Bourne Jr., in 1890. Bourne later moved to the Bourne Mansion after it was bequeathed to him by his aunt, Mrs. Maria Sewall, in 1894. The Porter House was next sold to Harry Lunge in 1910. Lunge constructed the brick commercial building that stands on the left side of the house today. He used it as his Hudson-Essex auto show room. Many other businesses have been located here over the years.

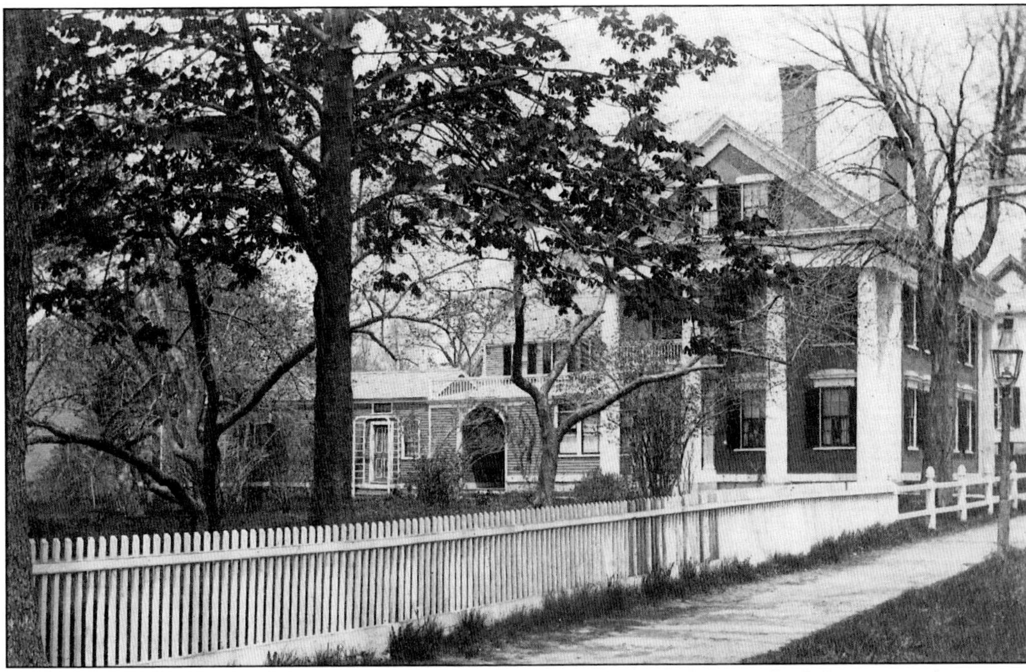

The Porter House, c. 1885. The side lawn ran down to the Stephen Furbish house on the corner of Bourne Street. The street light in front had not yet been replaced by an electric one. Before the advent of electric street lights, the town lamplighter would light each lamp at sunset, then return in the morning to put them out. During the day he would refill each lamp and trim the wicks. Being a lamplighter was a full time job; in 1915, the position was held by a Mr. Wells.

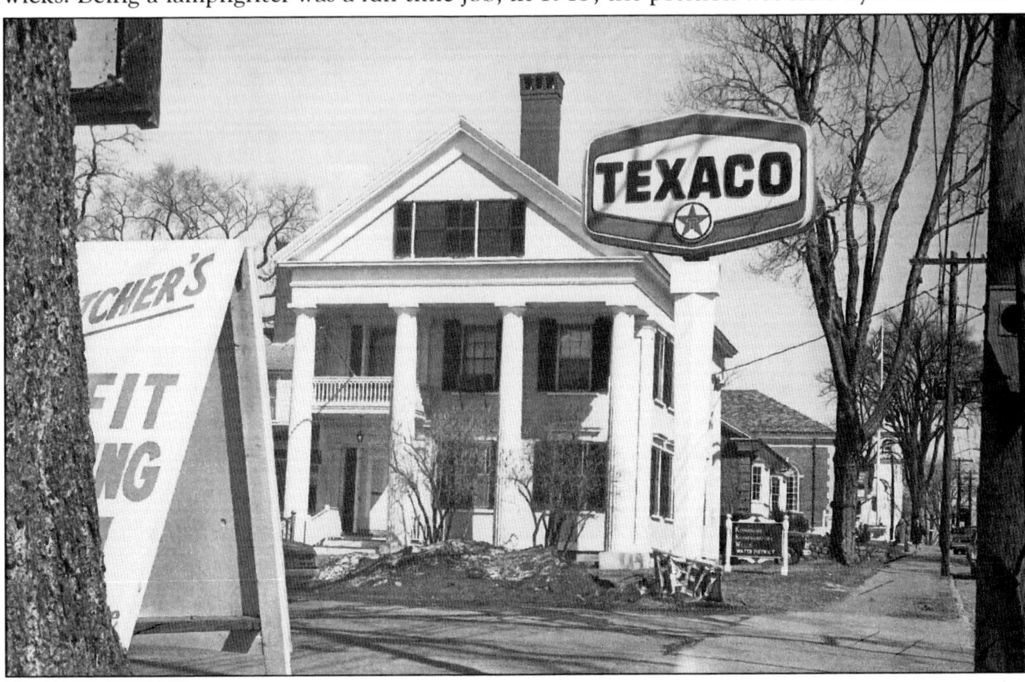

The Porter House, 1970. The Texaco Station replaced the Stephen Furbish House was razed in the 1930s for the Texaco Station.

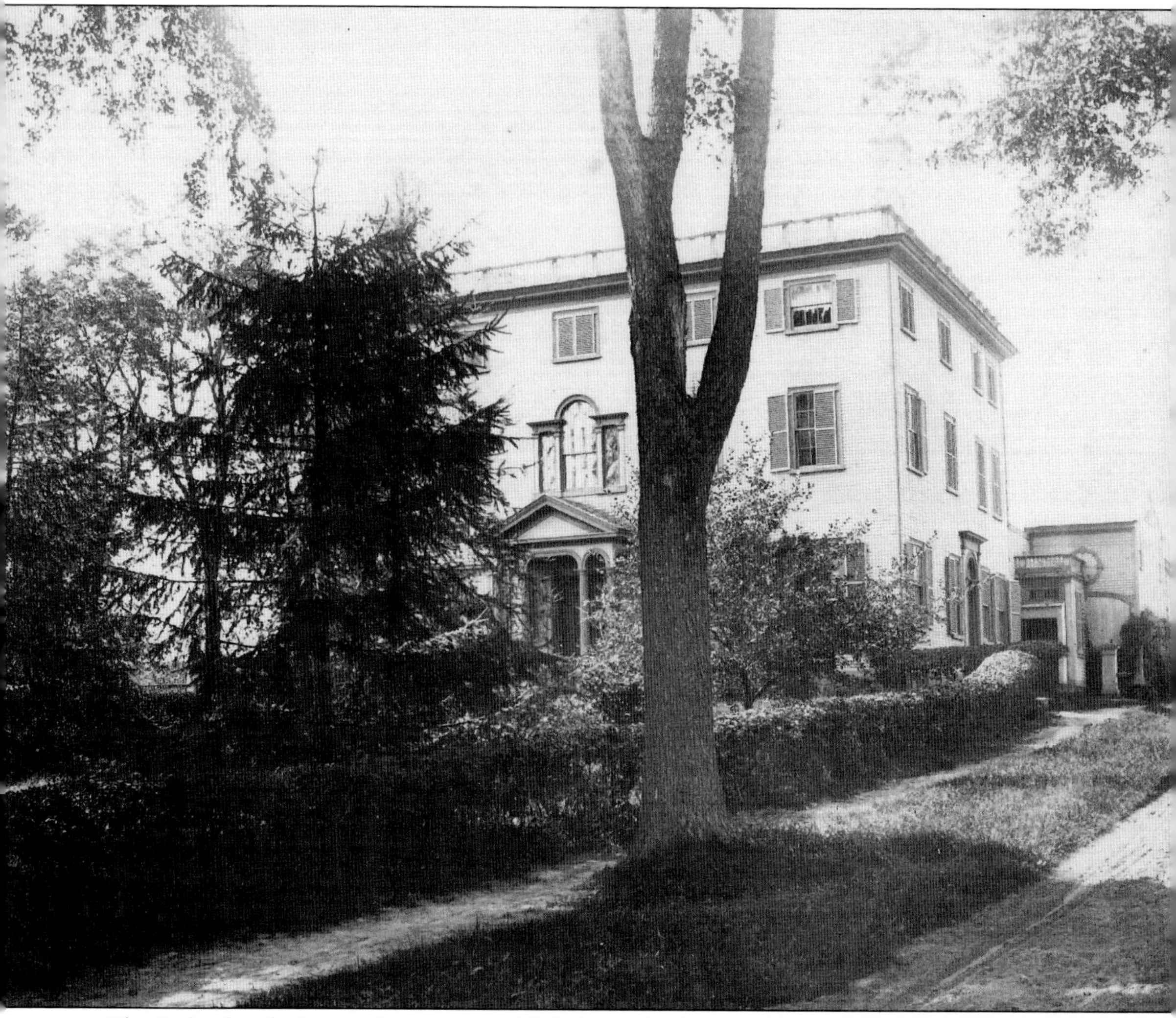

The Federal-style Bourne Mansion, *c.* 1895. It was built *c.* 1812–1814 for John Usher Parsons, who sold the house to Daniel Sewall on June 29, 1815. A carriage shed, similar to that of Wallingford House on York Street, extended from the right side of the house. Part of the shed still existed when this photograph was taken. The house was designed by housewright Thomas Eaton, who also designed many other buildings, including: Lexington Elms, Wallingford House, the Taylor-Barry House, and the Clark-Lord House (all located in Kennebunk); the 1803 renovations to Kennebunk's First Parish Church; and the Captain Lord Mansion in Kennebunkport. Edward E. Bourne inherited the Bourne Mansion from his aunt in 1894, and it remained in the Bourne family well into this century. Edward E. Bourne Sr. was a popular local lawyer and historian. He wrote *The History of Wells and Kennebunk*, published in 1875.

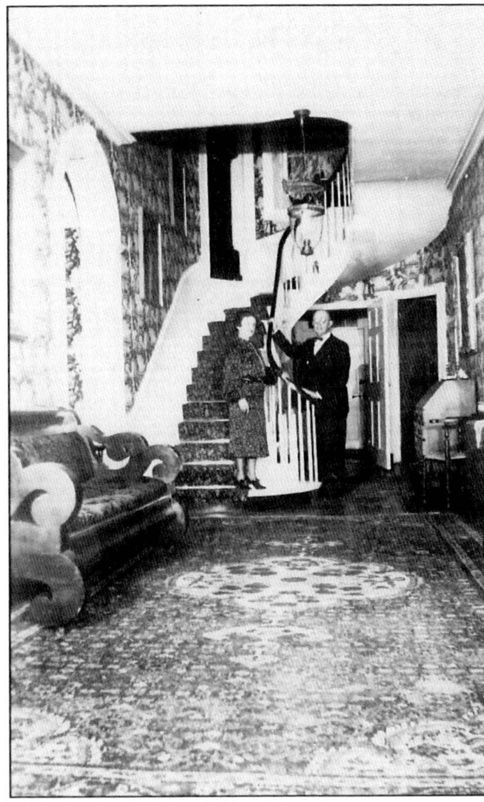

The front hall of the Bourne Mansion, 1937. Judge Harold H. Bourne and his wife Sally are standing at the bottom of the staircase.

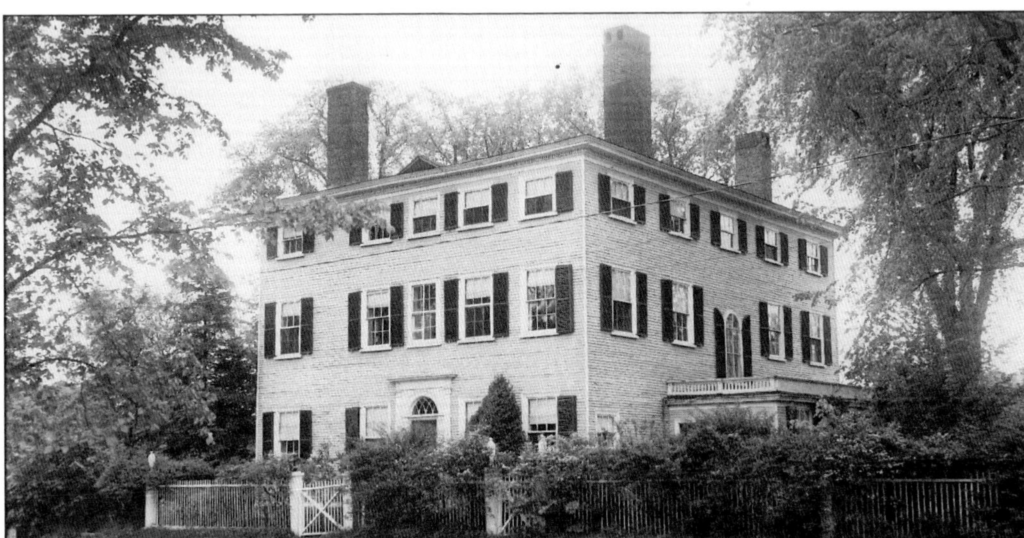

The Bourne Mansion, c. 1965. The carriage sheds were connected to the back of the house, where the single unshuttered window can be seen to the right of this picture.

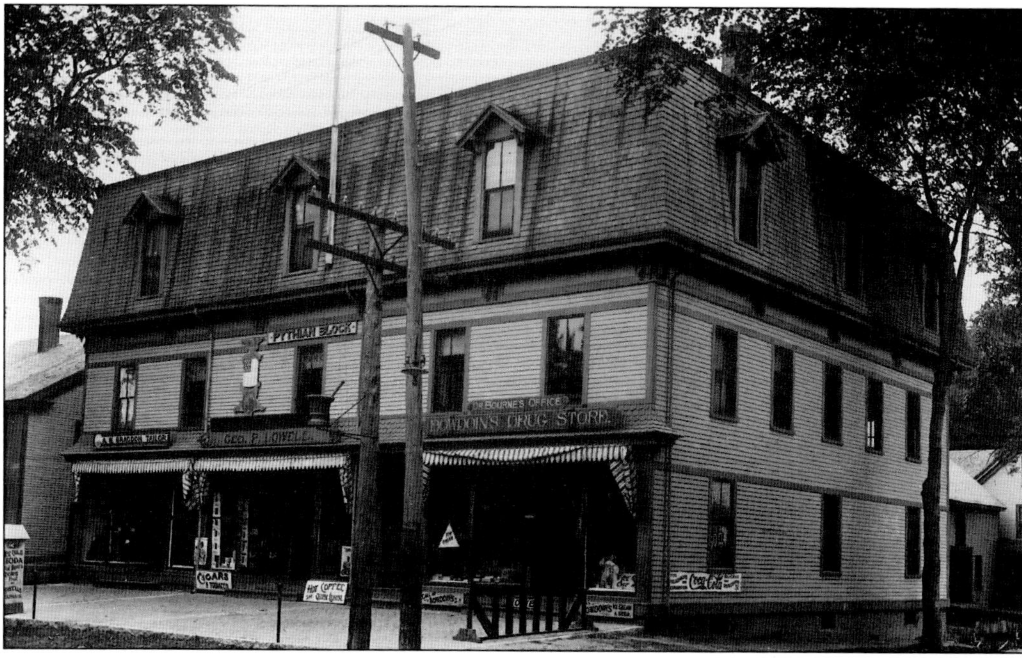

The Pythian Block, c. 1895. At the time this photograph was taken, A.W. Bragdon owned a tailor shop here (right), George P. Lowell had a cigar and coffee shop (middle), and John W. Bowdoin owned a drug store (left). The Knights of Pythias had their meeting hall on the third floor. The building was constructed in 1891 and was damaged by fire on March 6, 1919. It was rebuilt as it appears today.

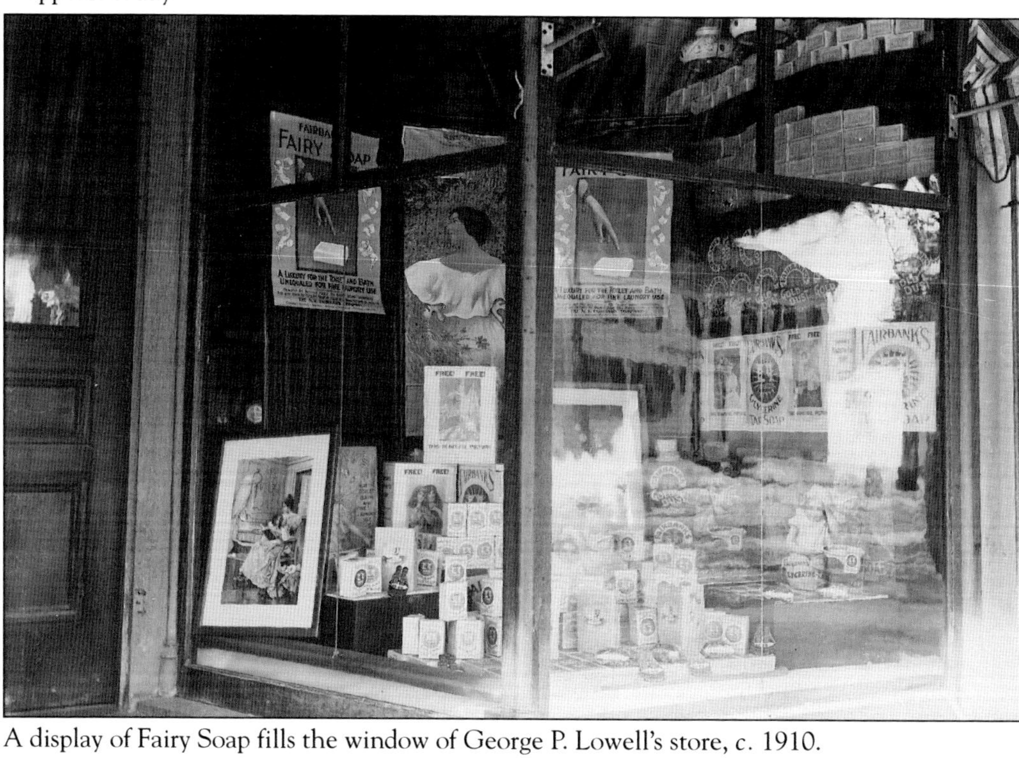

A display of Fairy Soap fills the window of George P. Lowell's store, c. 1910.

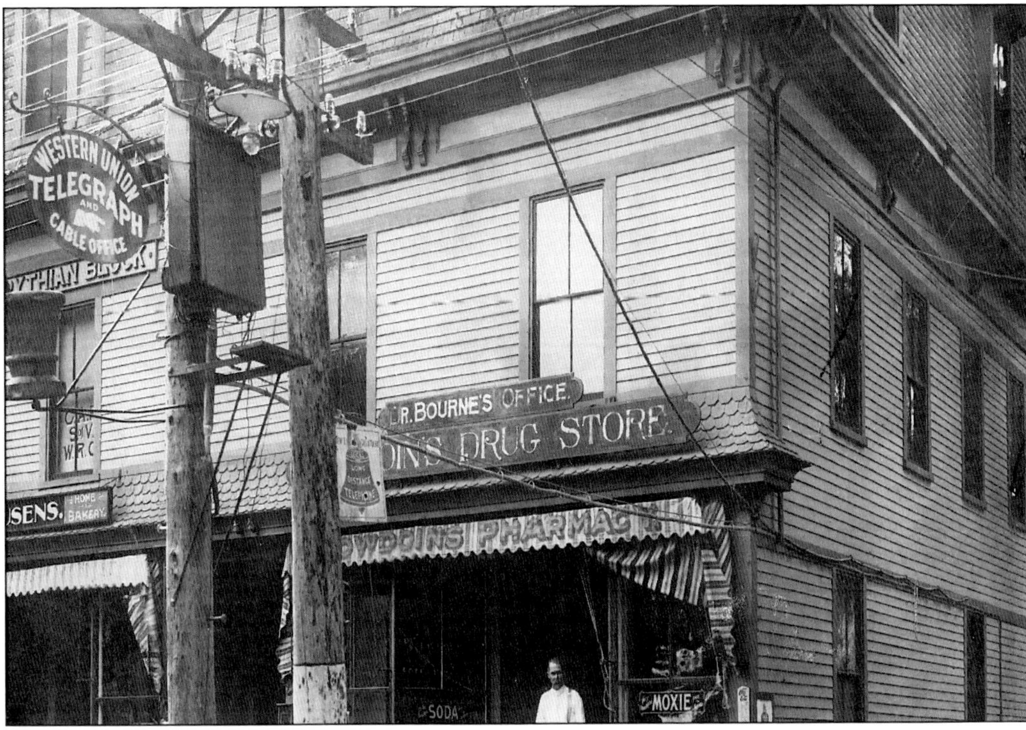

John Bowdoin stands in front of his drug store, *c.* 1900. Because John Bowdoin did not hold a Druggist's license, Dr. Bourne would come in once a day to fill prescriptions. That's why Dr. Bourne's name was over the Bowdoin pharmacy sign.

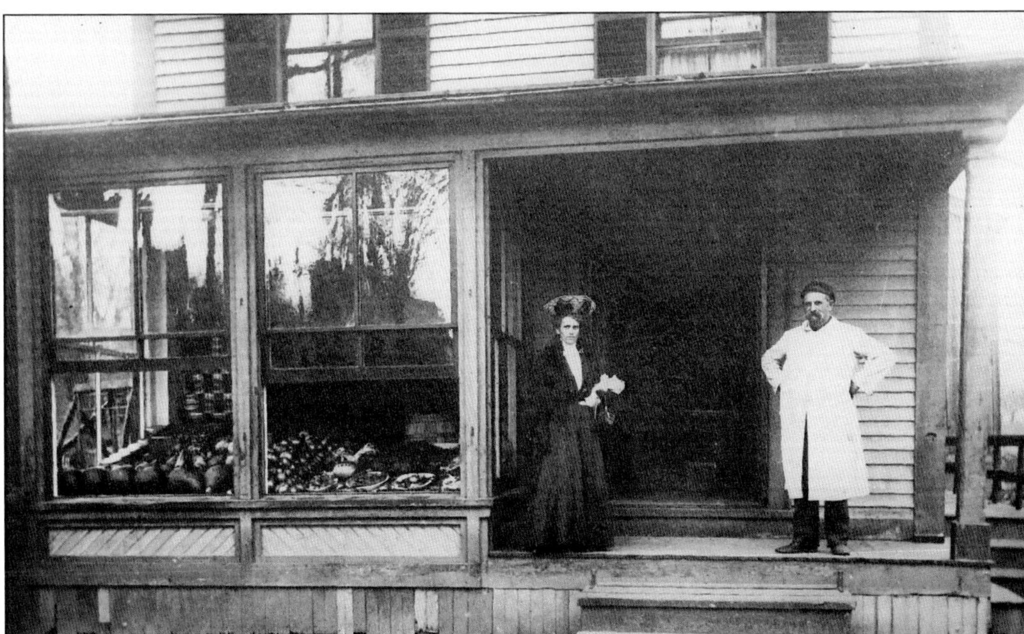
Charles "Cappy" Tarbox's meat market, *c.* 1910. The woman next to Cappy Tarbox is Mrs. Charles Hooper. Notice the open windows with no screens, and the unwrapped meat.

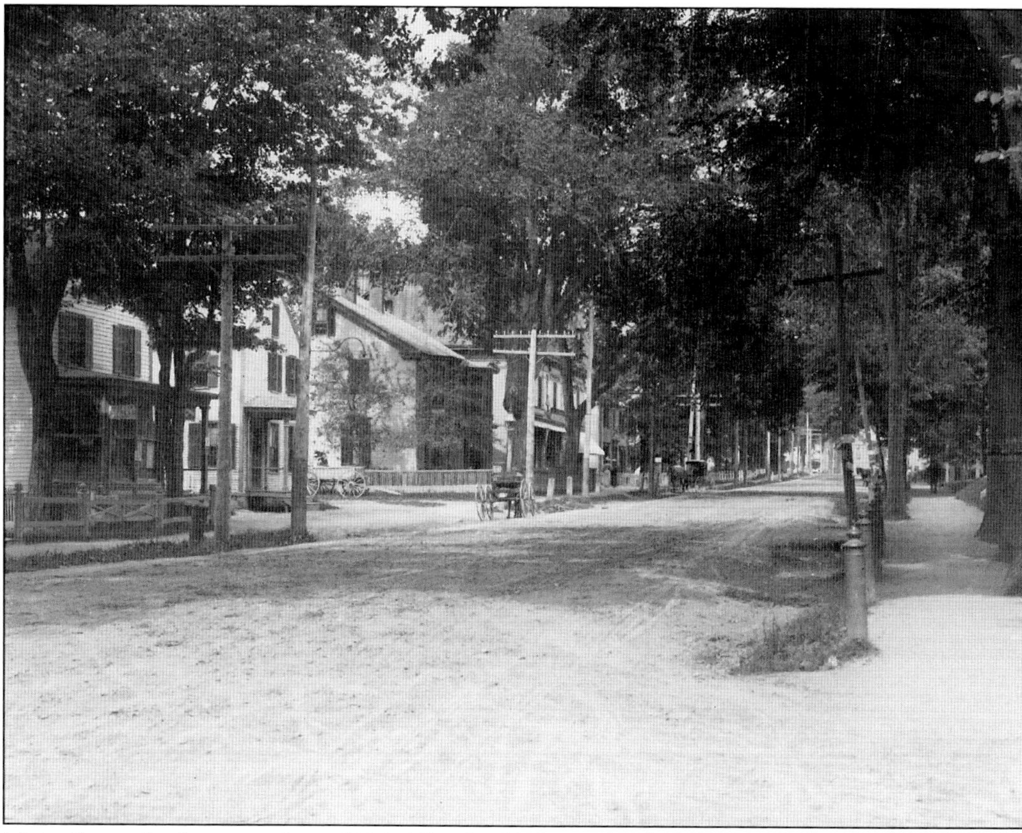

Main Street looking north, *c.* 1890. The building to the left of the photograph is the meat market of Cappy Tarbox. In 1911, the Acme Theater was built next to it. Tarbox's market was razed in 1961 during renovations to the theater and the block. The house to the right of Cappy's was razed in the 1930s to make way for a filling station. The Kennebunk Convenience Store was the most recent business located on that site. Just beyond that is the Pythian Block.

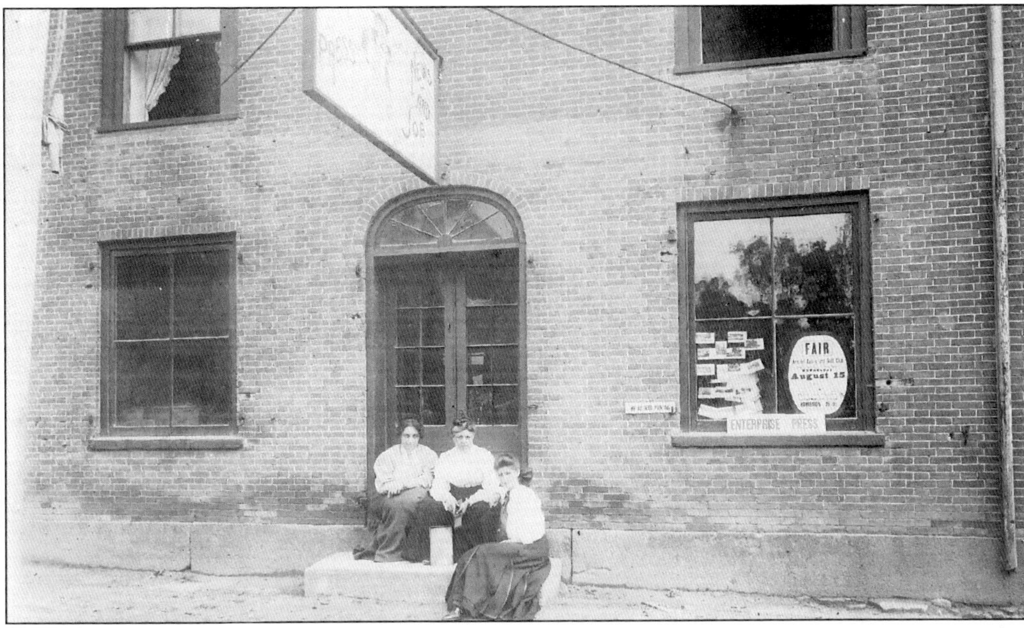

The Enterprise Press, at the Kelly Block on Green Street, c. 1910. The paper was started in this building in 1904 by Annie Joyce Crediford. The *Enterprise* wasn't afraid to take a stand on important issues. Annie could put the fear of God into any politician or local selectmen. Her editorials were the whole truth and nothing but the truth. At the turn of the century, downtown businesses dumped their sewer into Scotchman's Brook and the odor was more than noticeable. Annie led the fight for a town sewer system, and won. Annie Joyce Crediford was hardworking and intelligent, with a sharp eye for news. She was the first woman editor in Kennebunk, and the first woman to own her own newspaper. She was a prominent person in town and holds an important place in Kennebunk's history.

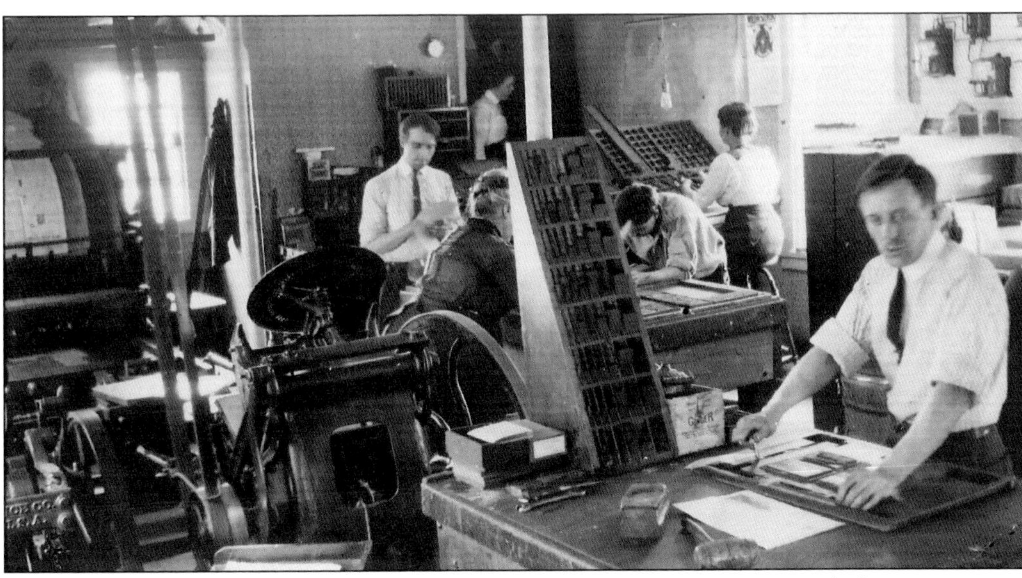

Note the traditional clutter of a newspaper office, the huge presses, and the storage trays for lead type.

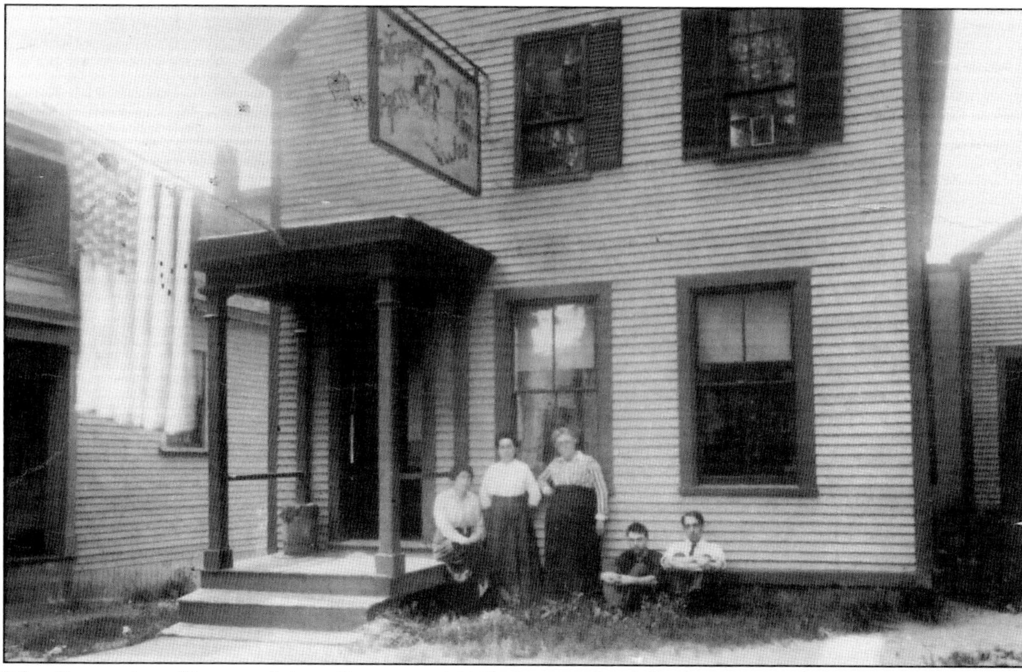

The *Enterprise* offices on Main Street, *c.* 1915. Annie Crediford is pictured third from left. This building was moved to Main Street from Summer Street, *c.* 1840. The post office was located here before it moved to the Ross Block in 1890. From 1913 to 1922, the *Enterprise* offices were housed here. The Square Toes restaurant now occupies the building.

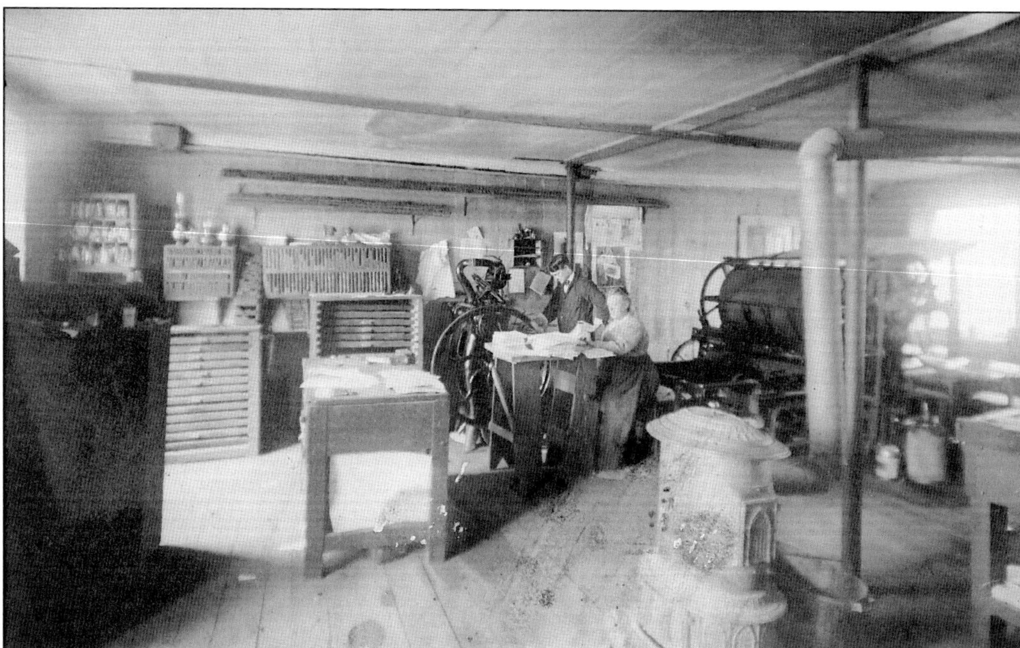

The *Enterprise* office, *c.* 1915. Notice the corner of the huge rotary press and the compositor assembling a page of lead type and locking it together.

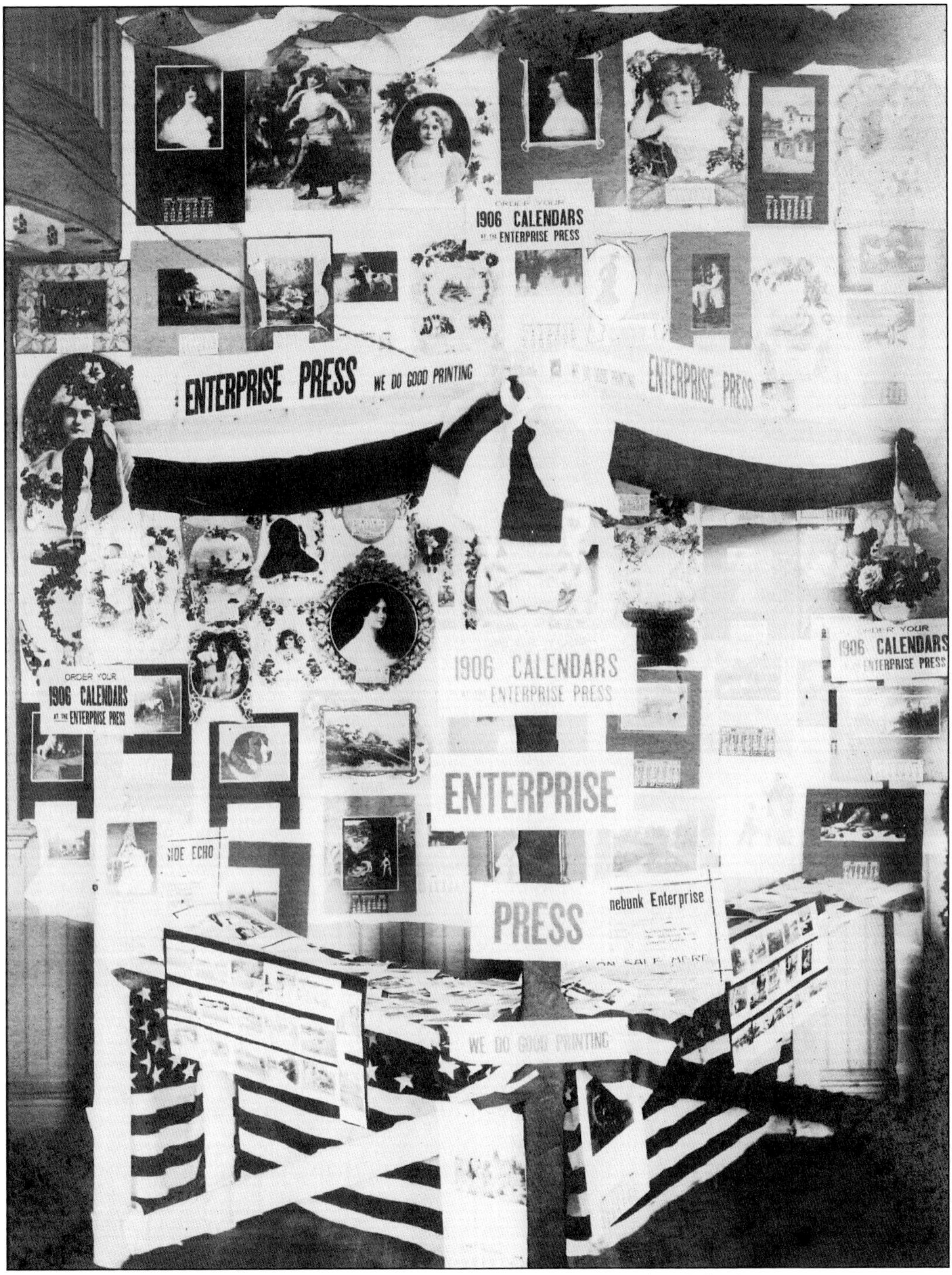

Annie Crediford, owner of the Enterprise Press and newspaper, also did job printing to augment the newspaper's income. Displays similar to the one in this 1905 photograph advertised her firm's capabilities.

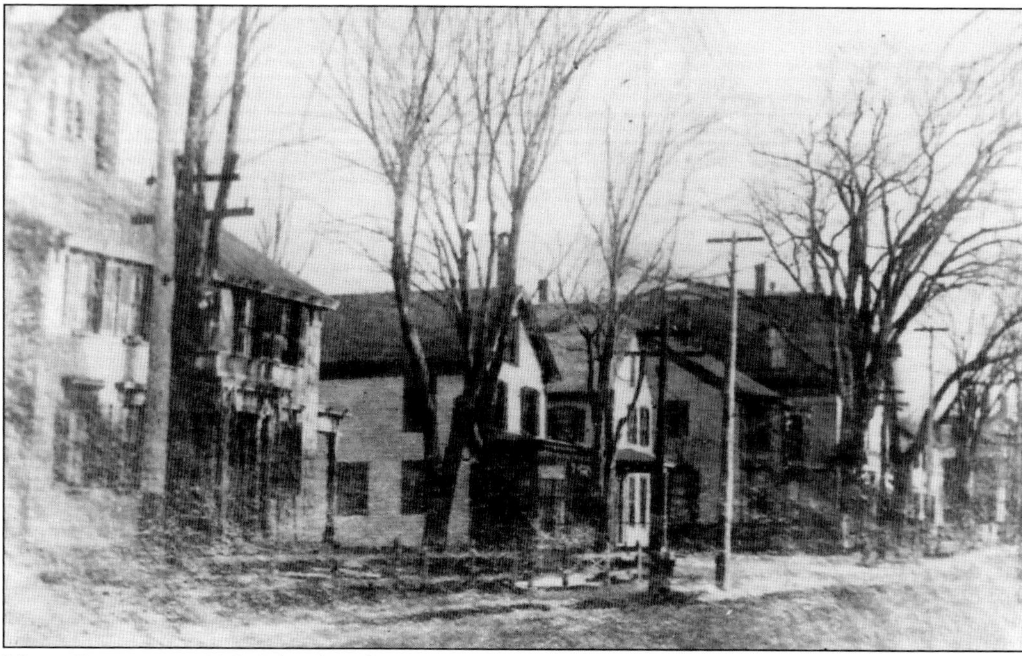

Main Street, *c.* 1895. The handsome and ornate house on the left was built *c.* 1800 by Captain Charles Perkins. It was owned for many years by Christopher Littlefield. John Bowdoin purchased the house in 1910, and raised it in 1912 to build a new commercial block under it. The post office was moved to this location from the Ross Block, and Bowdoin moved his drug store there from the Pythian Block.

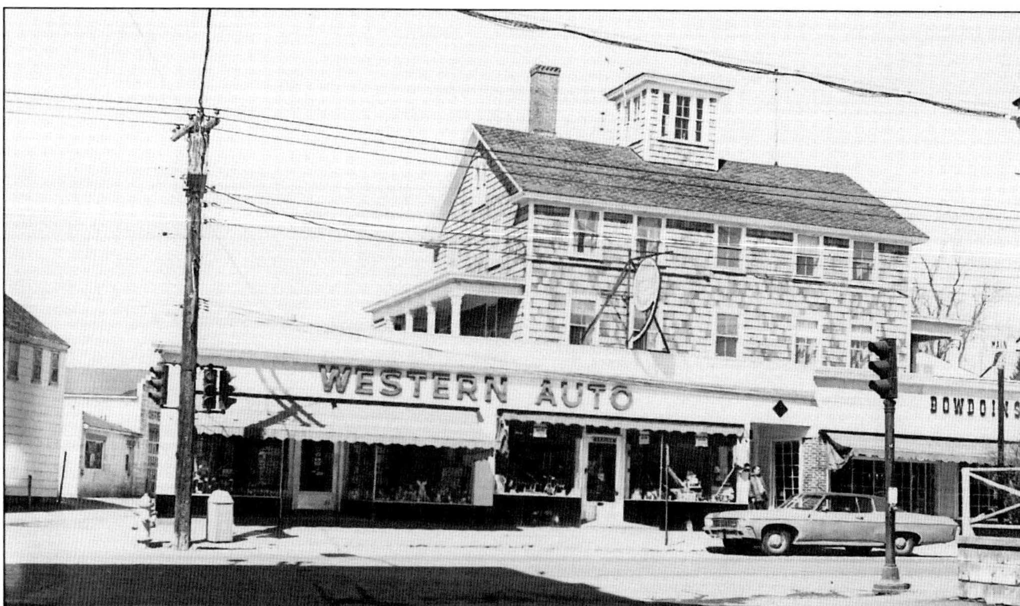

The Bowdoin Block, 1970. As we can see, the house has been stripped of all its ornamental trim. Arthur Jack operated the Western Auto Store and his wife Ruby ran a toy store adjoining it.

Two

Post Office Square

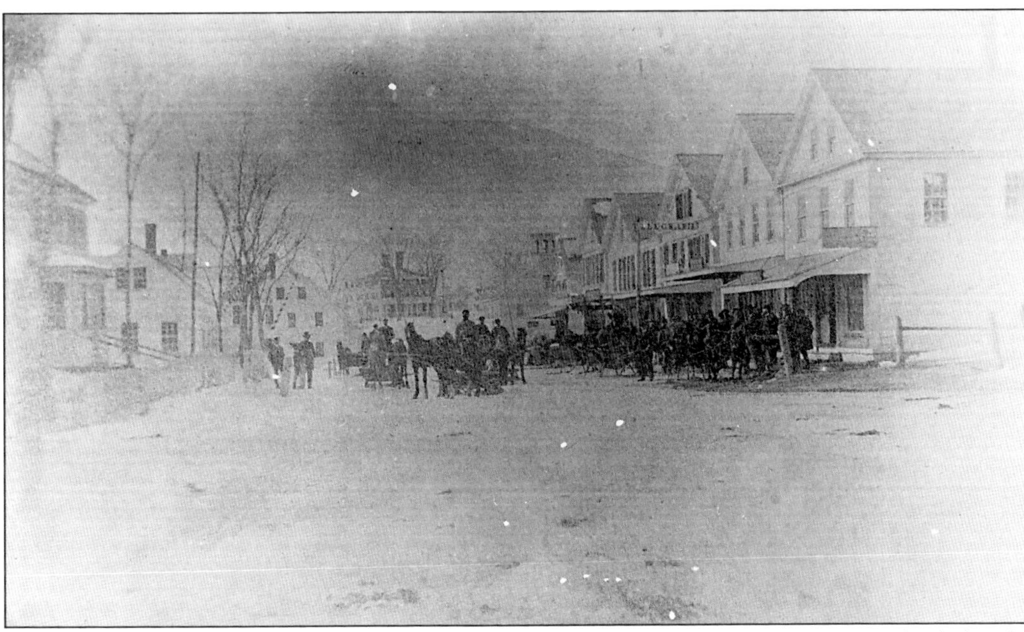

Main Street, looking south, *c.* 1880. The Michael Wise House can be seen on the left. The building next to it is the Downing Block, built in 1878 by Frank Mason. The Grist Mill and the Mousam House are just visible in the distance.

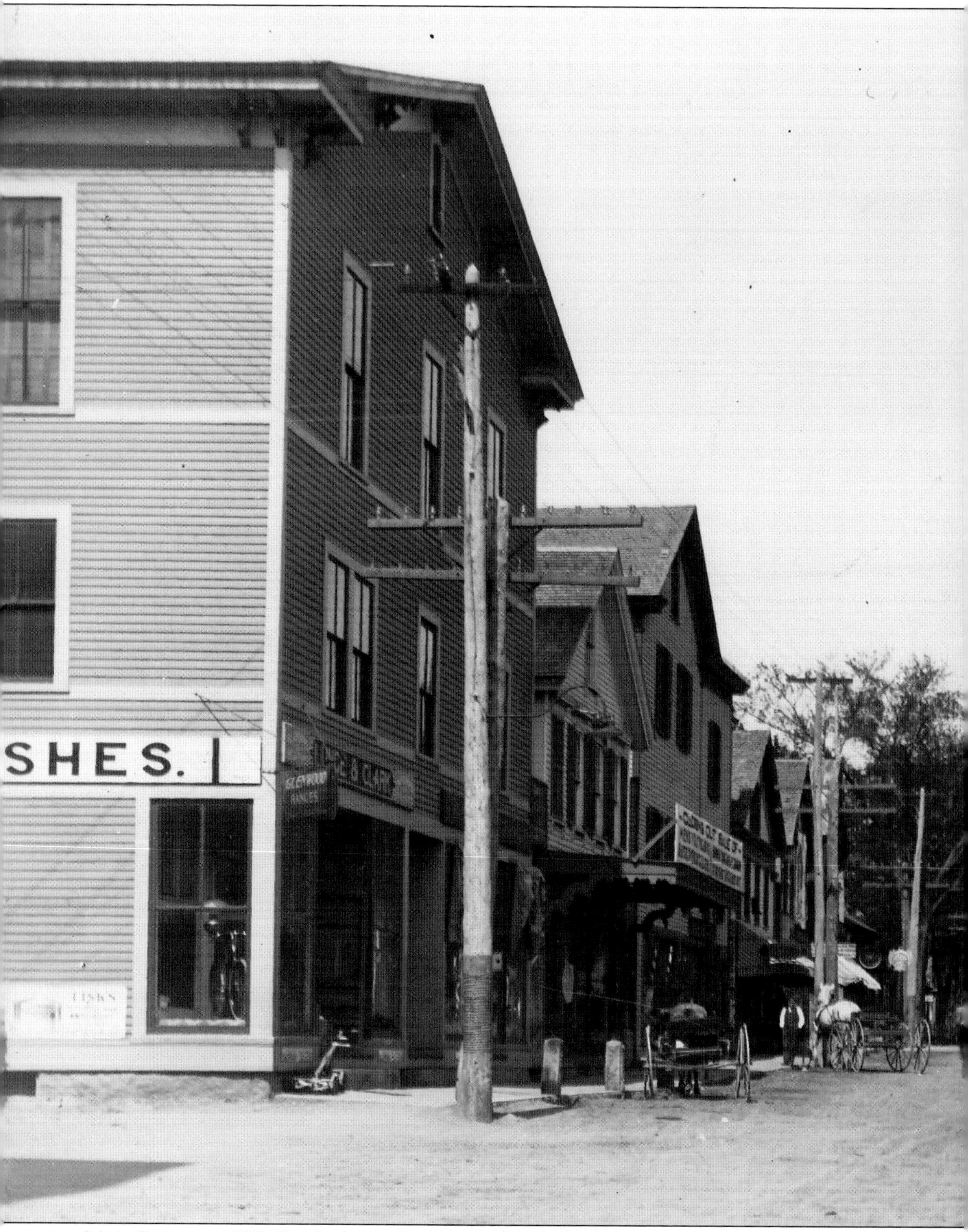

Main Street, *c.* 1895. On the left is the Parsons Block, built in 1888. On the right is the Old

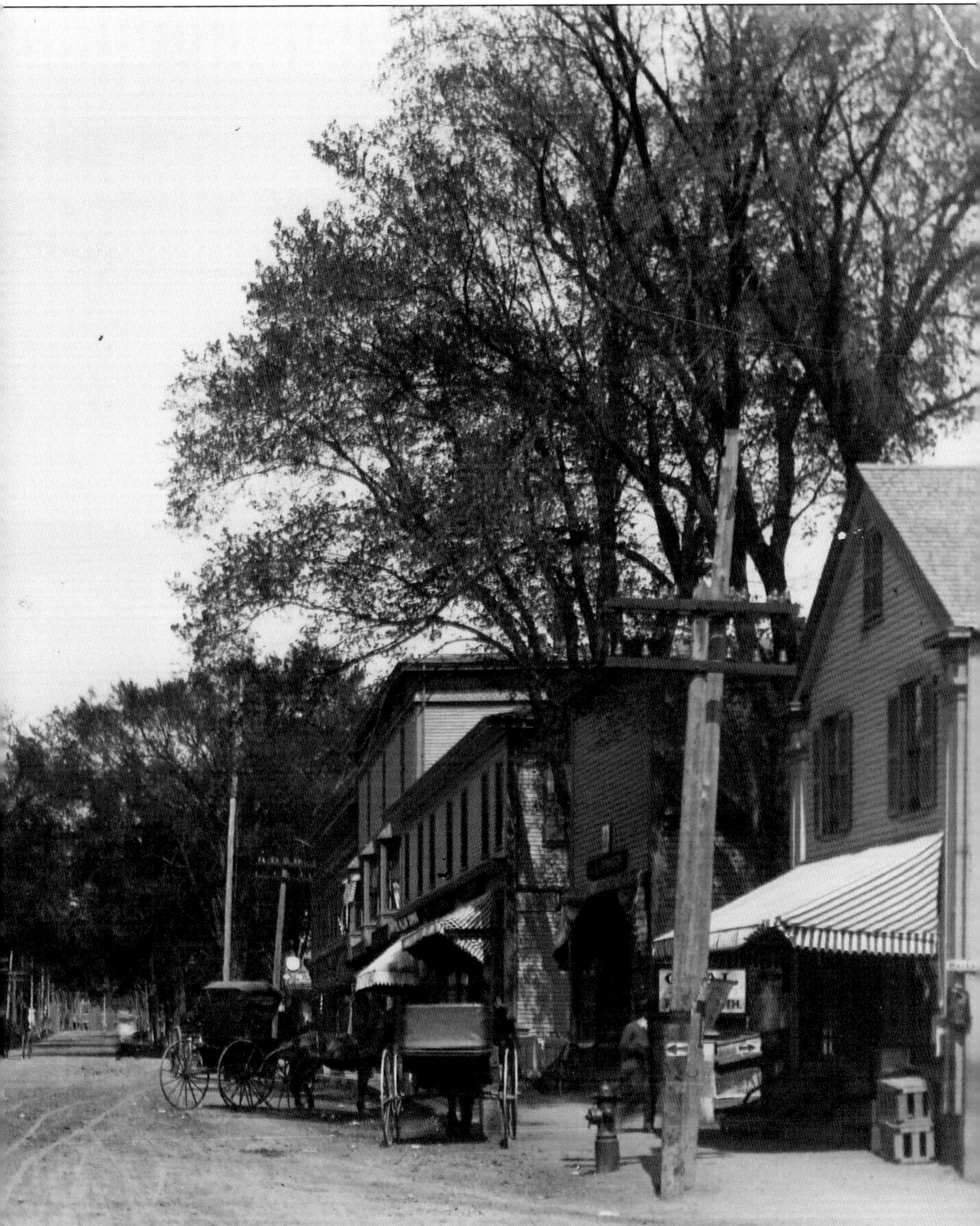

Corner Grocery, owned by George Cousens.

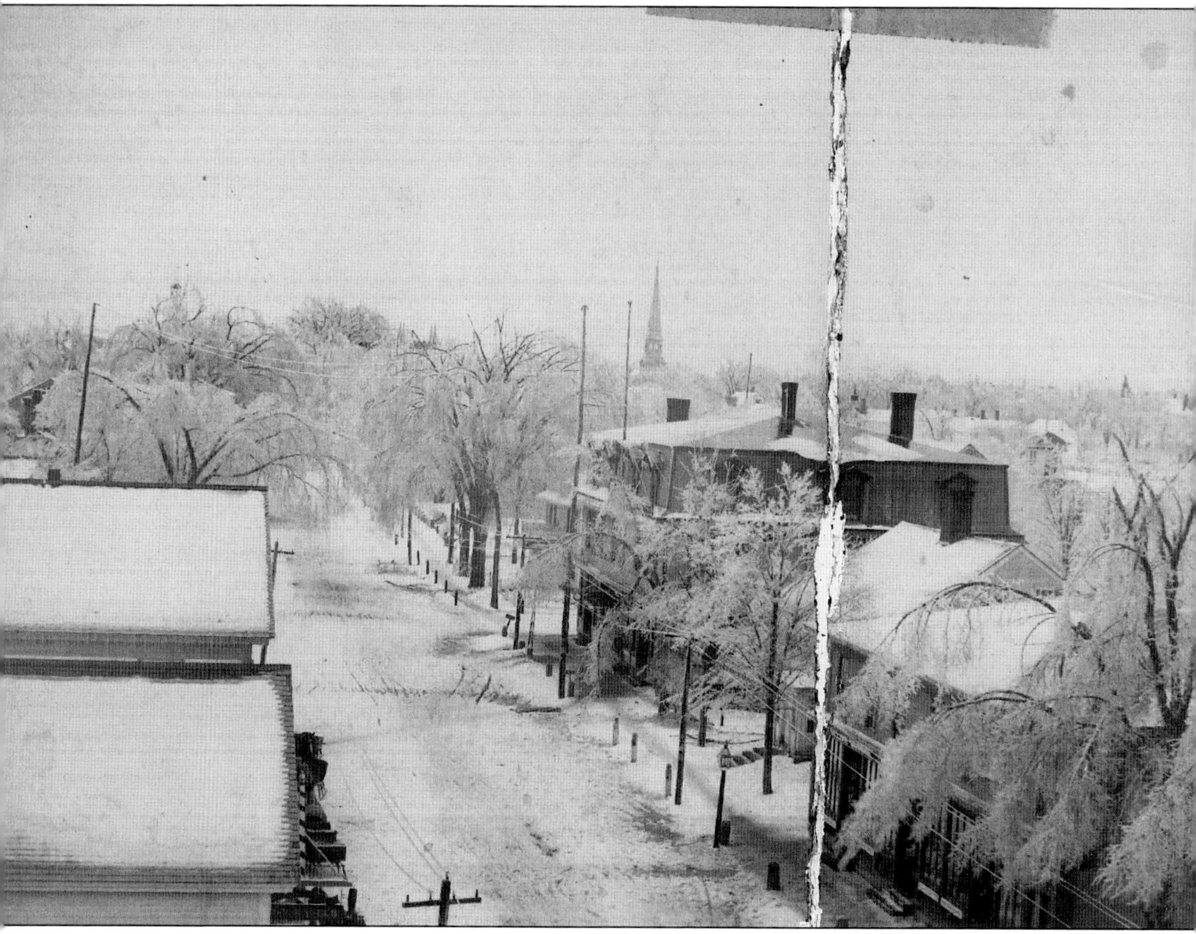

Main Street, 1886. Although damaged, this early photograph is important because it gives us a rare view of the Michael Wise House, pictured second from the right. Built in 1792, the Michael Wise House was moved to the rear of the lot in 1895, when the Odd Fellows Block was built. The house was later razed for parking.

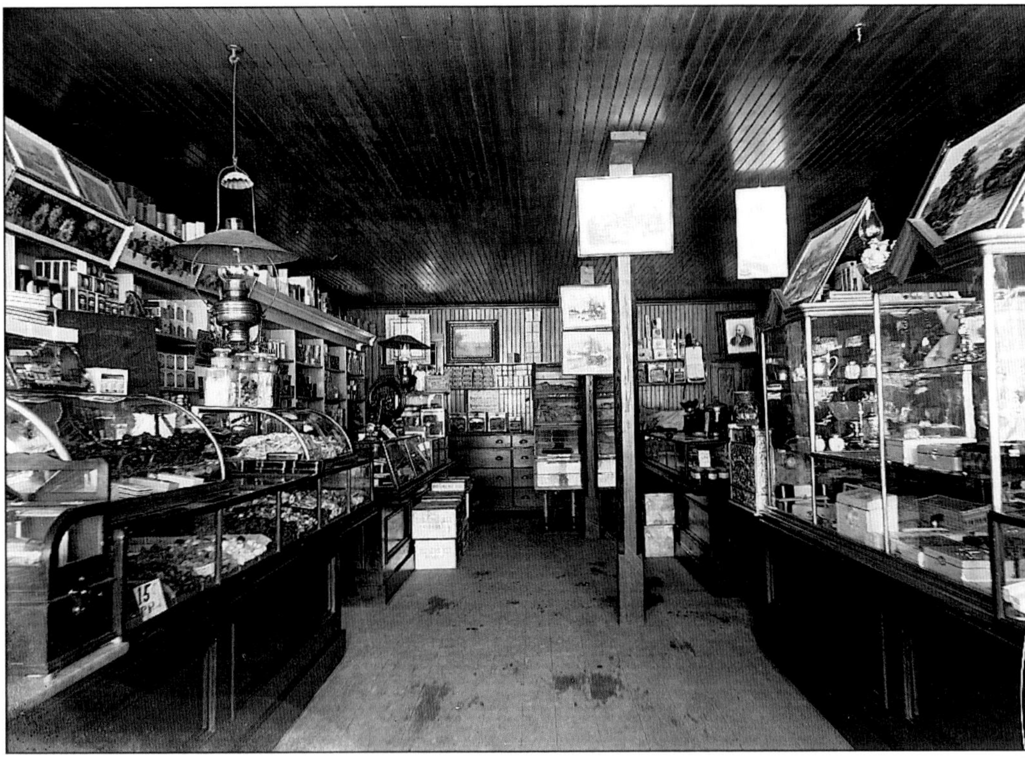

The interior of a Main Street store, *c.* 1905, showing a range of items from candy to framed prints.

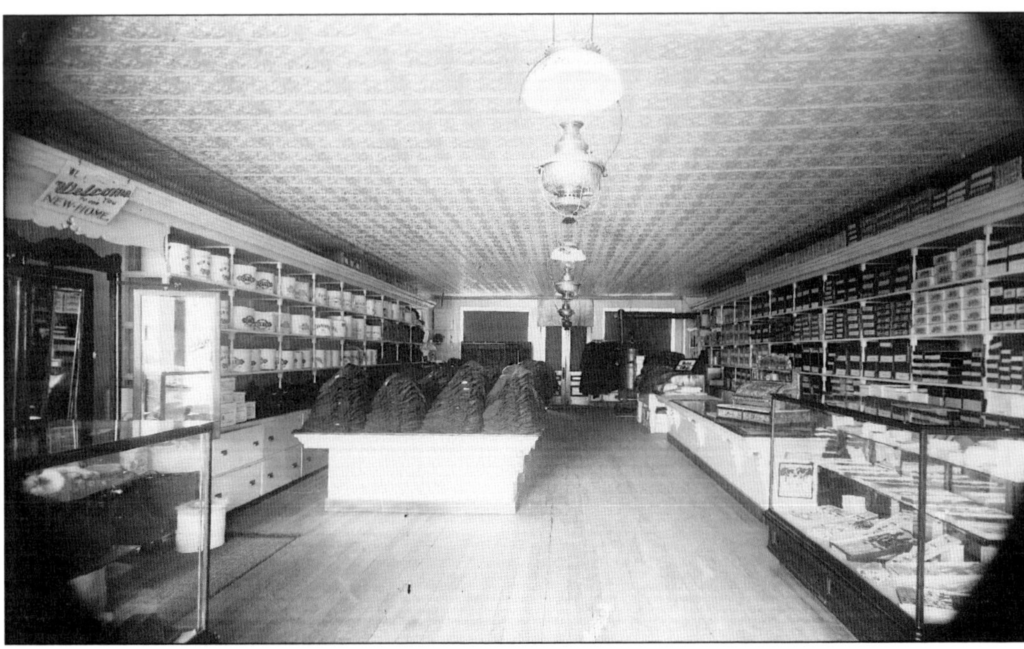

The interior of a men's clothing store, *c.* 1905. The location is unknown.

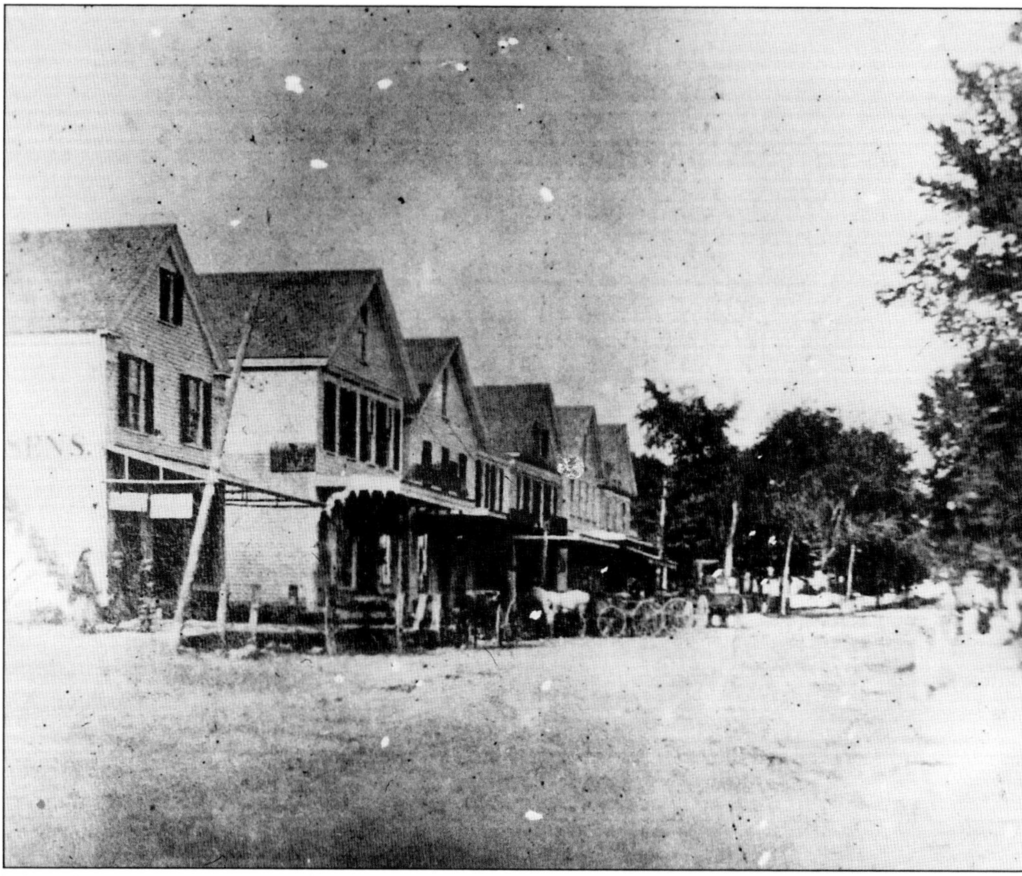

Main Street, c. 1875. Bounded by Main, Garden, and Storer Streets, the triangle has housed many different businesses. The building on the left in this photograph was moved to Pleasant Street in 1886 when the Parsons Block was built. Next to it is Charles Dresser's store, built in 1858. The building third from the left was built in 1870 by Samuel Clark. The building fourth from the left was called the Blue Store. It was once painted blue, at a time when it was common for buildings on Main Street to be painted yellow. It still stands today, the only surviving building in this block. Winston Realty is located there now.

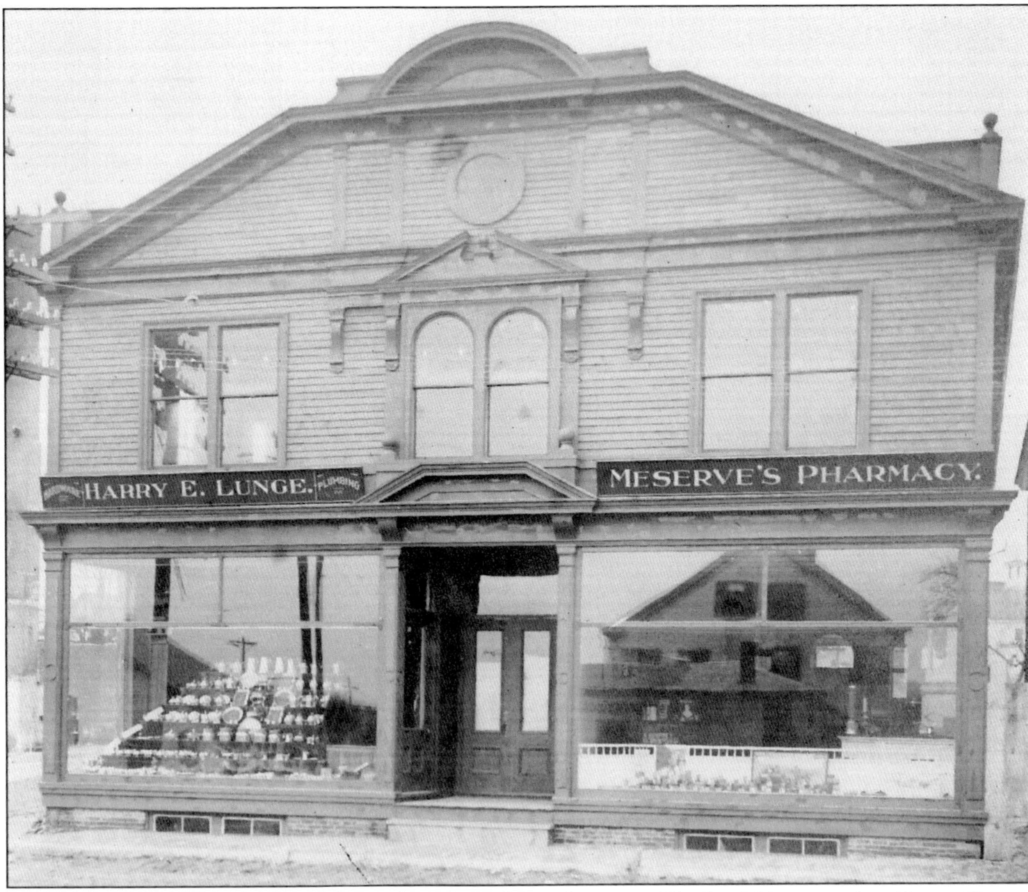

This building was constructed on the site of the Parsons Block, following the Great Fire of 1903. It may have been designed by local architect William Barry. Chadwicks clothing store is located there today, and the current owners have recreated the exterior to appear approximately as it would have in 1903.

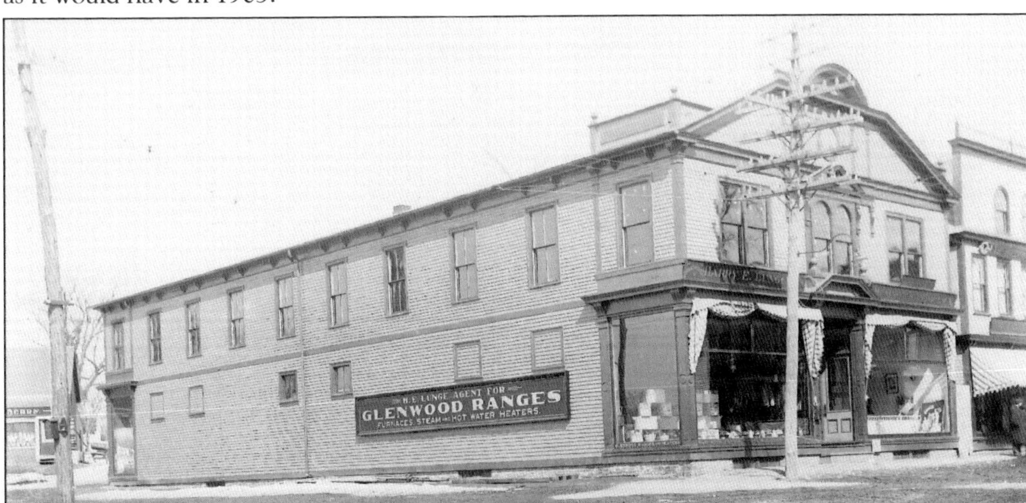

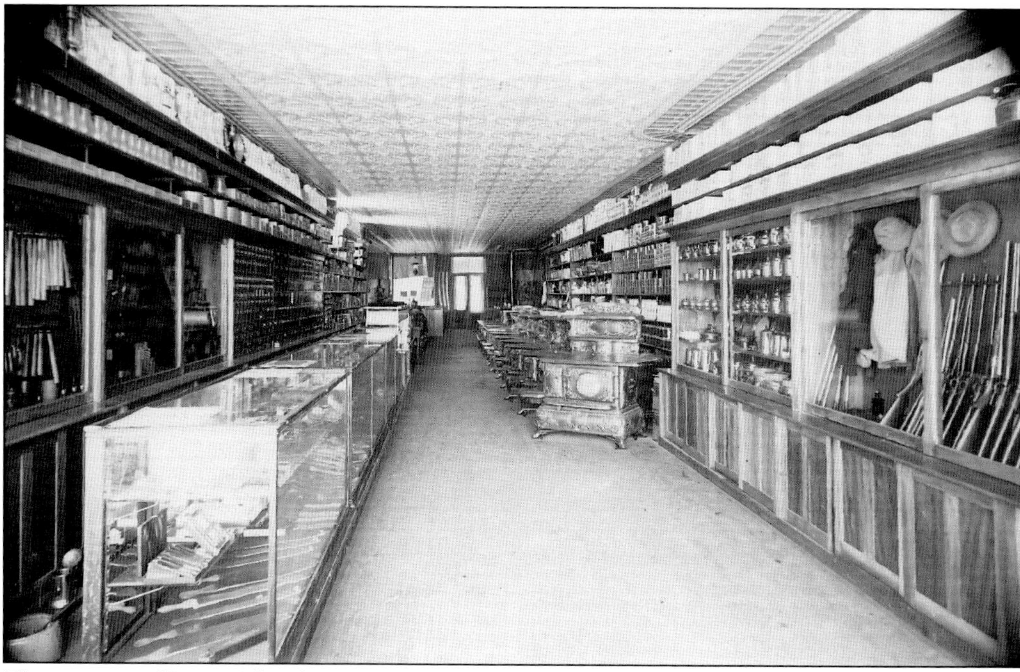

The interior of Lunge's hardware store, looking toward the back, 1903. Everything was kept on shelves or in glass cases, and each customer was waited on personally by the store clerk.

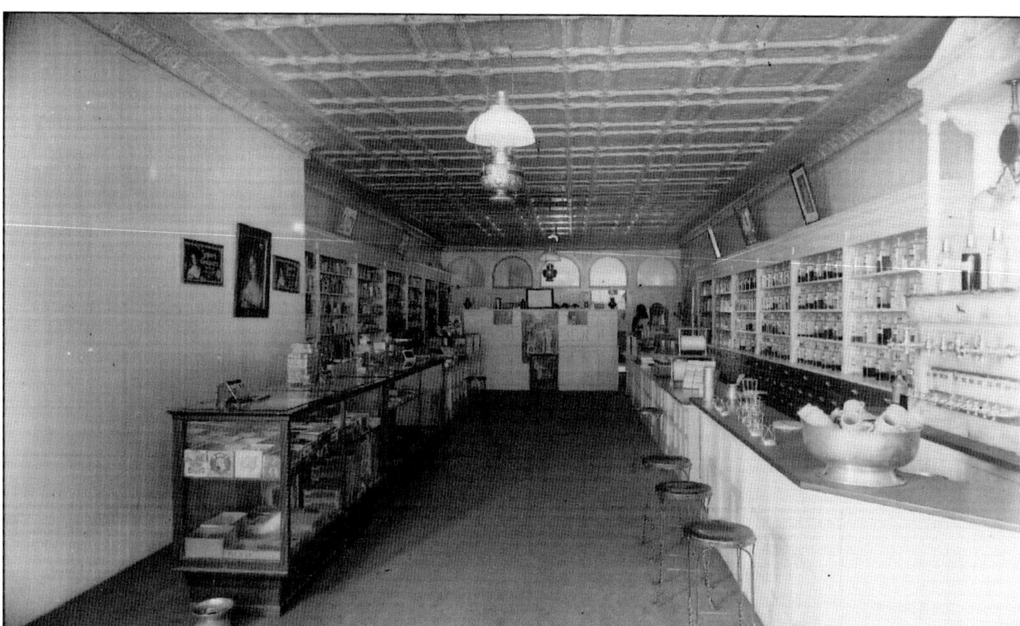

The interior of Meserves Drug Store, looking toward the back, 1903. The soda fountain can be seen on the right, and on the left are cigars and chewing tobacco. Notice the spittoon beside the counter.

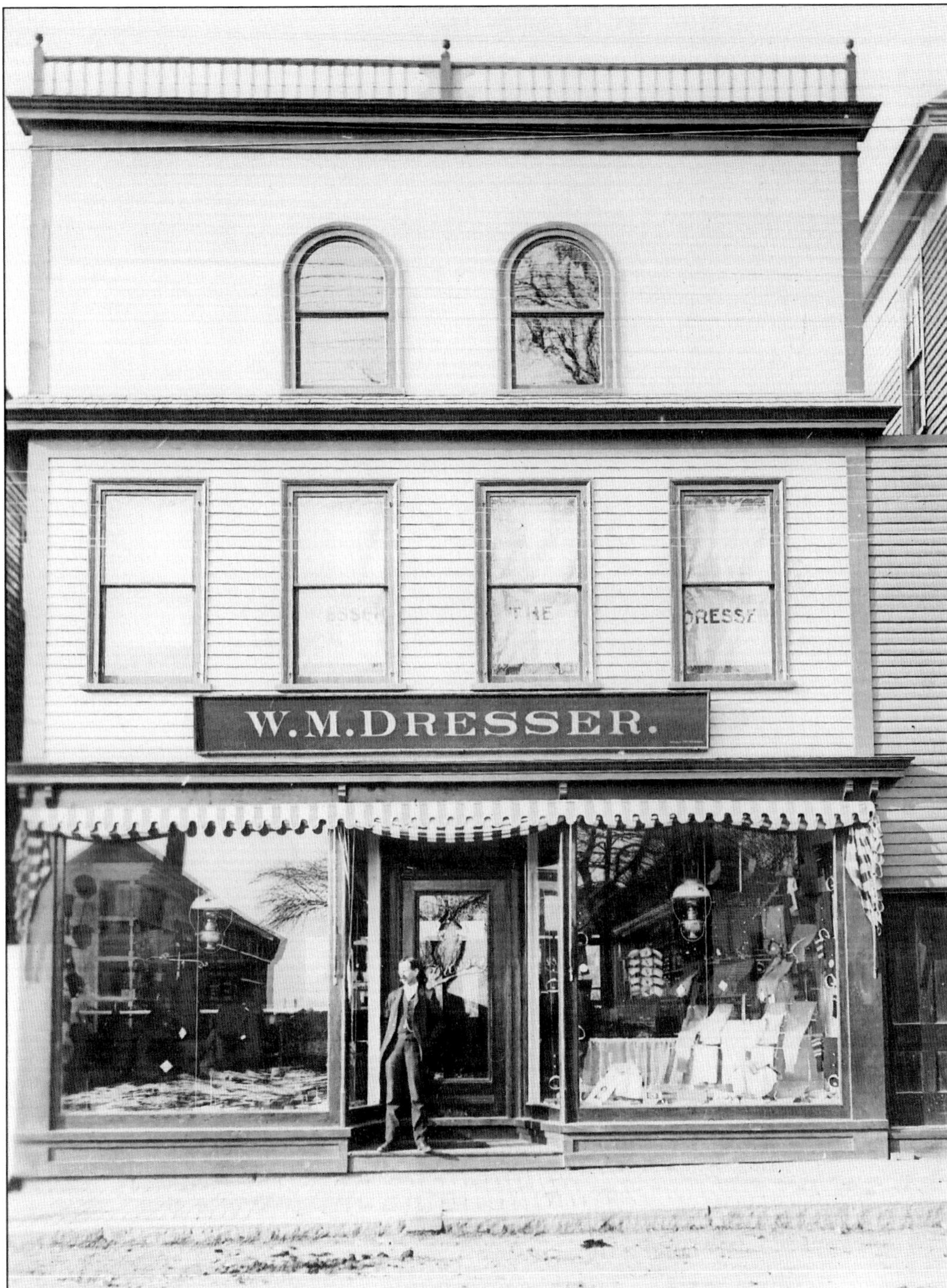

William M. Dresser and his store, c. 1910. The store was rebuilt after the Great Fire of 1903. Dresser sold men's clothing. Customers called him "Dresser the Dresser," as can be seen on the second-floor window shades.

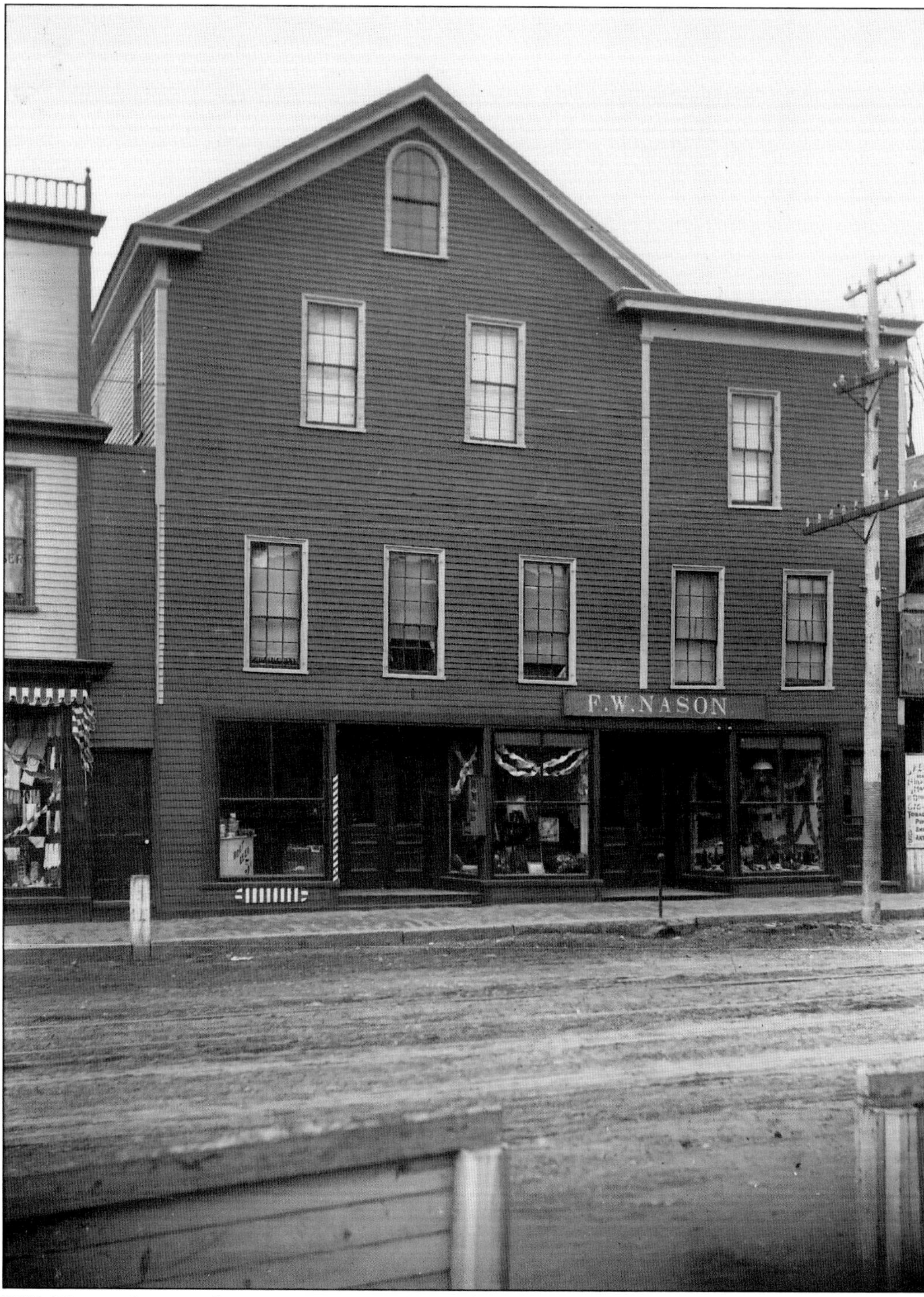

F.W. Nason china and variety store, c. 1910. The Mousam Lodge met in this building before the third floor of the Ross Block was finished. Nason sold everything from wallpaper to toys. The store closed in 1936, and the building was razed shortly afterwards. It was replaced with the present building, now part of the Kennebunk 5 & 1.00.

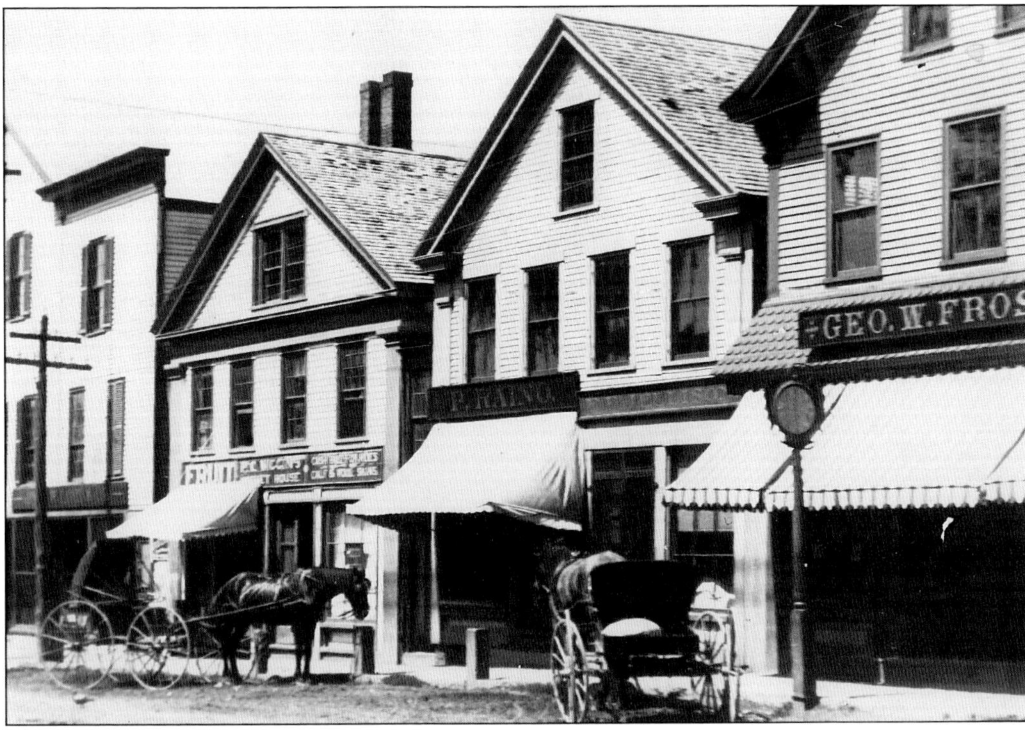

This detailed photograph of the shops on the triangle was taken *c.* 1880. The building pictured third from the right was the Blue Store, today Winston Realty. The building just visible on the left is the Clark Block (see p. 44). The two first stores were razed after fire damaged them in 1923. They were replaced by the brick building, where the Hole In The Wall restaurant is now located.

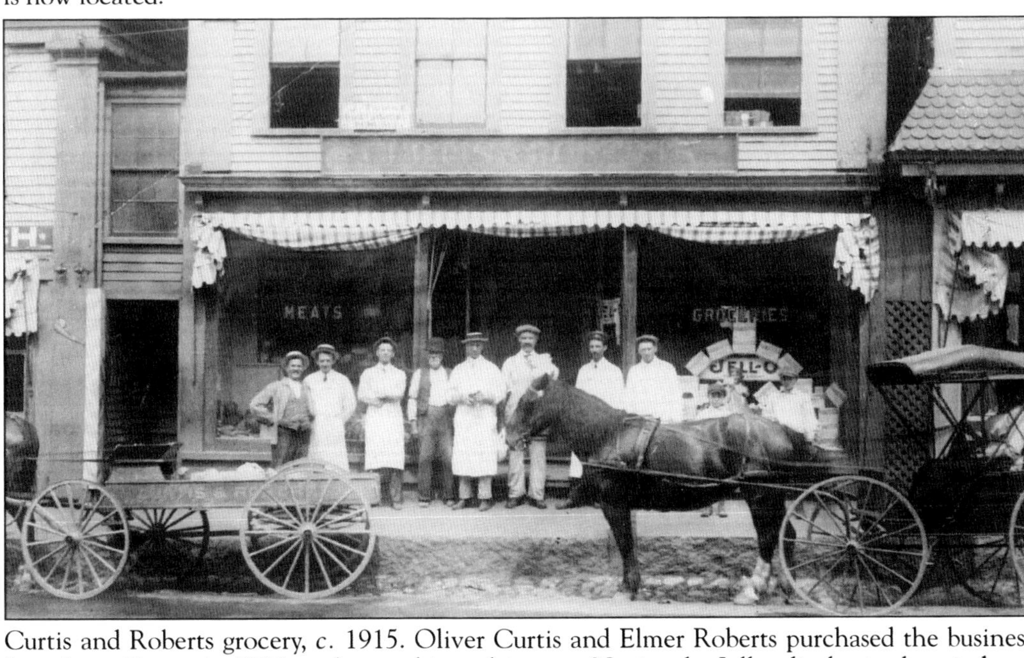

Curtis and Roberts grocery, *c.* 1915. Oliver Curtis and Elmer Roberts purchased the business from Jonas Emery in 1898, and moved it to this store. Notice the Jell-o display in the window.

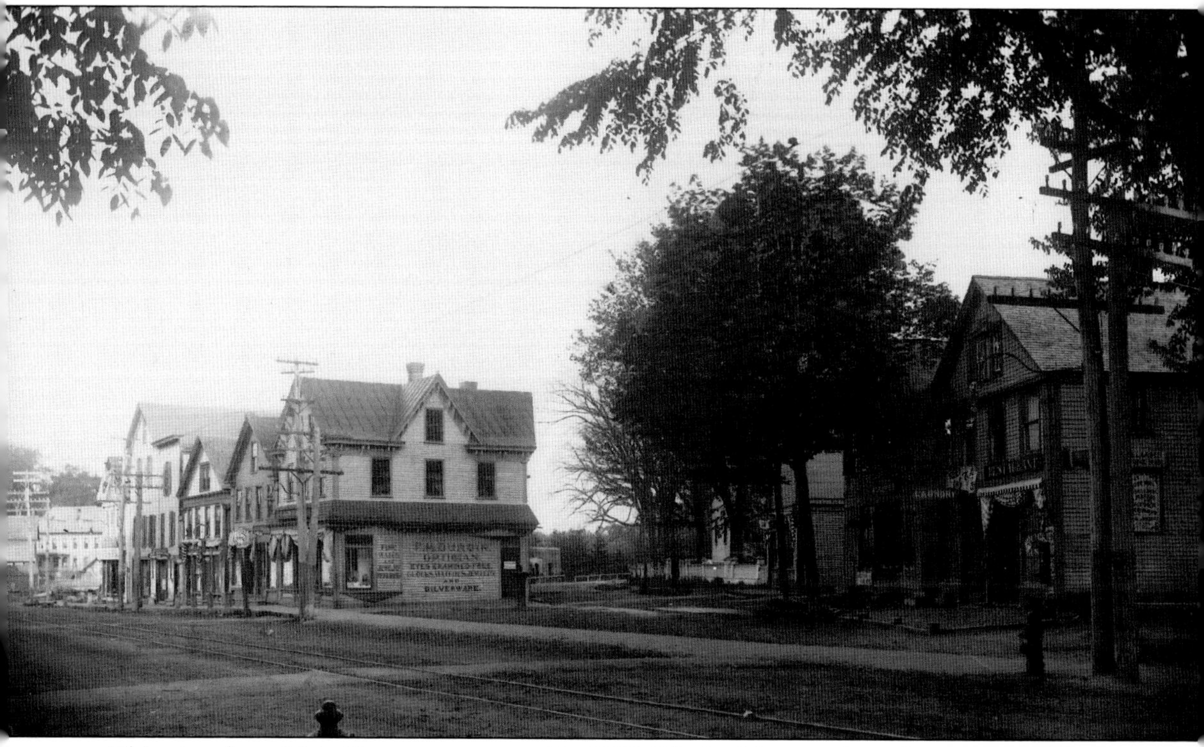

This view down Main Street was captured in 1903. The building on the right was moved there in 1842. The store next to it was built *c.* 1792 by Joseph Parsons, and was occupied by John Lord's hardware store at the time this photograph was taken. The next occupant was Reginald Libby, who remained there for many years. The building third from the left was the John Cobby store, and behind the tree there was an alley called Cobby's Lane. It was in this store building that the Kennebunk Library began in 1881. Just visible right of center is the Orrin Ross House.

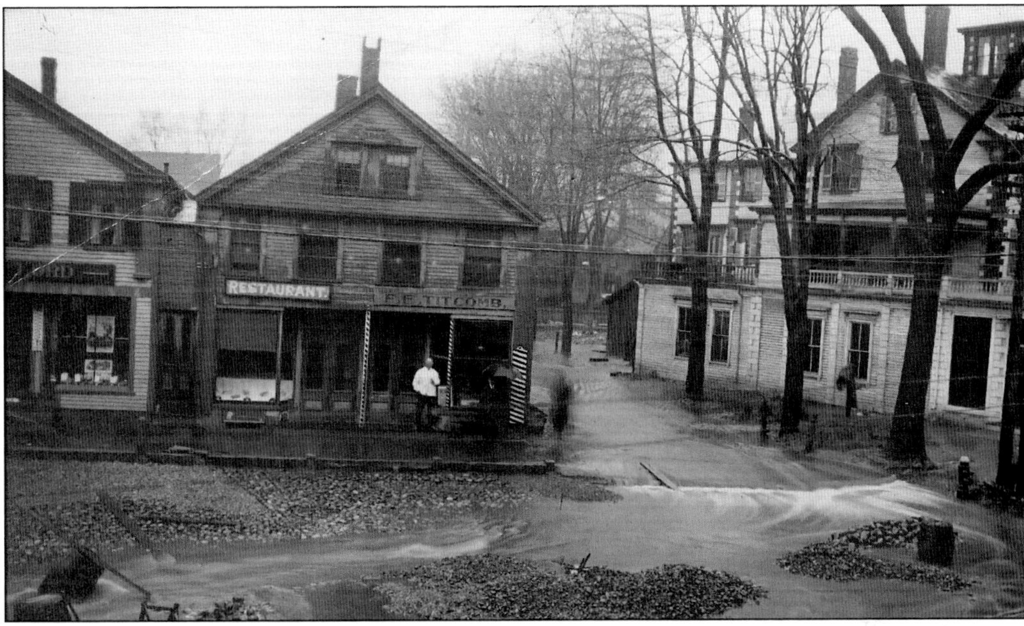

Post Office Square, looking towards Curtis Lane, 1936. The building in the center is the Beam House of the old Scotchman's Brook tannery. It was moved to this site in 1842. Scotchman's Brook, shown here flooding the street, was named for two men who were the first to operate a mill in Kennebunk, on the Mousam River, in 1680. The tannery was located on Grove Street behind the Kennebunk Inn.

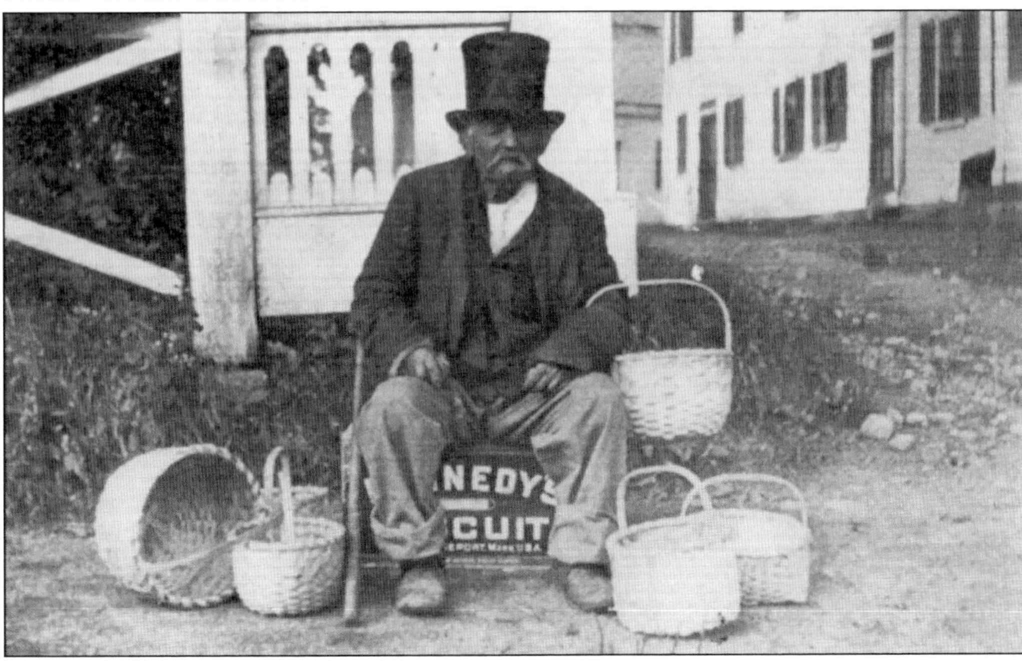

Calvin Plaisted, the basket man, pictured here in an undated photograph. He made baskets and sold them to support himself in his old age. He is sitting in front of the Orrin Ross House on Garden Street, which was razed in 1963 to make way for the entrance to the new Red and White, now Shop 'n Save.

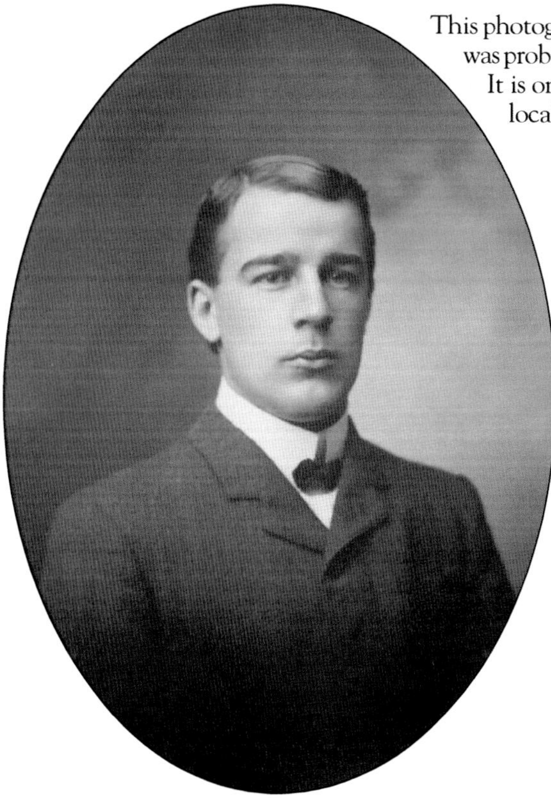

This photograph of Frank Barrett, a Kennebunk merchant, was probably taken when he graduated from high school. It is one of many turn-of-the-century photographs of local residents in the Joy collection.

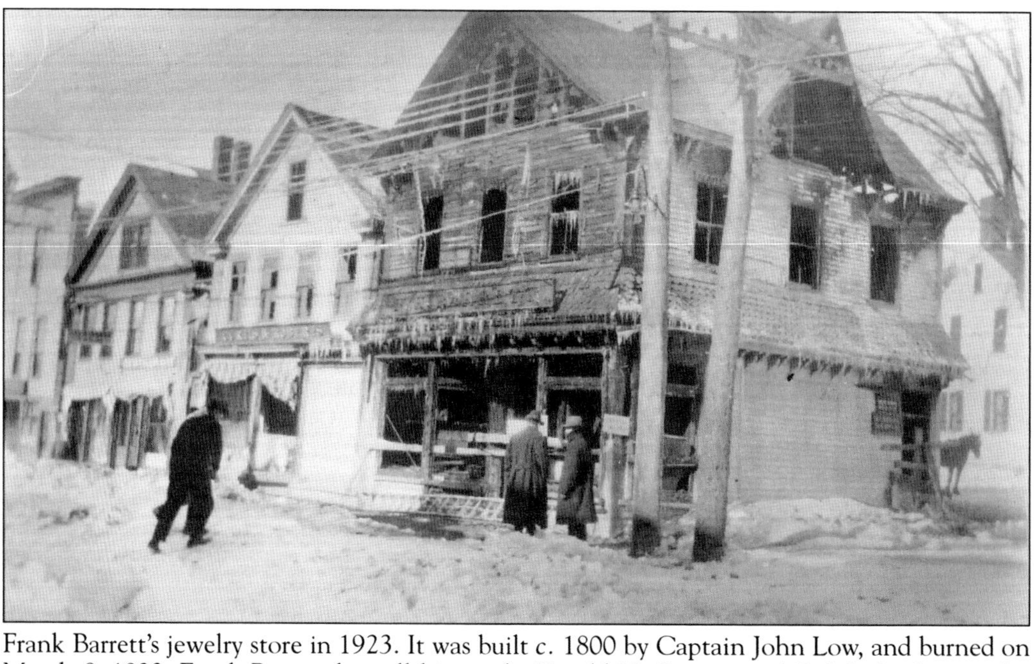

Frank Barrett's jewelry store in 1923. It was built *c.* 1800 by Captain John Low, and burned on March 8, 1923. Frank Barrett lost all his stock. Harold H. Bourne and Ralph Andrews, who had their law offices on the second floor, lost valuable papers and law books. After the fire, Oliver Curtis and Elmer Roberts bought the building and razed it.

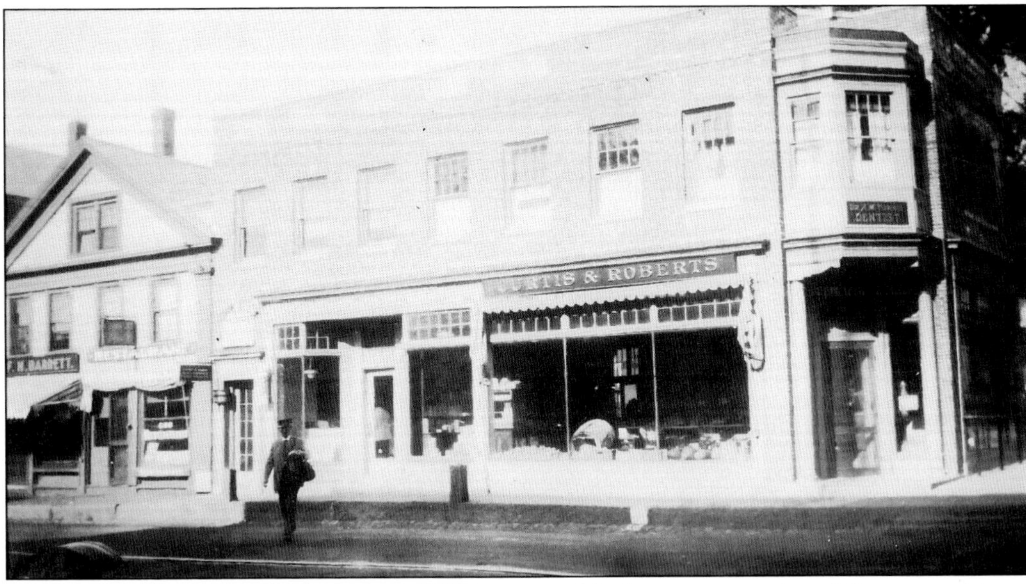

The new Curtis and Roberts store, 1925. Curtis and Roberts commissioned Boston architects Kroklyn & Brown to design their new brick building. The plate glass windows, elaborate interior fittings, refrigerated meat storage, and display cases were the talk of the town. The mailman seen here is Bent Hill.

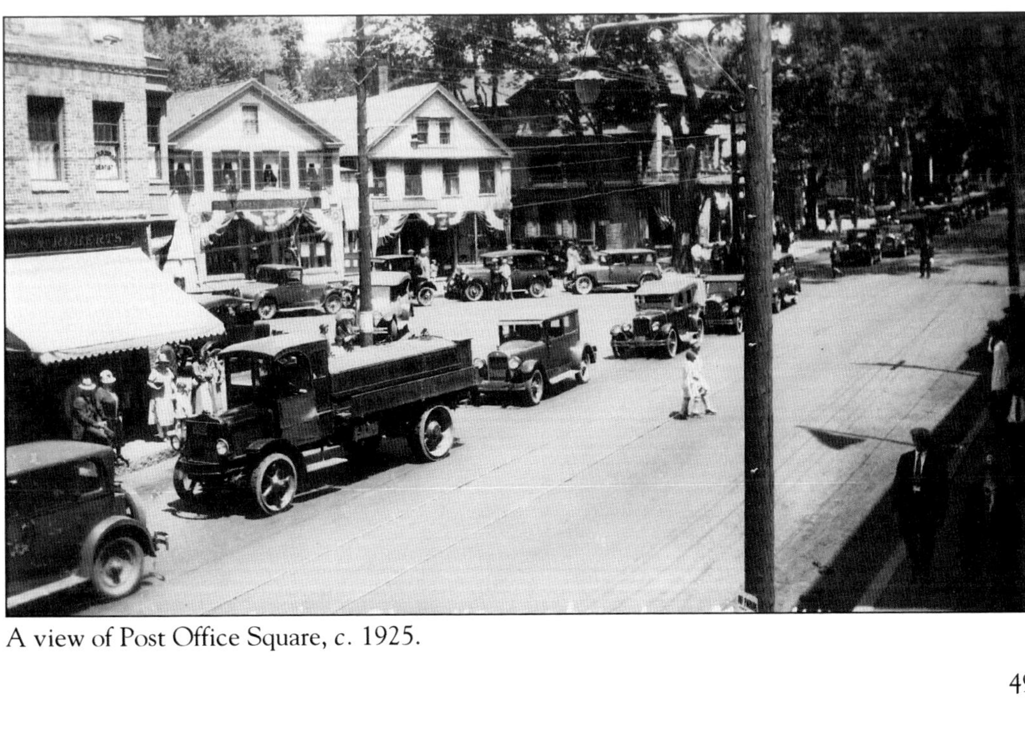

A view of Post Office Square, *c.* 1925.

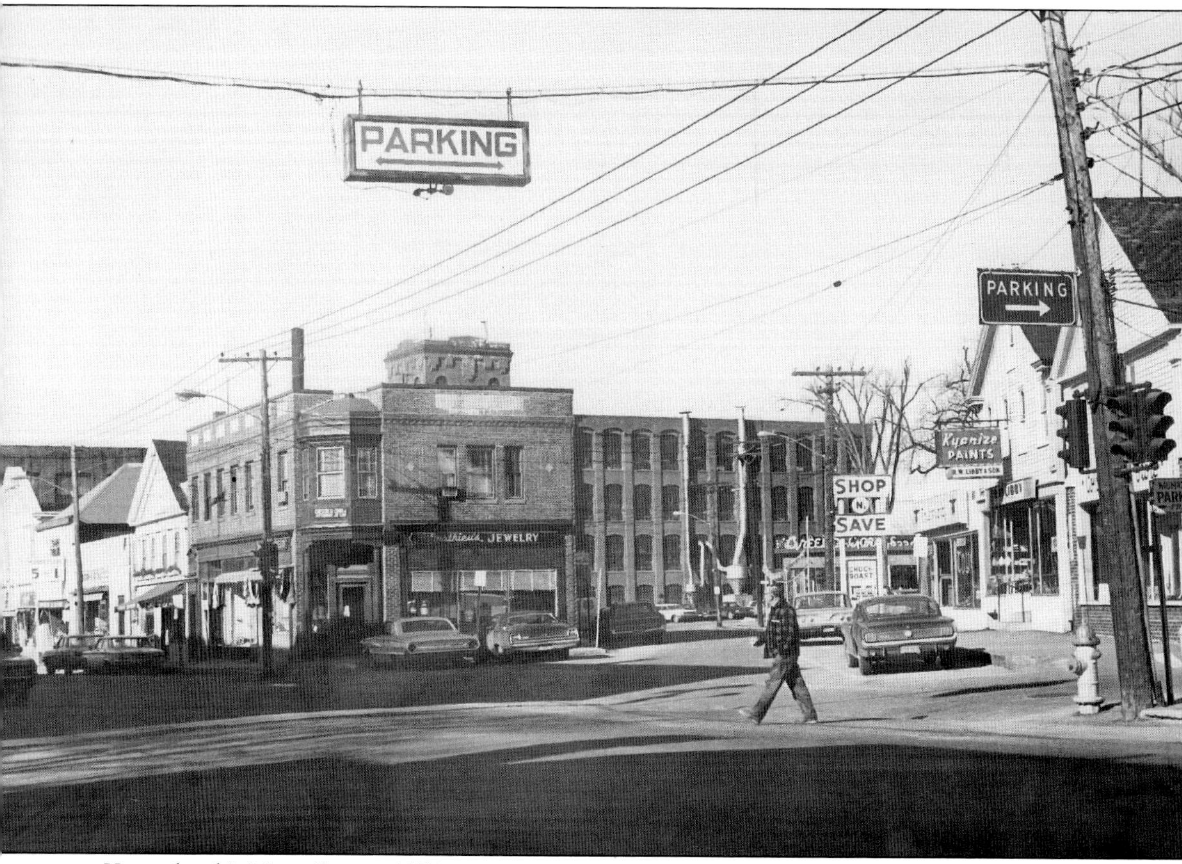

Kennebunk's Main Street, 1970.

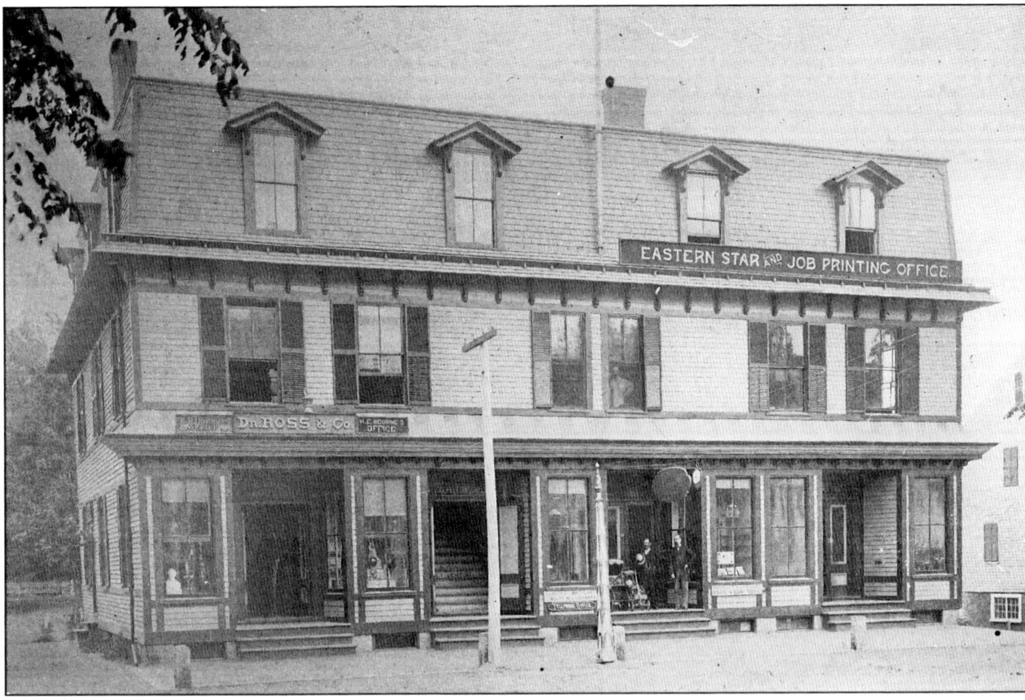

The Ross Block, c. 1885. This is the second wooden building built by Dr. Ross on this site. The first, which was similar, burned in 1881. The building pictured here burned in 1895. Dr. Ross, whose former home now houses the Kennebunk Inn, had his office and pharmacy in the store to the left in this photograph. The building in the center was a barber shop, while the store on the right looks vacant. The *Eastern Star*, later the *Kennebunk Star*, was located on the second floor.

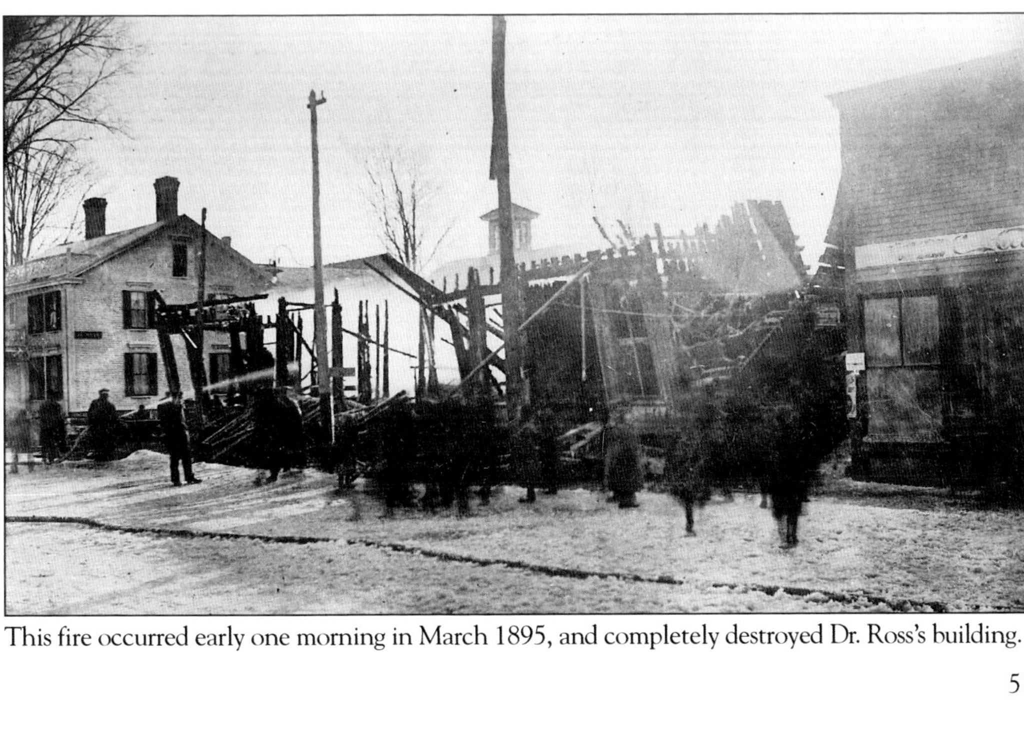

This fire occurred early one morning in March 1895, and completely destroyed Dr. Ross's building.

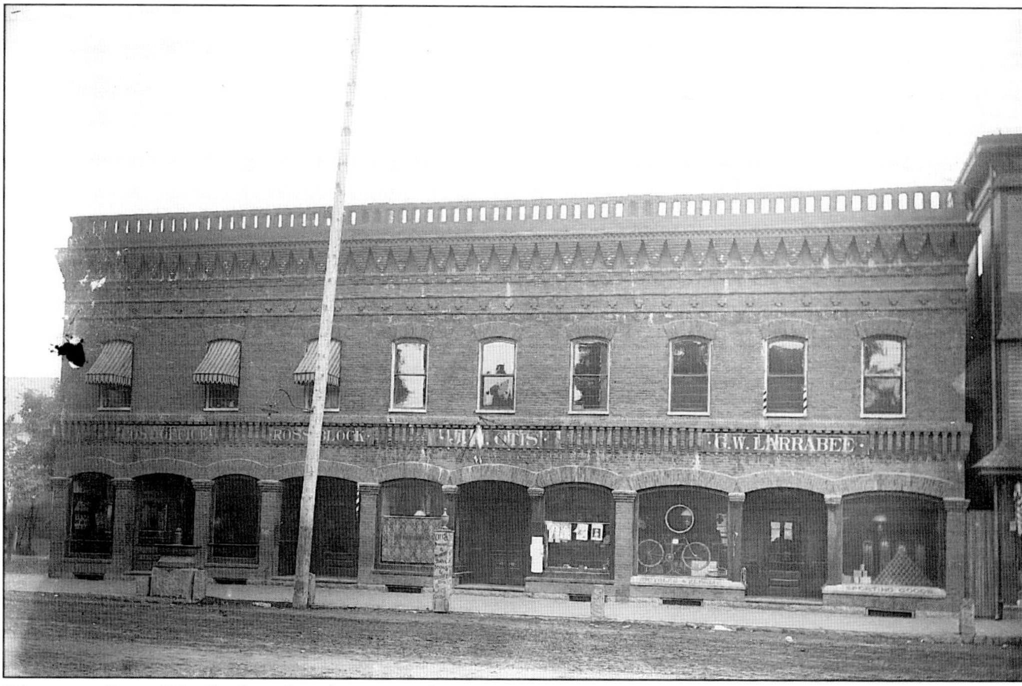

The new Ross Block shortly after completion. Apparently Dr. Ross was taking no chances this time, as the third block was built with brick. On the left is the post office; next to it stands J.H. Otis' store, and on the right is G.W. Larrabee's hardware store. Notice the horse trough in front of the post office.

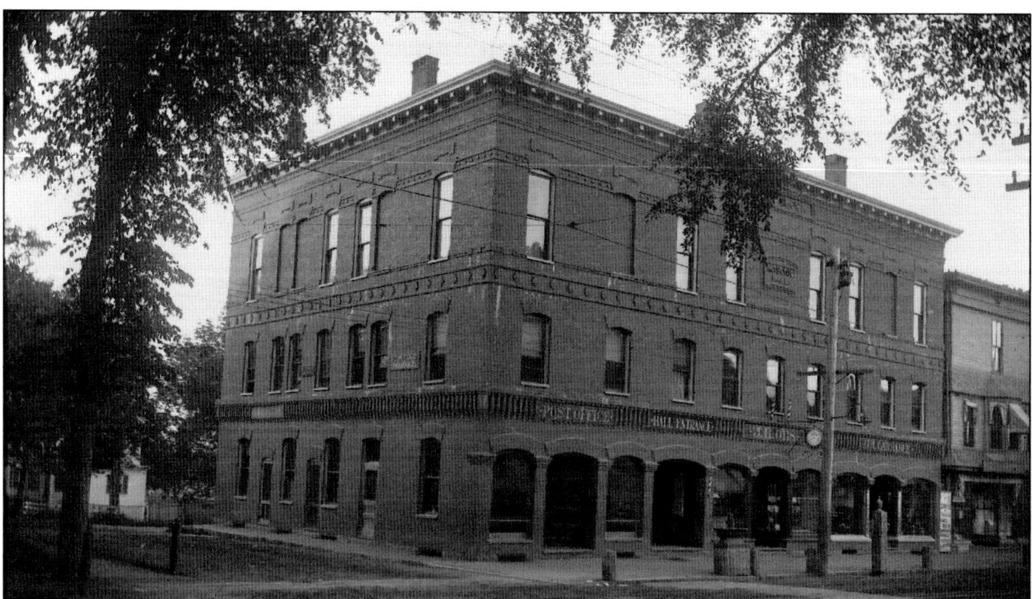

The Ross Block, following the completion of the third-floor Masonic Hall.

Virgil Fiske, *c.* 1910. In 1912, Fiske opened a drug store in the Ross Block, in the store left vacant by the post office when it moved across the street. Eventually, Willis Gowen took over from Fiske in 1954 and remained in business until 1975.

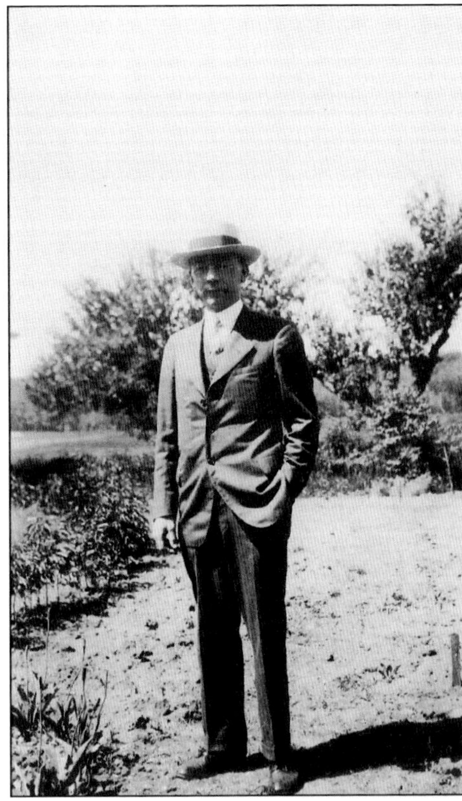

This photograph, dated July 1909, shows a paper boy on Main Street in front of the "1810 House."

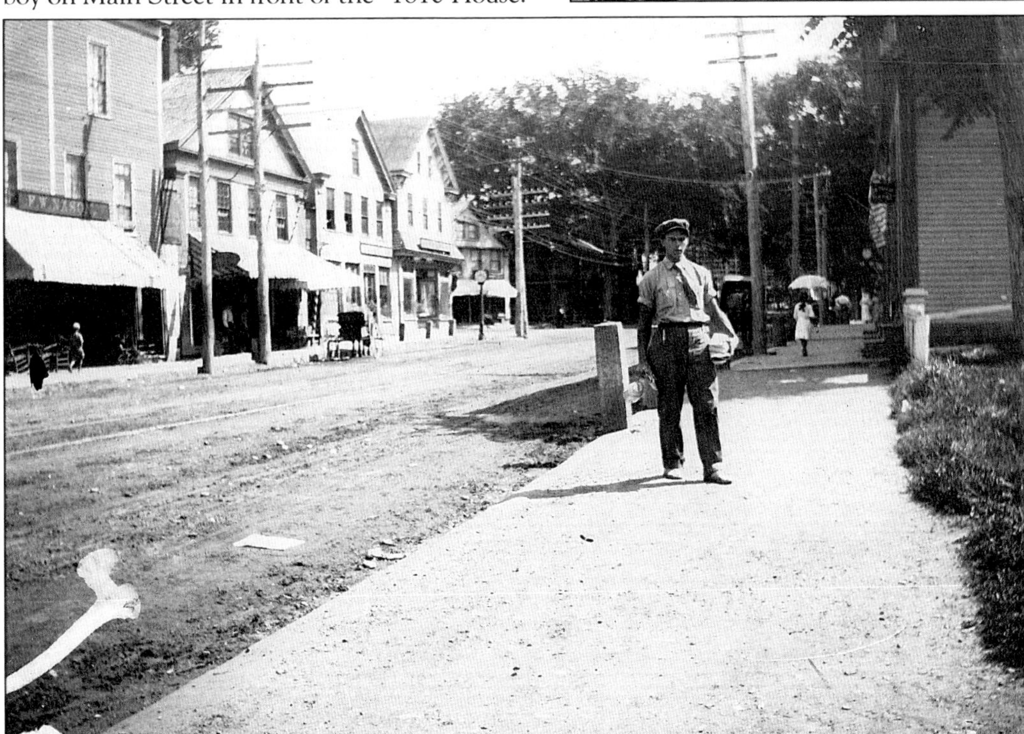

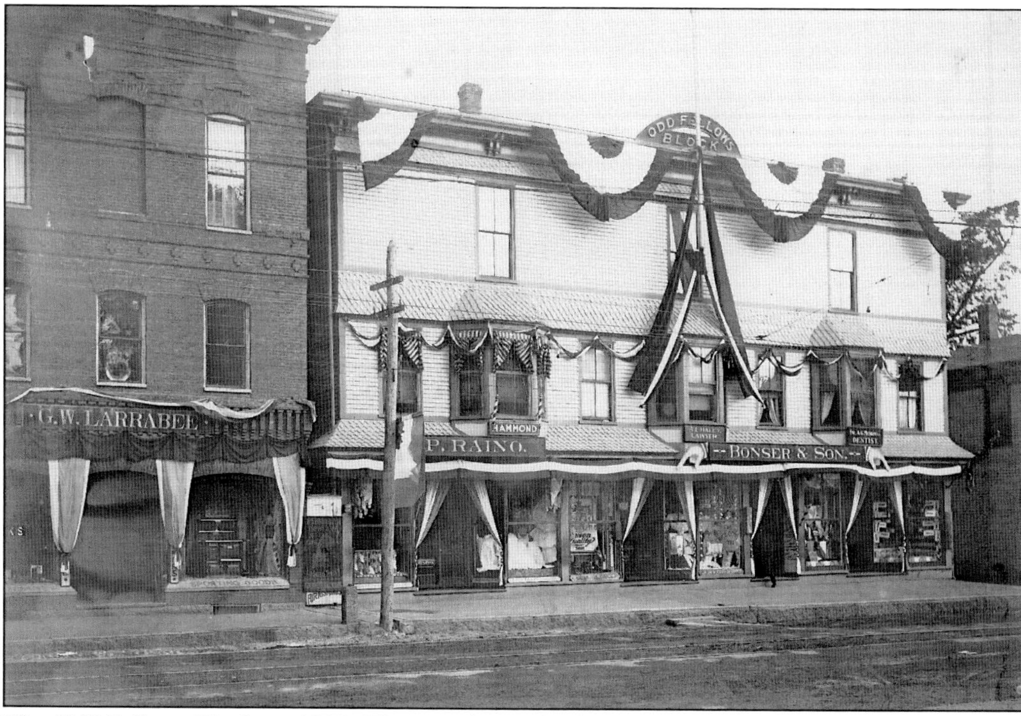

The Odd Fellows Block, c. 1920. This was formerly the site of the Michael Wise House, which was moved in 1895 to make way for this block. In this photograph, you can see the original, decorative shingle work.

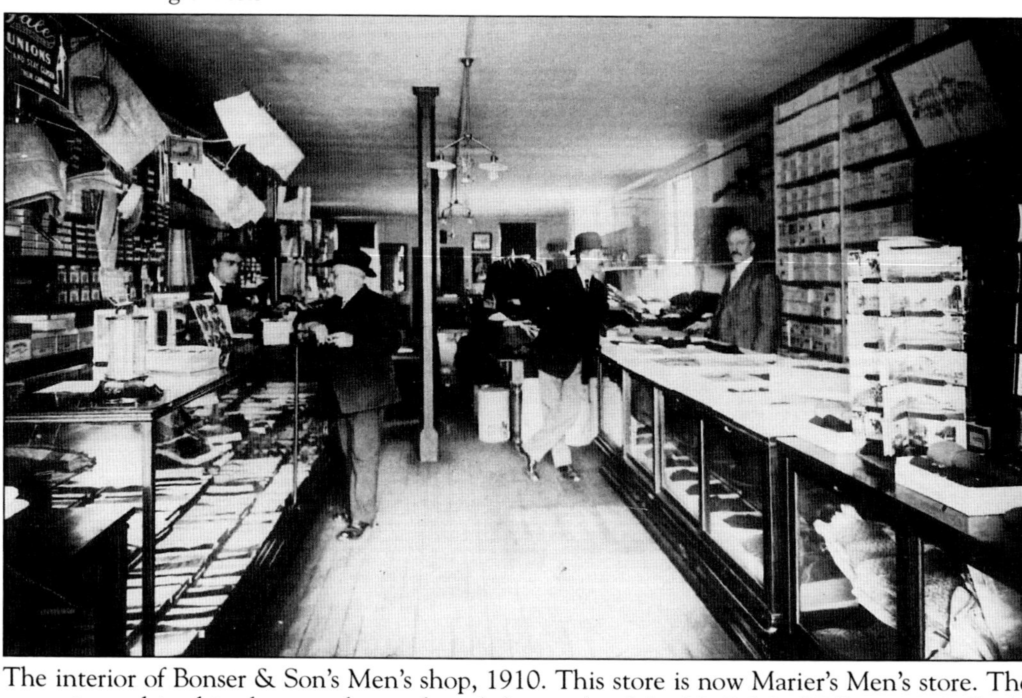

The interior of Bonser & Son's Men's shop, 1910. This store is now Marier's Men's store. The men pictured in this photograph are, from left to right, John N. Balch, William McCulloch, unknown, and Frank Bonser.

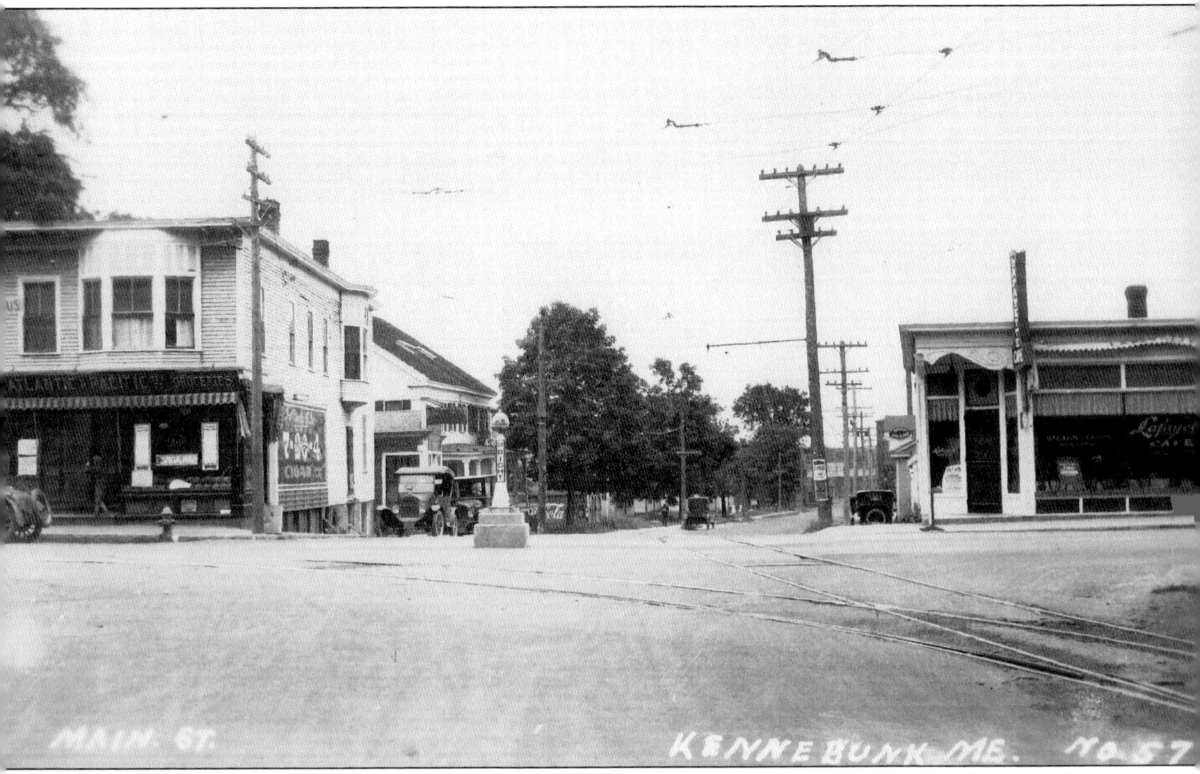

Looking down Water Street, *c.* 1925. The blinker was installed in 1925. The building on the right was constructed in 1912 by Nathaniel Thompson Jr., who set up an ice cream and soda shop there called Thompson's Spa. In 1915 S.M. Parillo bought it; he operated a fruit stand here, but eventually sold the building to George Baitler, who opened the Lafayette Cafe (shown in this photograph). Baitler later purchased the Ross Home and opened the Kennebunk Tavern, now the Kennebunk Inn. The building on the left was built after the Great Fire of 1903. The offices of Reagan and Adams are located there today. The first building on this site was moved to Storer Street *c.* 1858. The next building was built by Mark Ford, who moved it to Pleasant Street, where it still stands. In the mid-1880s a third building, which became the Old Corner Grocery store (owned by George Cousens), was moved onto the lot. This building originally sat on the site of today's Lafayette Center; it was then moved across the street to the present site of the Rotary Park, before it was moved to its final site. George Cousens owned the grocery until it was bought by the A&P Company, which left Kennebunk in 1969.

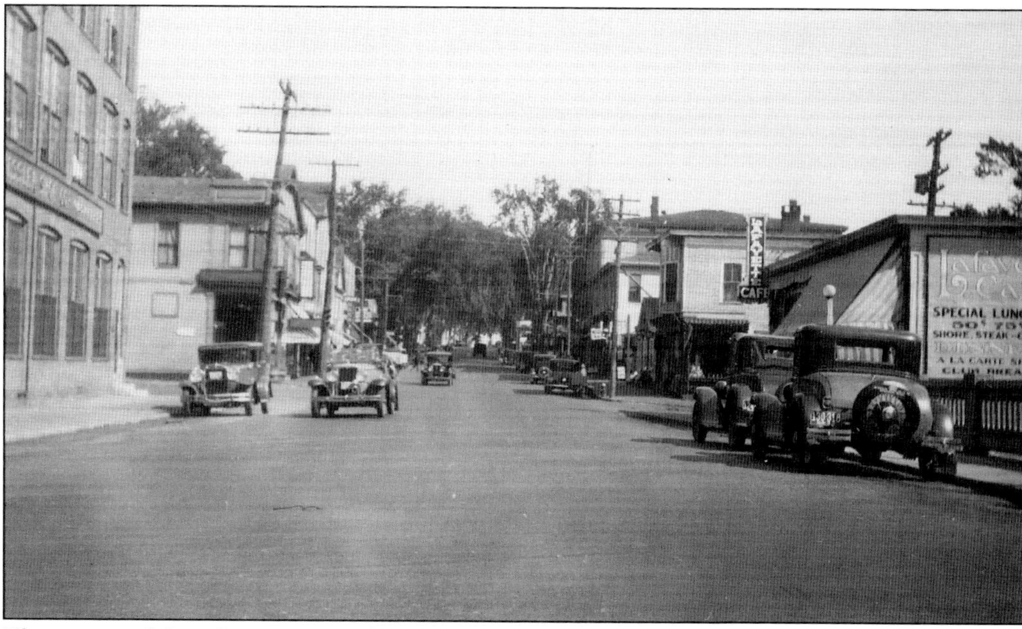

This view up Main Street, across the Mousam River Bridge, was captured *c.* 1925.

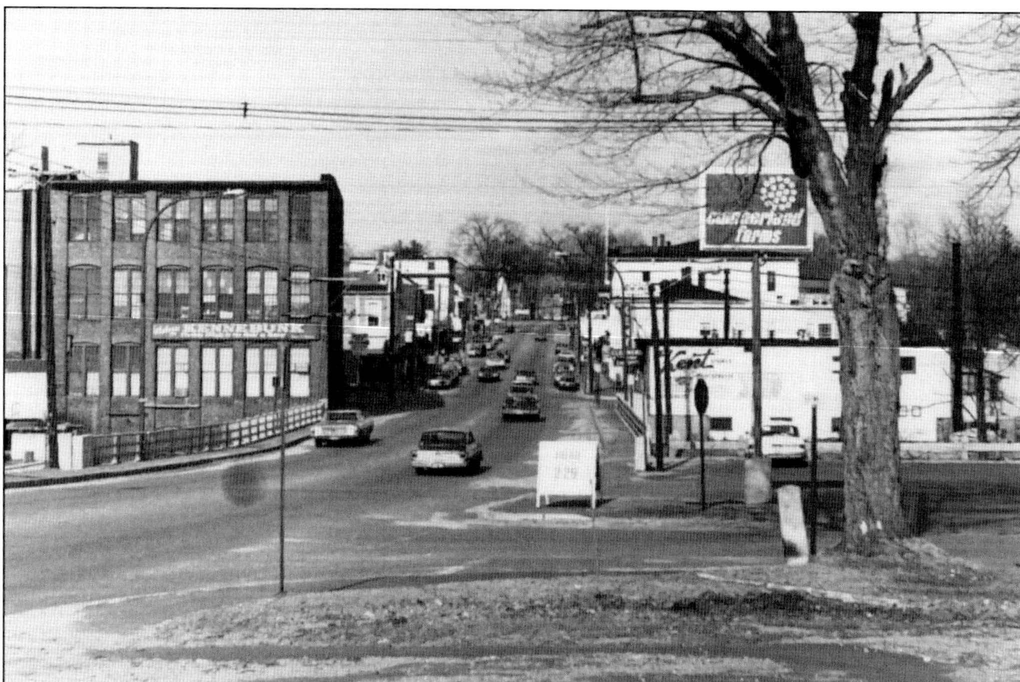

This photograph was taken in 1970. Kents Cleaners opened in 1939, and was later owned by Jack and Gussie Ephross, who ran the laundry business for thirty-three years until retiring in 1972. That building, and the old Kennebunk Steam Laundry behind it, were razed in 1976 to create the Rotary Park.

Three

Mills and Factories

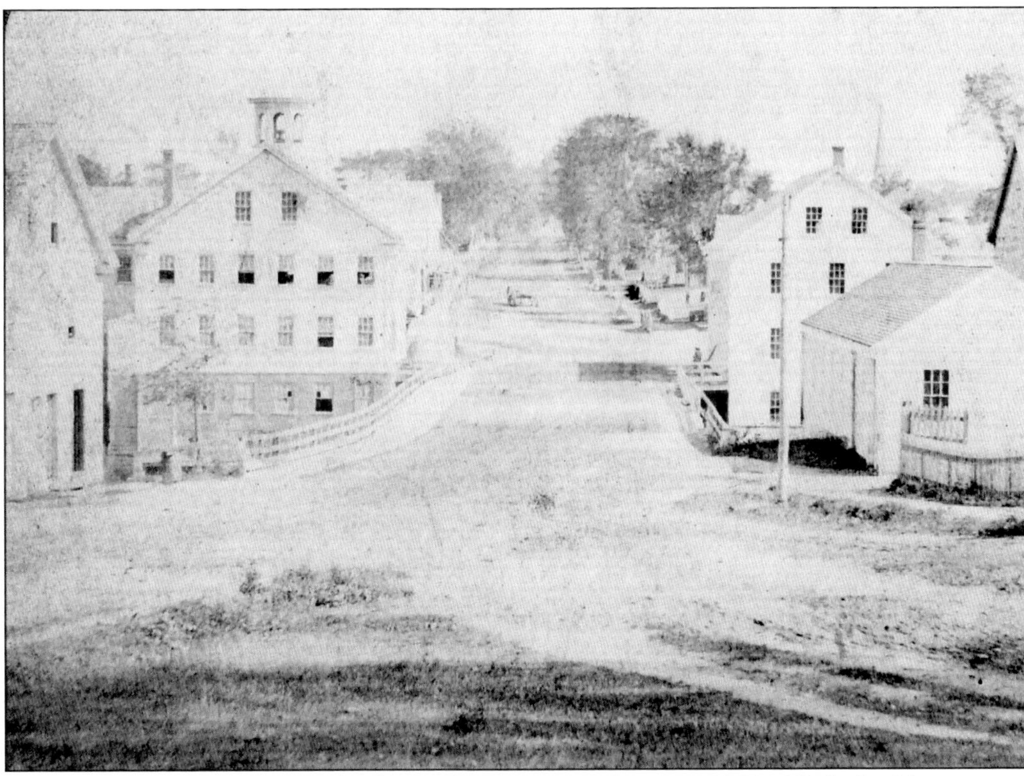

Looking up Main Street from the front of the Mousam House, *c.* 1871. All the buildings appear to have been painted white, and seem well-kept and orderly. Kennebunk's early mills on the Mousam River were water-powered. Dams held back the mill ponds, and the height of the dams created the "fall" and the pressure needed to operate the water wheels and turbines. The three-story Hewitt Mill, with its bell cupola, was constructed about 1825 and later moved to Water Street in 1877. The small, single-story building on the right of the photograph was a counting house. The Grist Mill can be seen across the bridge.

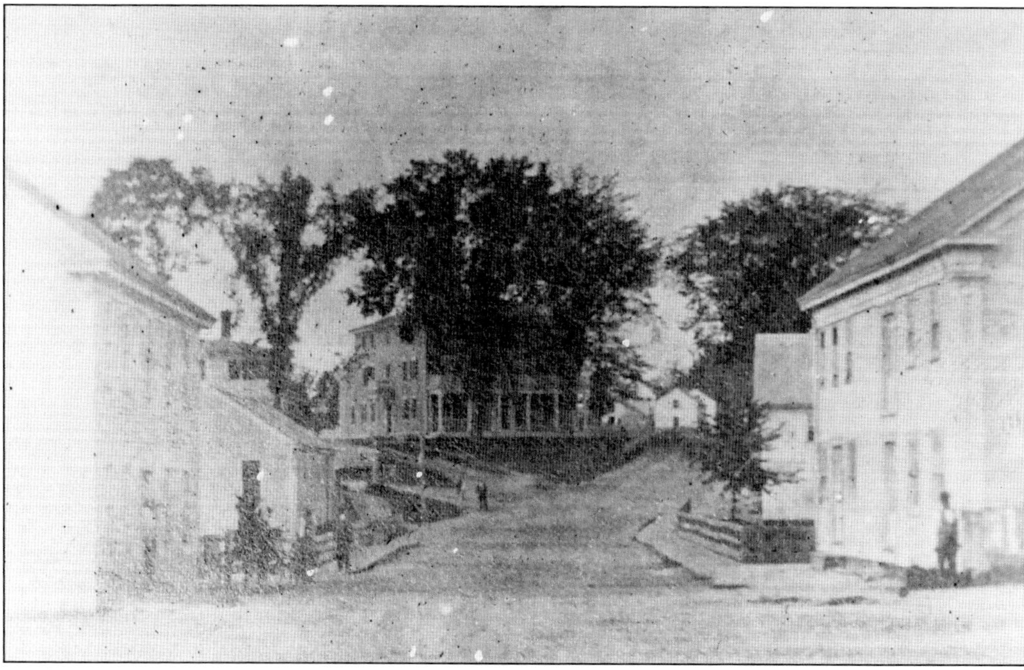

Looking towards the Mousam House on Tavern Hill, c. 1870. The Hewitt Mill is on the right, with the Grist Mill on the left.

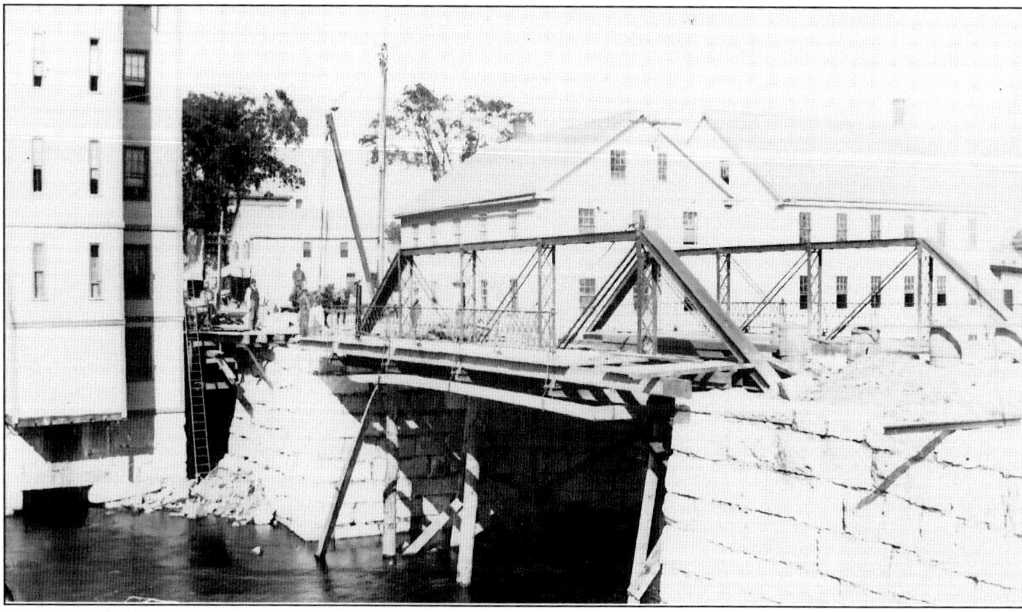

A view of the new iron bridge under construction.

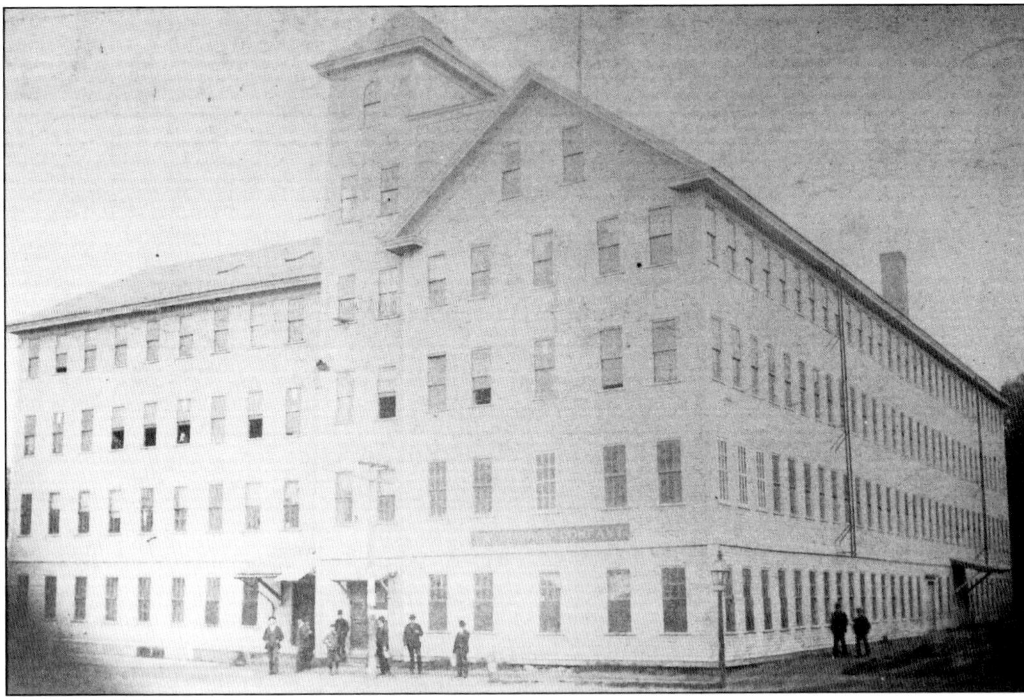

The Davis Shoe Co. building, *c*. 1890, at the corner of Main and Storer Streets. Oliver Littlefield and John A. Lord built a factory on this site in 1825. They manufactured window sashes and doors. In 1851 the Warp Mill Co. took over the mill and refitted it for textile work. The Hewitt Manufacturing Co. leased the building to spin cotton in 1865. In 1877 the mill shown above was built and leased to the Mechanic Falls Shoe Company. In 1885 the Hewitt Mill was moved to Water Street and another addition was made to the factory, on the Main Street side facing the river. The Davis Shoe Factory failed in 1891 and the building was next occupied by Mason Cobb. That company was followed by the Rice and Hutchins Shoe Co., who occupied the building until 1902. The building was empty when it burned in 1903. After the fire, the town of Kennebunk, which owned the site, built a brick factory in its place.

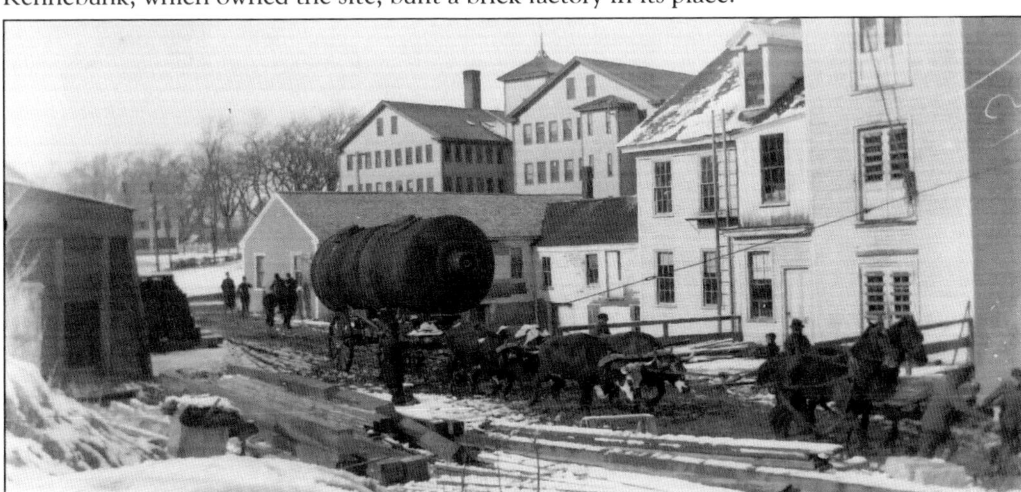

The Davis Shoe Factory under construction.

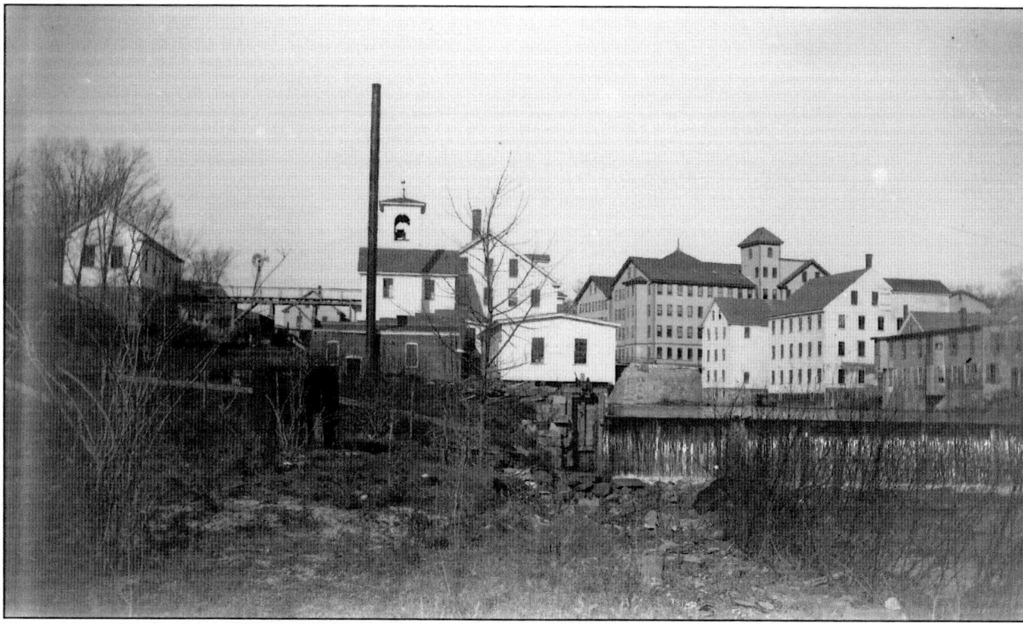

A view of the Mousam River, looking upstream, *c.* 1890. The paper mill can be seen in the center of this photograph. The small, white frame building is the dam control house.

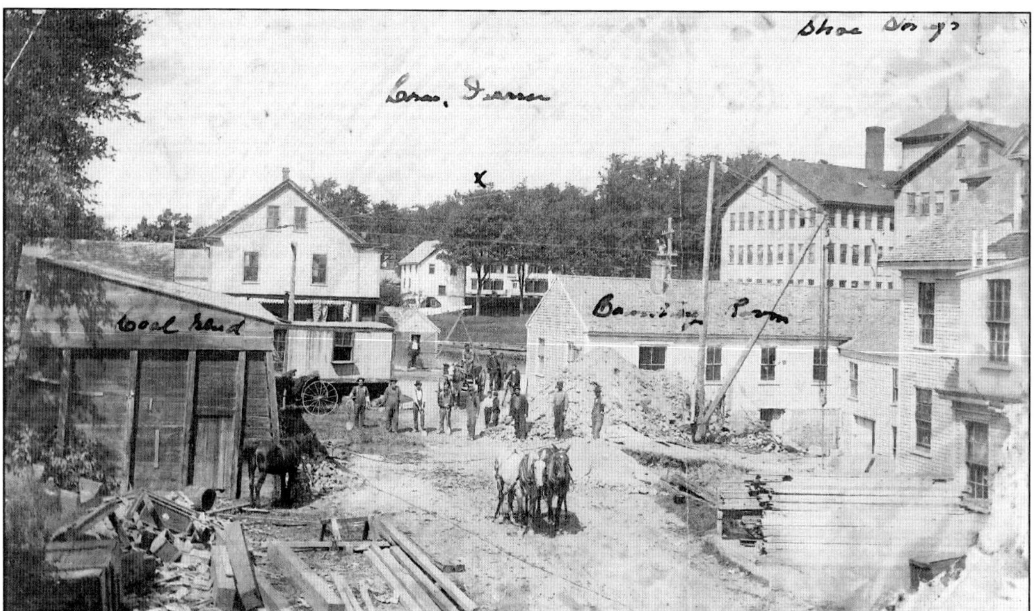

The paper mill complex, at the corner of Brown and Main Streets, *c.* 1885. It was built in 1868 for the Union Lace Co., which made shoe laces. The building was razed in 1922 and replaced by the Jones Diner. In 1969 Cumberland Farms built a store on this site. The horses seen in the center of the photograph are standing on a town-approved road called Eagle Street, which ran parallel to Brown Street and down to the river, where building bricks were made and an iron foundry operated. The single-story counting house was razed in 1922. The Davis Shoe Factory and other buildings can be seen above the lower dam.

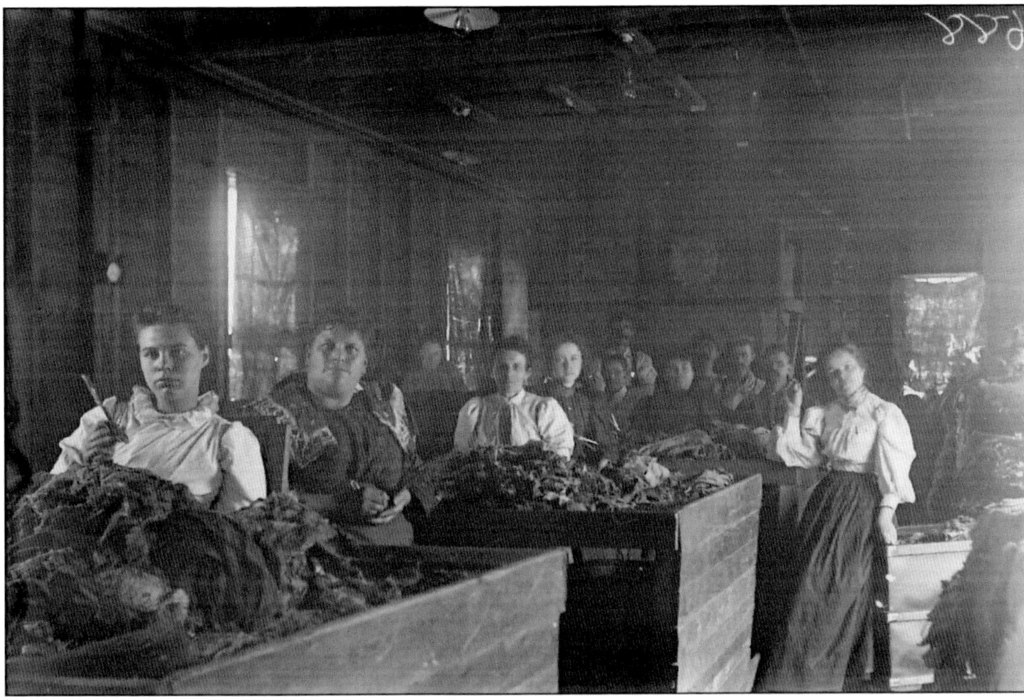

Women sorting and cutting rags for the paper mill. The date of the photograph is unknown. Local children would collect old rags and bring them to the mill, which paid them by the pound. The rags were recycled and used in the manufacture of paper.

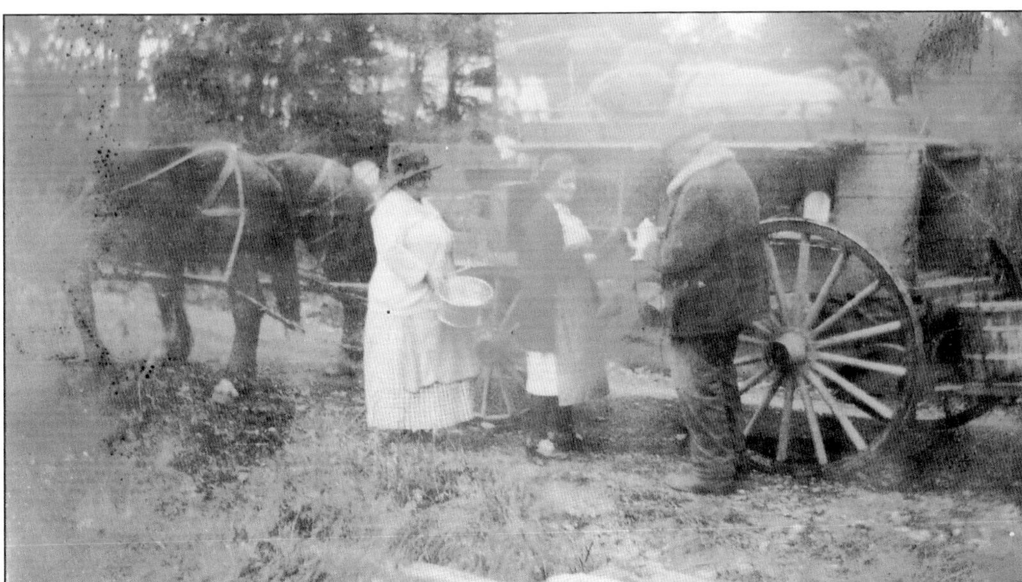

T.S. Bachelder, the local tin peddler and rag collector. In this photograph he is collecting rags from housewives. Bachelder paid them in merchandise from his assortment of tinware and kitchen utensils.

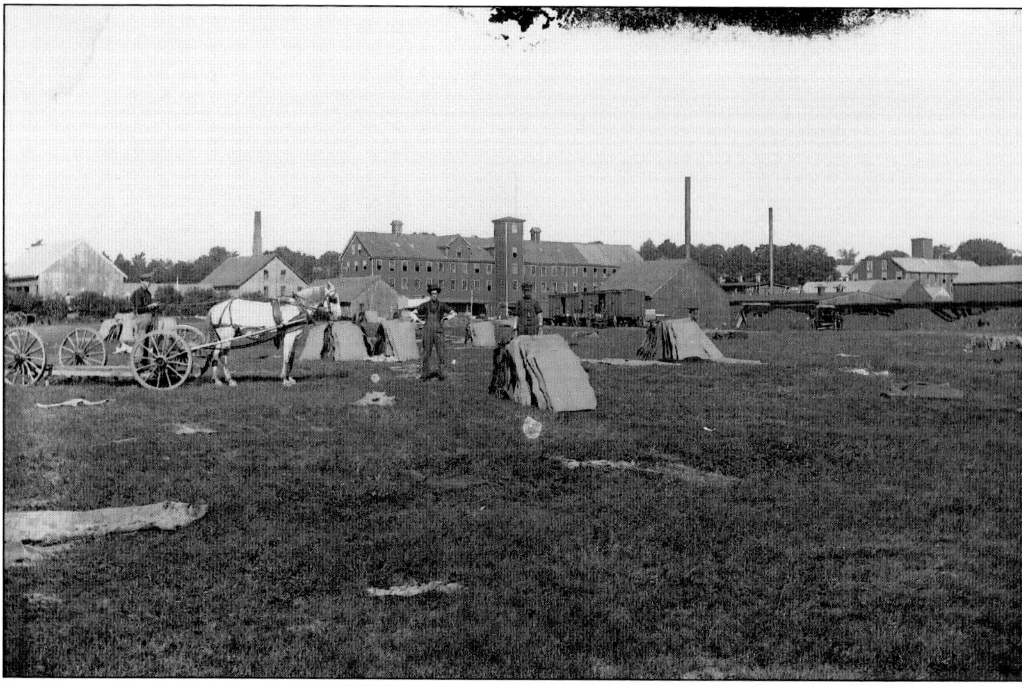

Leather piles dry in the fields off Water Street, *c.* 1895. The leather was used to manufacture steamer trunks and other products.

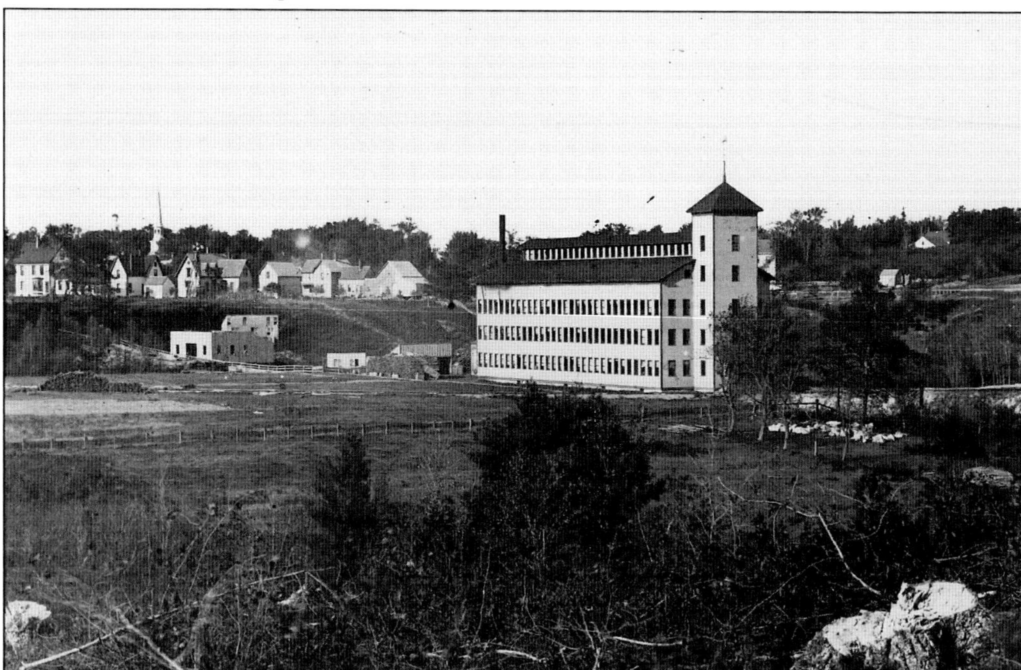

The Shoe Counter Shop, shortly after its construction in 1889 for the Kimball Brothers of Haverhill, Massachusetts. They stayed just a few years before the Mousam Counter Co. took over the building. The building was destroyed by fire in 1932. Shoe counters are the small piece of leather or fiberboard, at the back of shoes or boots, which support the heel of your foot.

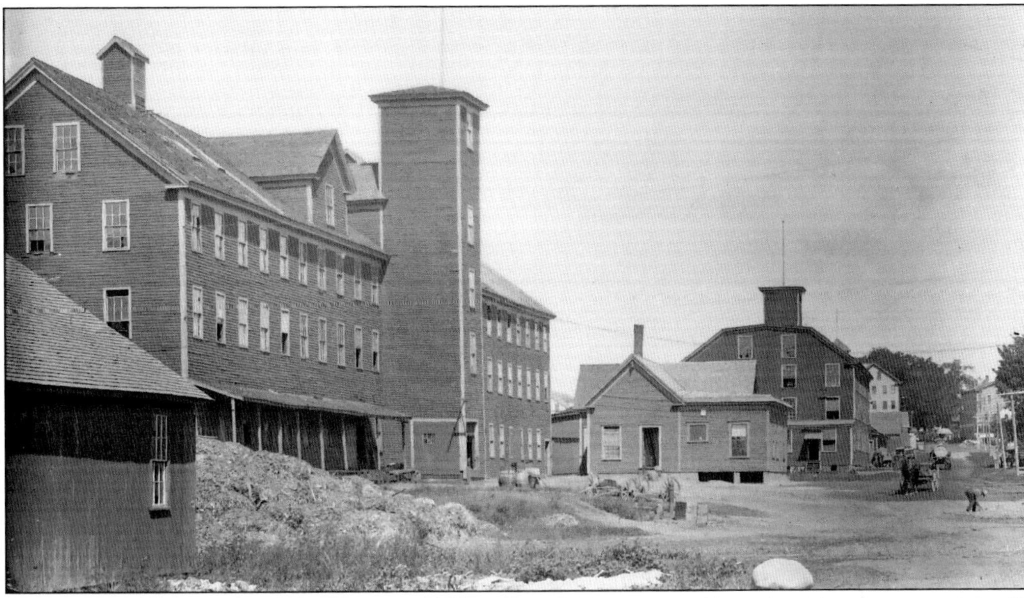

A c. 1895 photograph of the National Fibre Board Company. These buildings were originally built in 1875 for the Mousam Manufacturing Company. In 1881 National Fibre was founded and moved their operations into these buildings. In 1915 National Fibre became the Rogers Fibre Company. They ceased operations in 1958. The Leatheroid Co., the Counter Shop, and National Fibre were the largest employers in town.

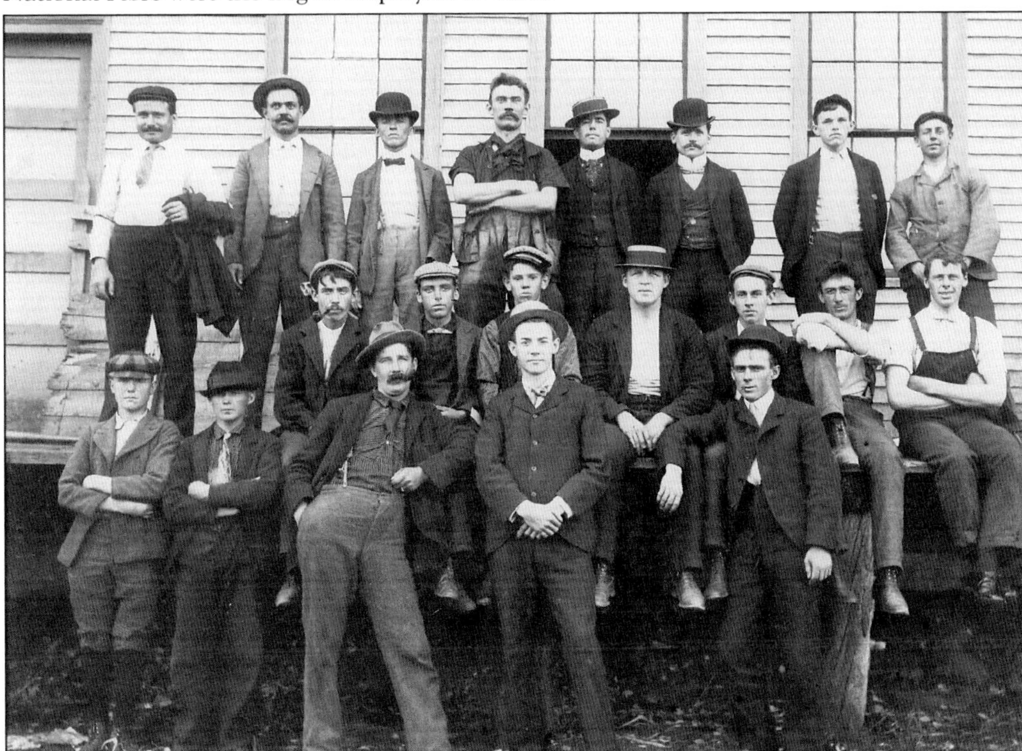

A group of workers from the Leatheroid Co. pose for a photograph, c. 1895.

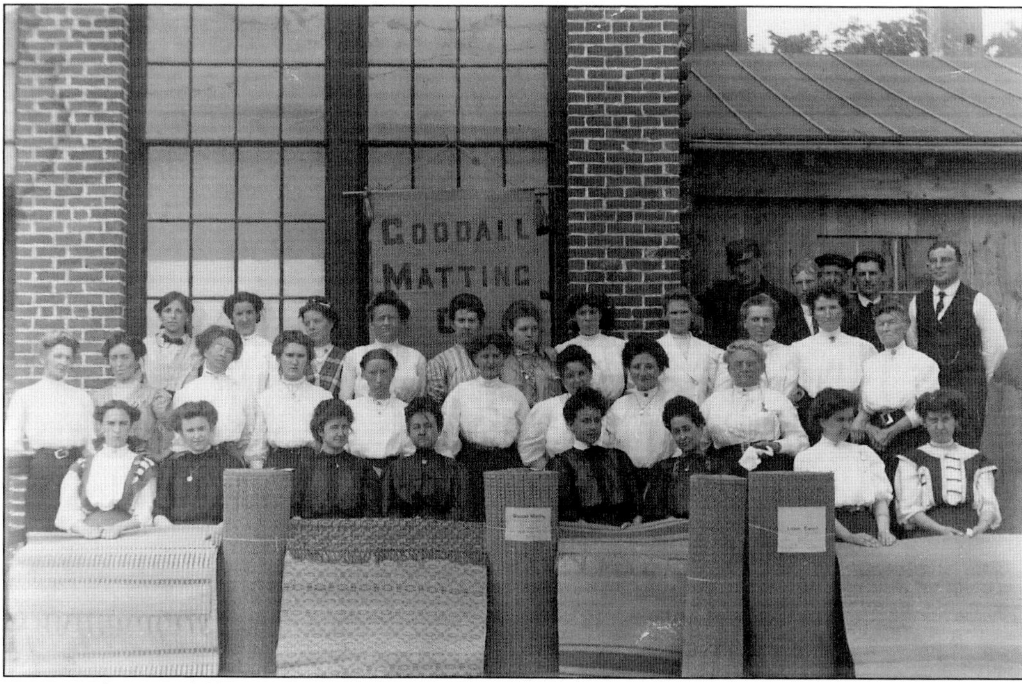

In 1904 the Goodall Matting Co. of Sanford leased the new brick factory built on the site of the burned Davis Shoe factory. This photograph dates to about 1910 and shows the different mats the company manufactured.

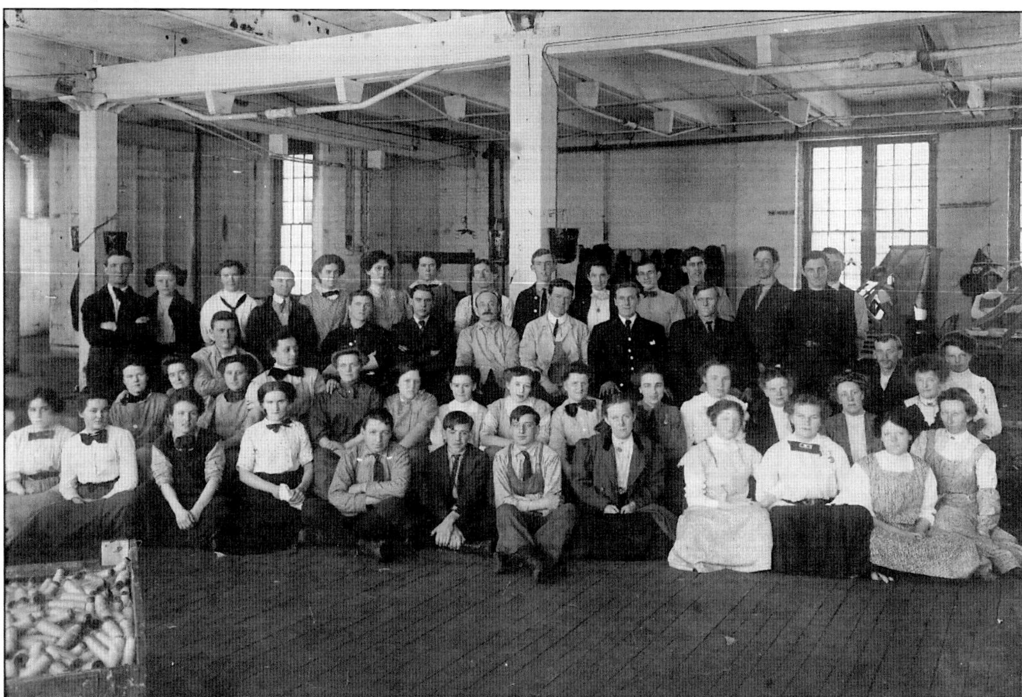

This photograph was taken *c.* 1915 and shows the interior and the employees of the Goodall Worsted Co.

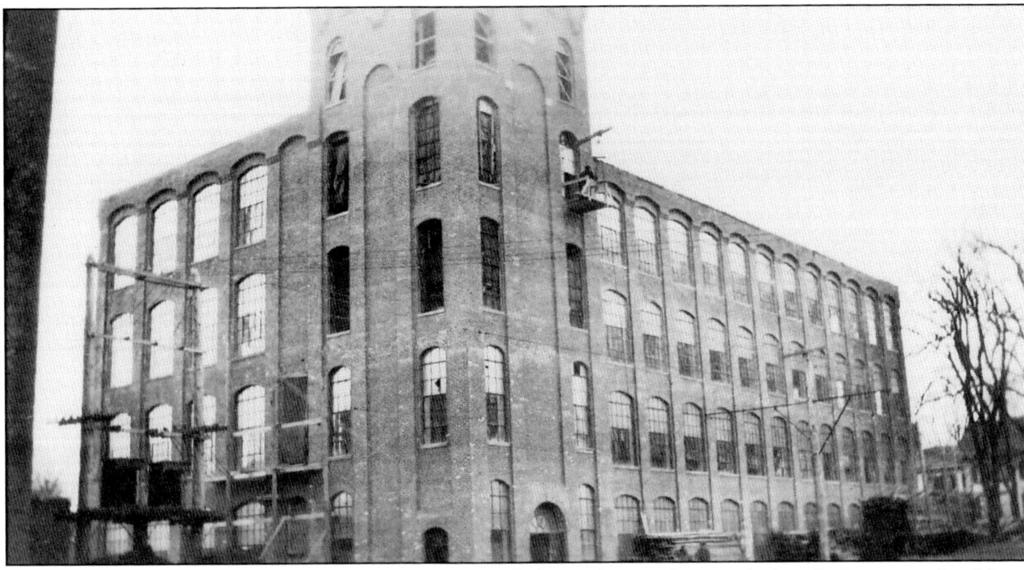

In 1918 the Goodall Worsted Co. was expanded on Storer Street, behind the main building. The new building included a four-story tower. These two photographs show the construction of this addition to the old building. In 1926 the company left Kennebunk and the Kesslen Shoe Company moved into the building.

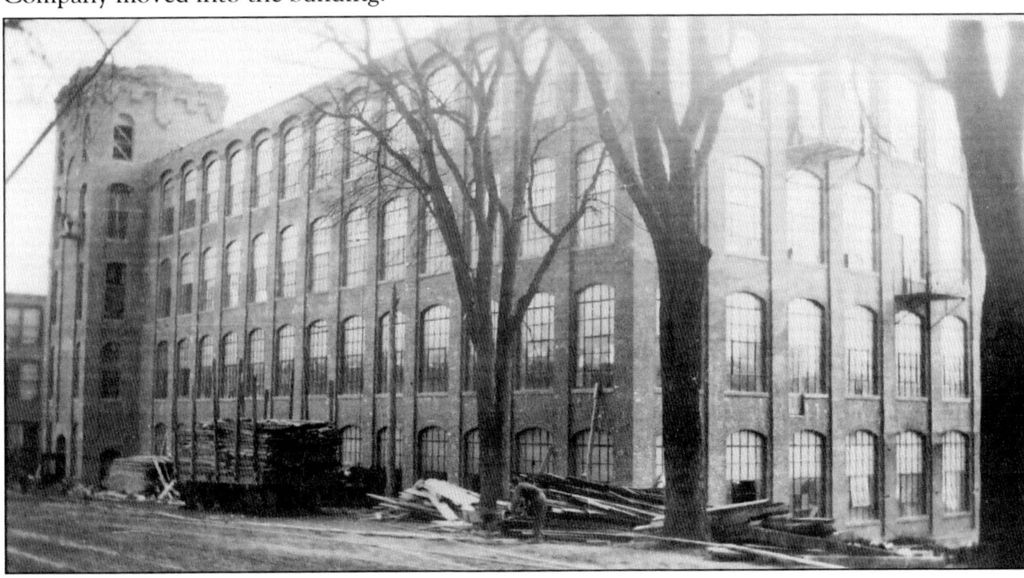

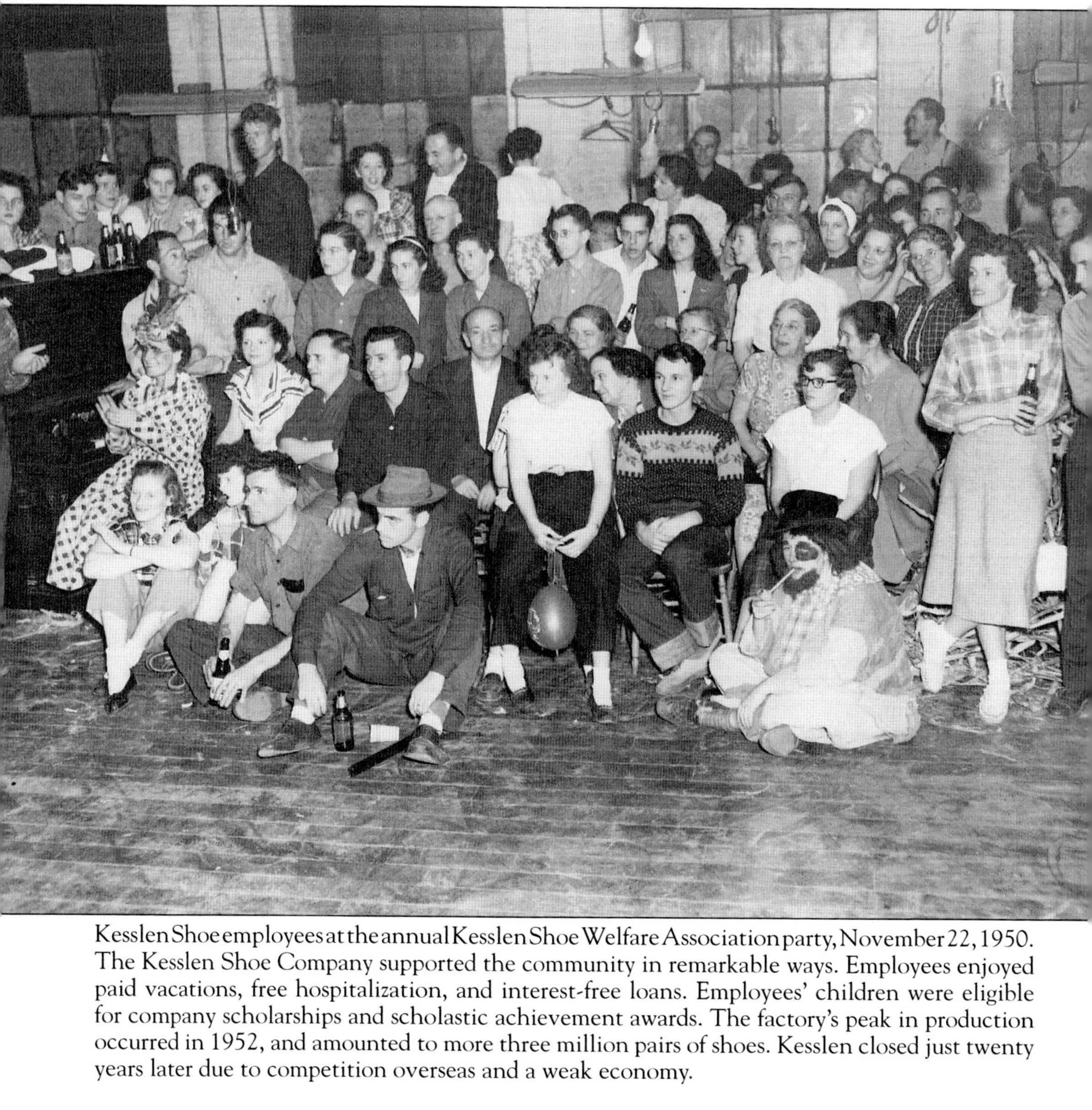

Kesslen Shoe employees at the annual Kesslen Shoe Welfare Association party, November 22, 1950. The Kesslen Shoe Company supported the community in remarkable ways. Employees enjoyed paid vacations, free hospitalization, and interest-free loans. Employees' children were eligible for company scholarships and scholastic achievement awards. The factory's peak in production occurred in 1952, and amounted to more three million pairs of shoes. Kesslen closed just twenty years later due to competition overseas and a weak economy.

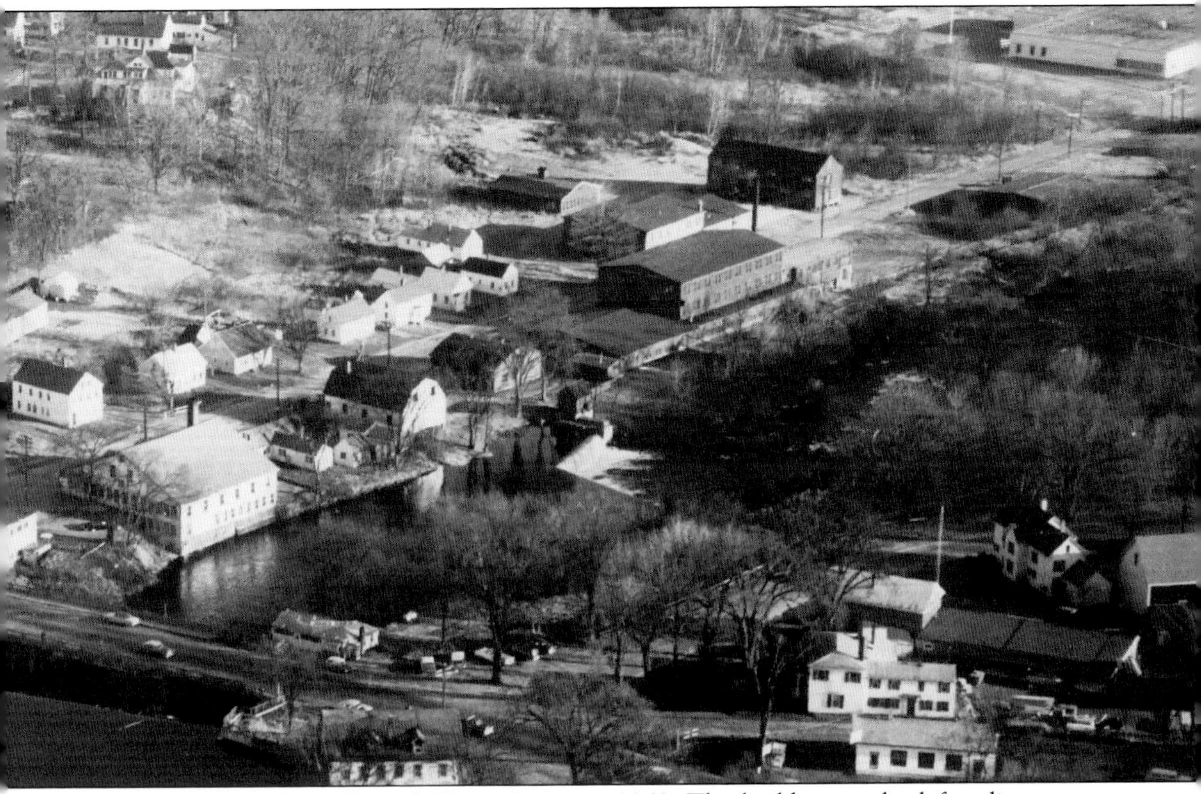

An aerial view of the mills and Water Street, *c.* 1960. The building to the left, adjacent to the river, is the old Kennebunk Steam Laundry. The large building with the smoke stack, further along the edge of the river, is the Rogers Fibre Company. It has since been converted to apartments. Jones Diner is visible on the opposite side of the river, next to the bridge. The large building to the right of the photograph was constructed in the early 1950s as the Holyoke Worsted Mill. A few years later it was bought by the Keuffel & Esser Co. from Hoboken, New Jersey. The small building to the right of the photograph occupies the former site of the Mousam House. Above it is the Jefferds House.

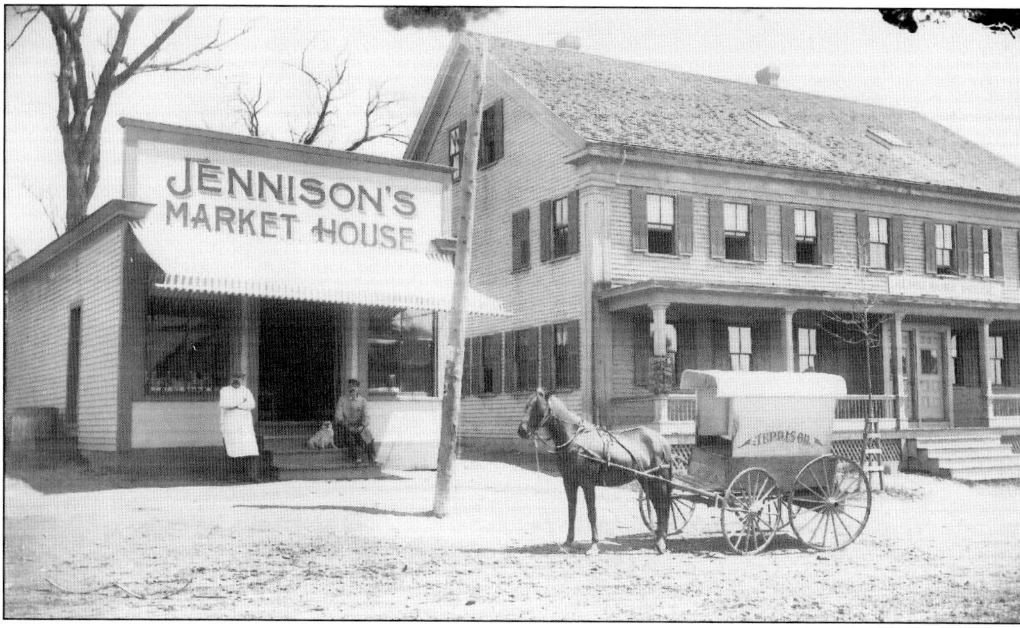

Jennison's Market and the Kennebunk House, c. 1900. The Kennebunk House Hotel was the former Hewitt Mill which was moved to Water Street in 1877. Underground pipes from the Davis Factory supplied the new hotel with steam heat and hot water. The name was later changed to the Riverside Hotel. In this photograph, the hotel appears unpainted and the tree in front has probably just been planted.

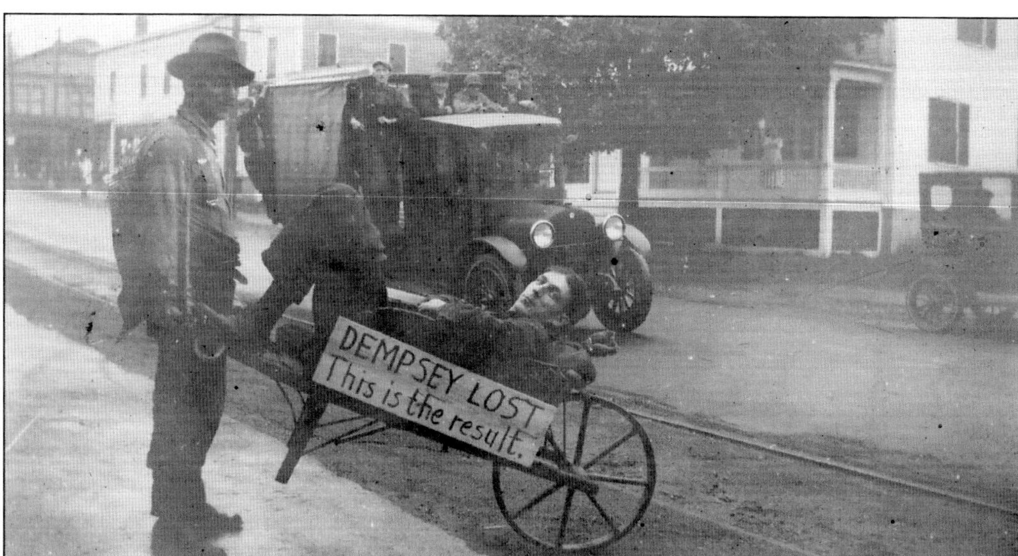

The same scene as the previous photograph, on September 15, 1923. Look at how the tree has grown! The Kennebunk House has also been spruced up and painted. This photograph was taken the day after Jack Dempsy lost his heavyweight title to Luis Angel Firpo. These two unidentified men most likely gambled, and lost, on Mr. Dempsey's reputation in the ring.

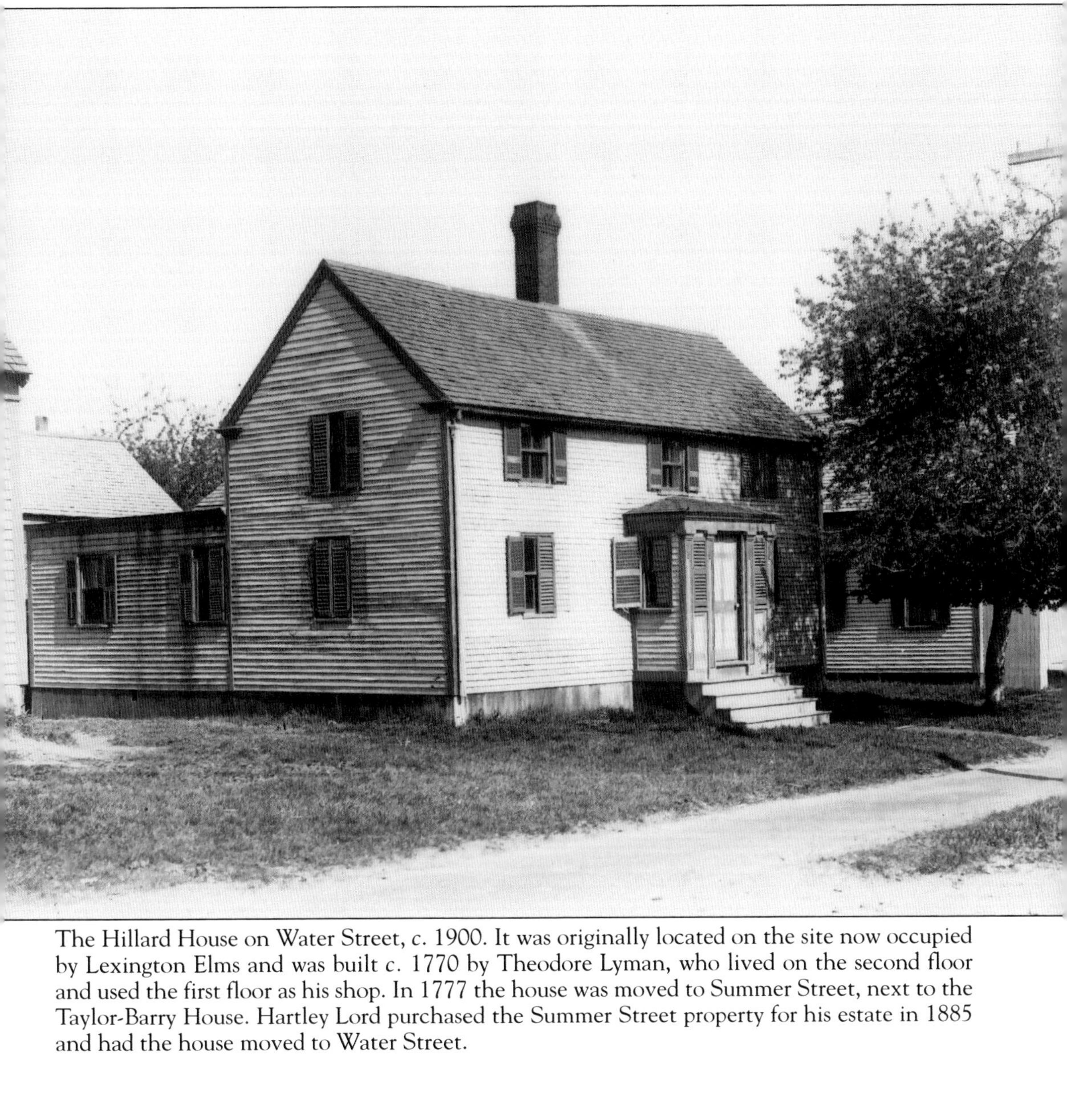

The Hillard House on Water Street, *c.* 1900. It was originally located on the site now occupied by Lexington Elms and was built *c.* 1770 by Theodore Lyman, who lived on the second floor and used the first floor as his shop. In 1777 the house was moved to Summer Street, next to the Taylor-Barry House. Hartley Lord purchased the Summer Street property for his estate in 1885 and had the house moved to Water Street.

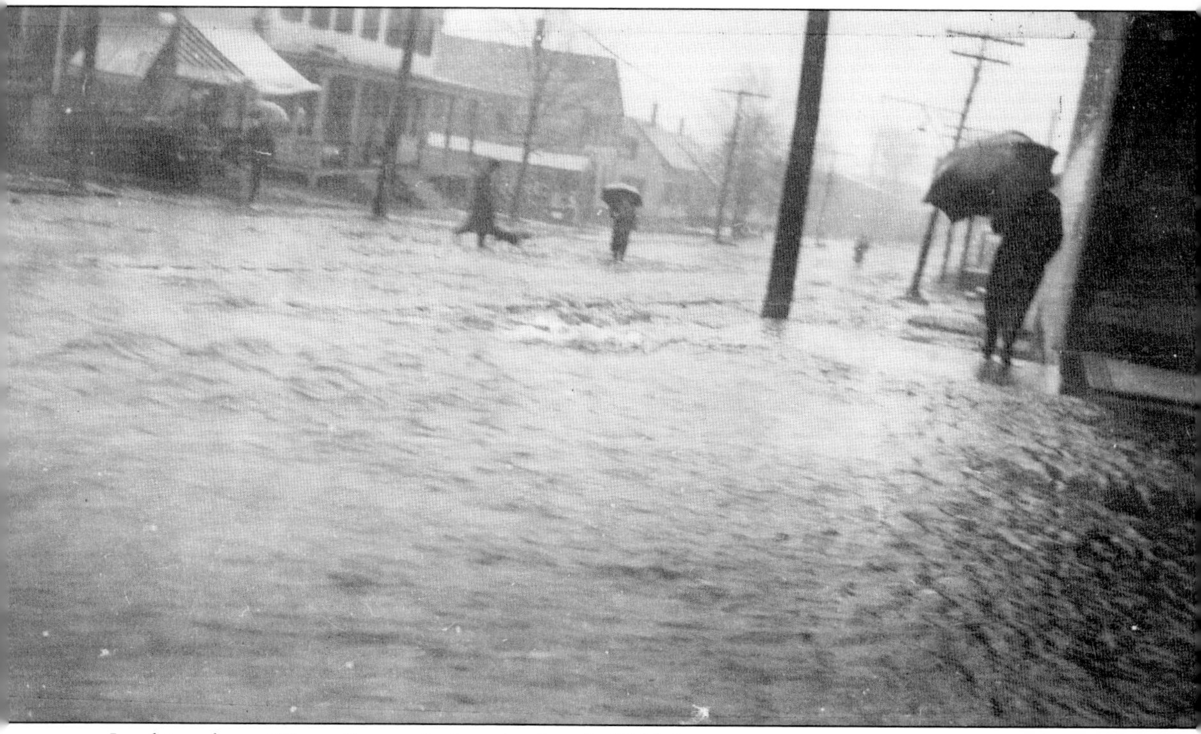

Looking down Water Street during the flood of 1936.

Four

The Great Fire of 1903

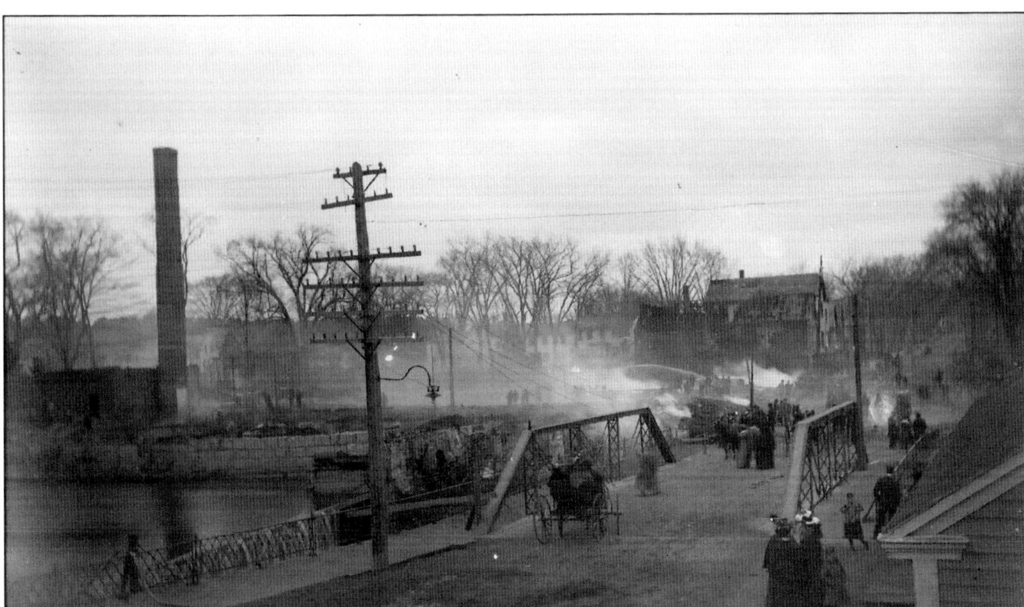

Early on the Sunday morning of May 3, 1903, residents watch as the fire department wets down the smoldering ruins of the Davis Mill, at the corner of Storer and Main Streets.

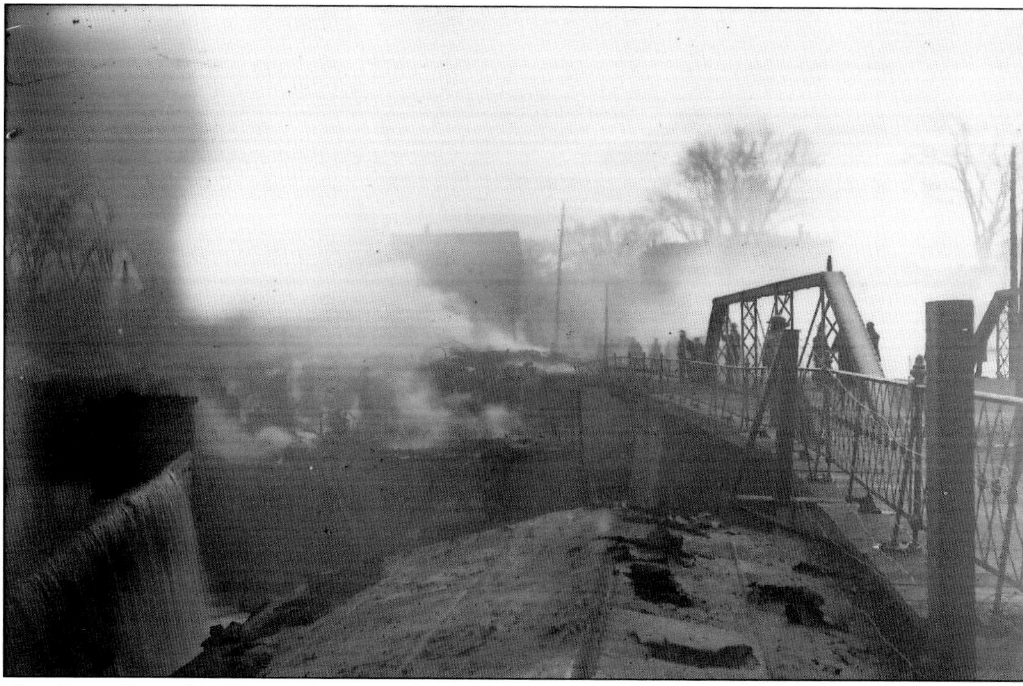

The Great Fire of 1903 was the worst fire in Kennebunk's history. The fire's origins were related in the *Eastern Star* newspaper the following morning by night watchman James A. Day and Officer Wentworth: "Around midnight as Day was making his nightly rounds [in the Davis Shoe Factory] he discovered a blaze had started in the shafting box located on the outside of the building and running from one wing to another. Day easily extinguished this fire. Shortly after 2 o'clock [a.m.] Officer Wentworth stepped into the dynamo room to eat his lunch; he heard what he thought to be water dropping, but on investigation discovered that a second fire was under way." The flames spread quickly, turning the mill into a blazing torch that lit up the sky and could be seen for miles. Sparks from the fire soon set the Grist Mill, the Old Corner Grocery, and the Parsons Block afire. Residents and business owners began taking their belongings and merchandise out to the streets. For a time it looked as if the fire might spread up Main Street. Through hard work, the firemen were able to contain the blaze. Lost in the fire was the town's electric plant, which had been located in the basement of the shoe factory. Fortunately there were no deaths or serious accidents. Although slightly singed, even the old gray and white mill cat survived. The cat, who had made his home in the mill for fifteen years, soon became a hero. His story spread quickly, and his picture appeared in an edition of the *Boston Herald*!

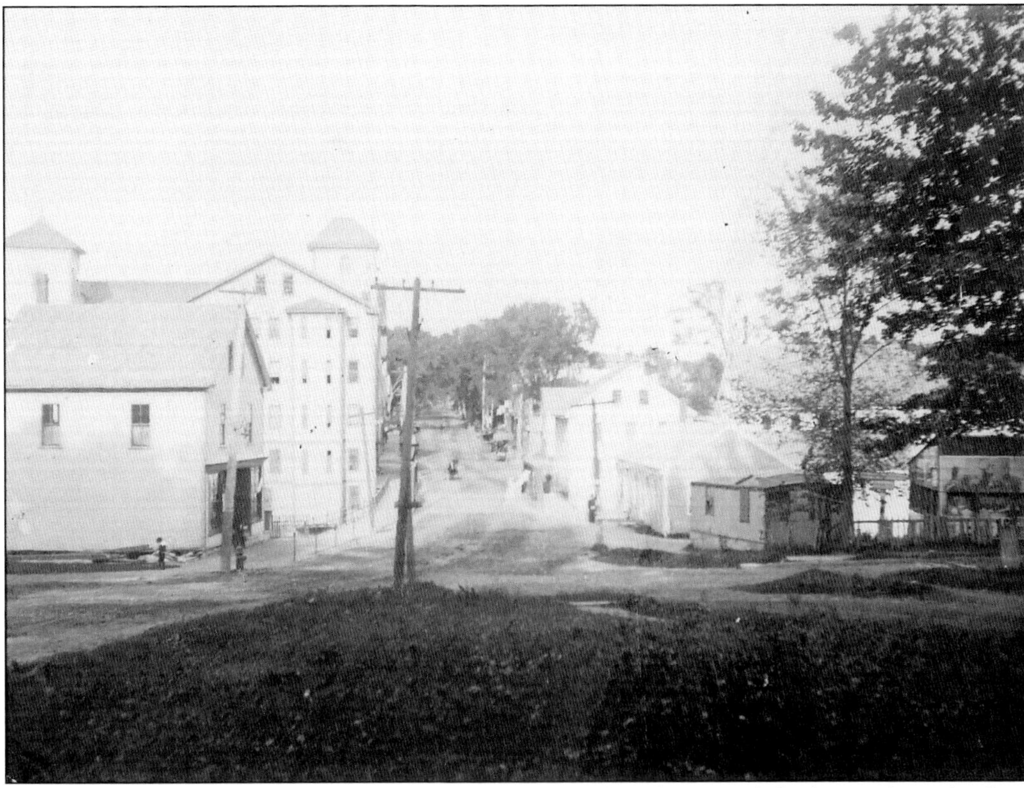

A view of Main Street before the Great Fire of 1903. This photograph looks out from the front lawn of the Mousam House, *c.* 1885. The Tomlinson store can be seen to the left, and beside it the Davis Shoe Factory. To the right is the old counting house, next to the Grist Mill.

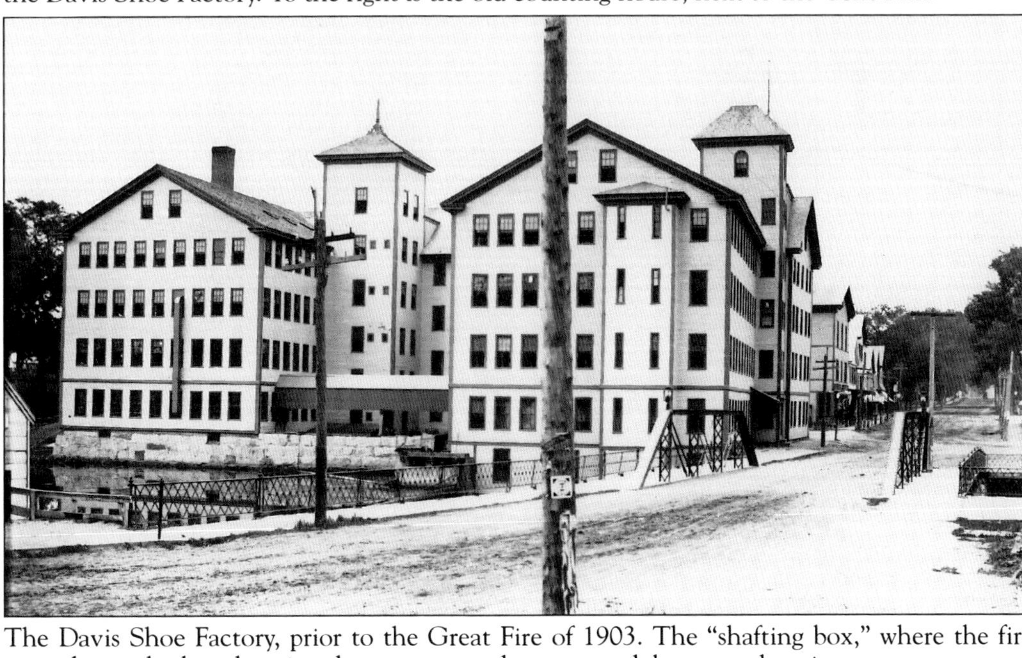

The Davis Shoe Factory, prior to the Great Fire of 1903. The "shafting box," where the fire started, was the long housing that ran across the courtyard, between the wings.

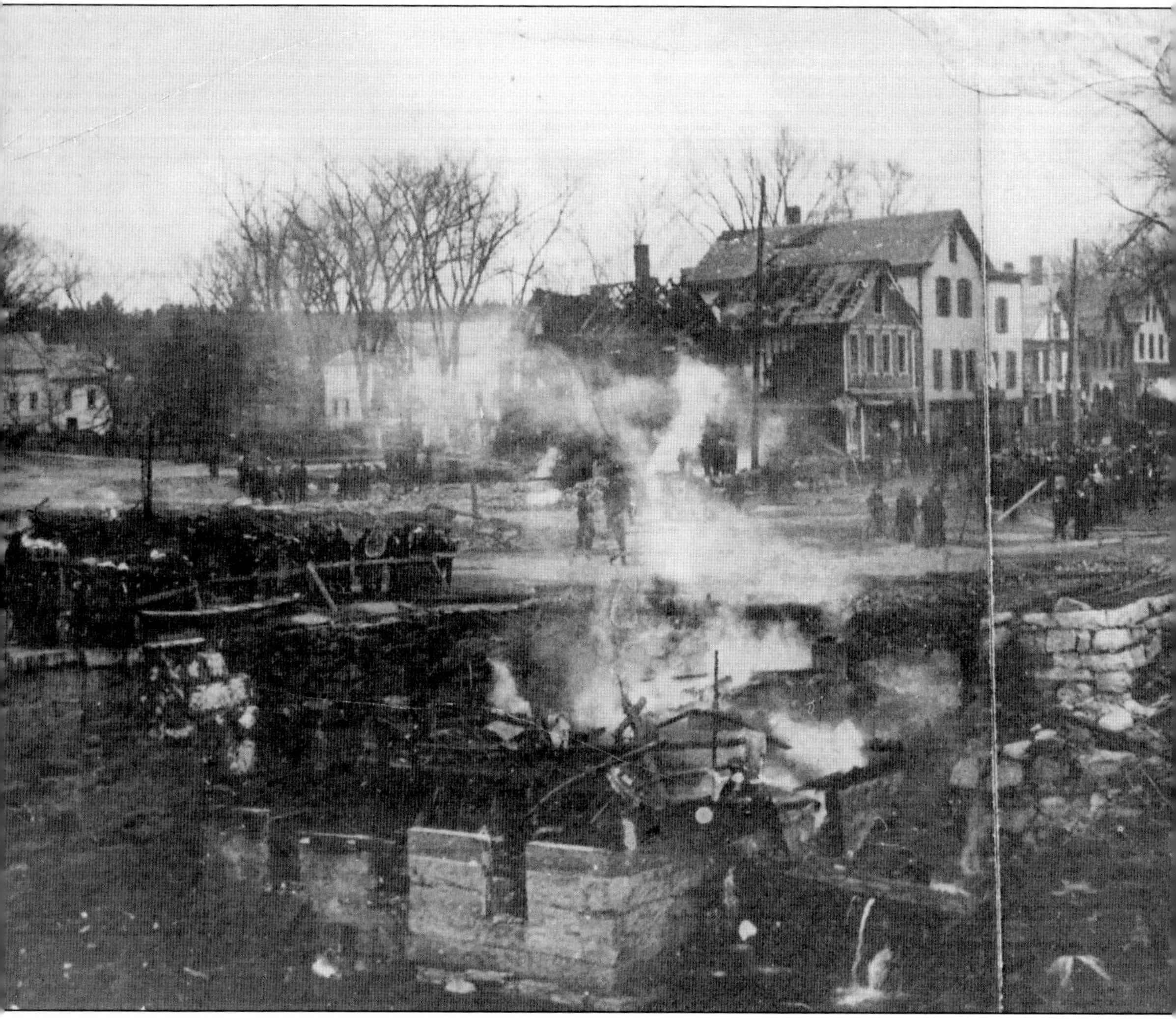

The Great Fire of 1903 burned all the corner buildings at the intersection of Main, Storer, and

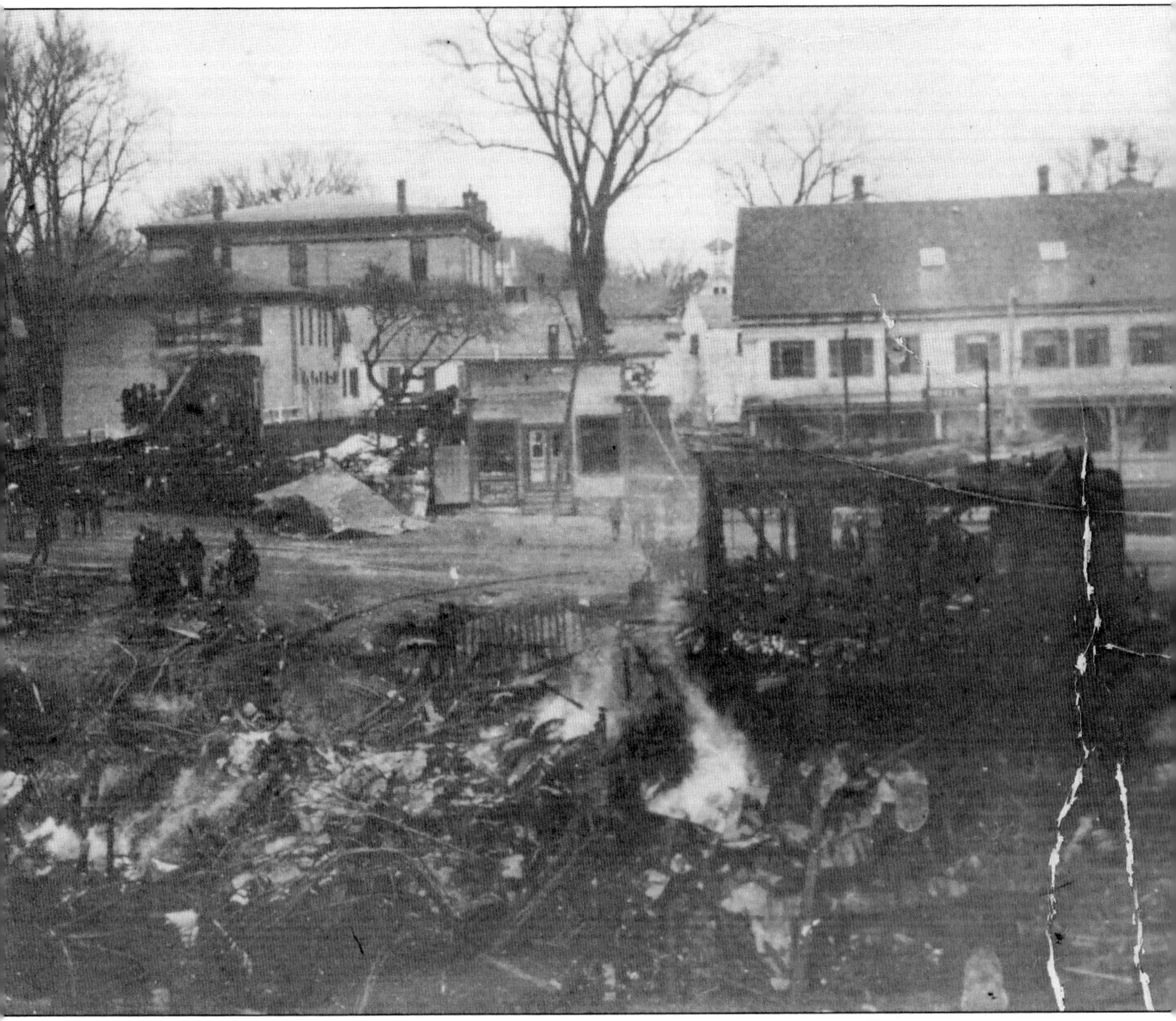

Water Streets. In this photograph smoke still rises from the ruined Grist Mill.

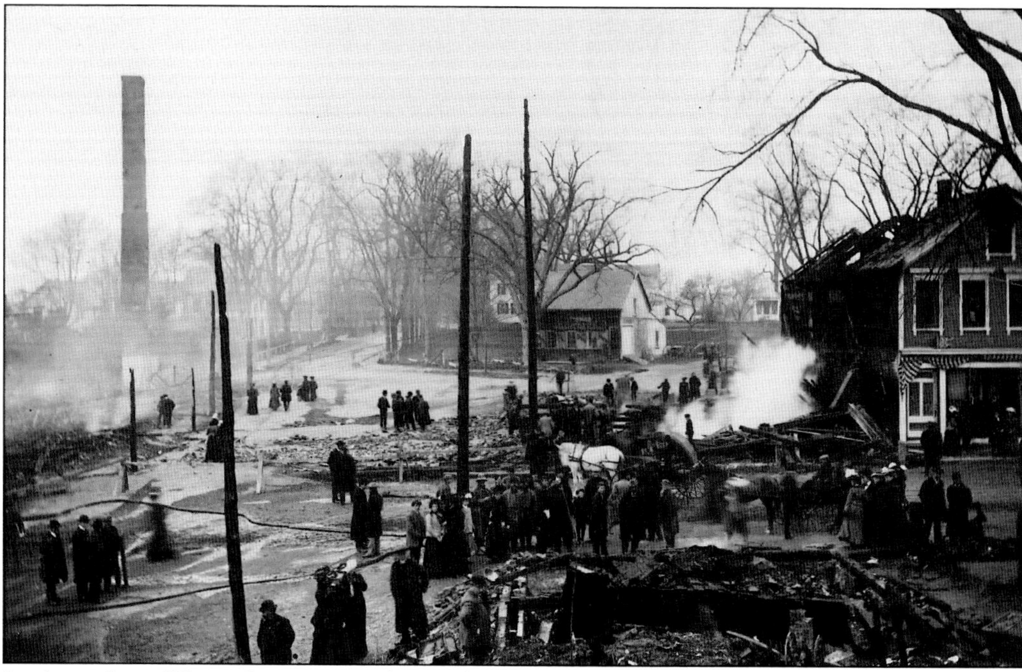

Looking from Water Street towards Garden Street. The Old Corner Grocery stood in the foreground, and the Parsons Block was across the street.

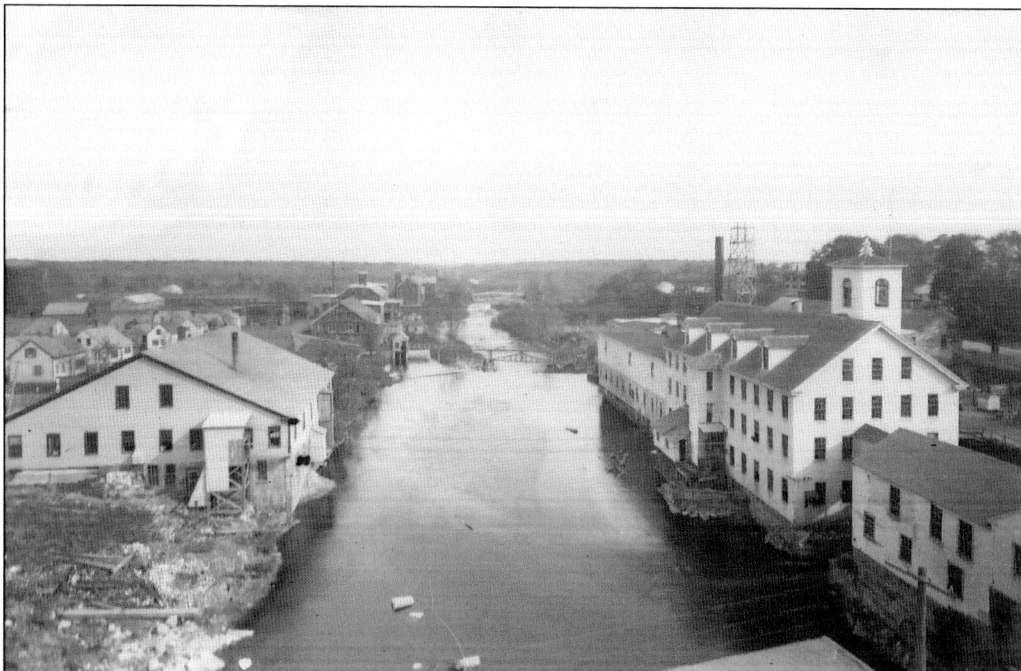

Looking down river after the fire, 1903. The Grist Mill stood on the left

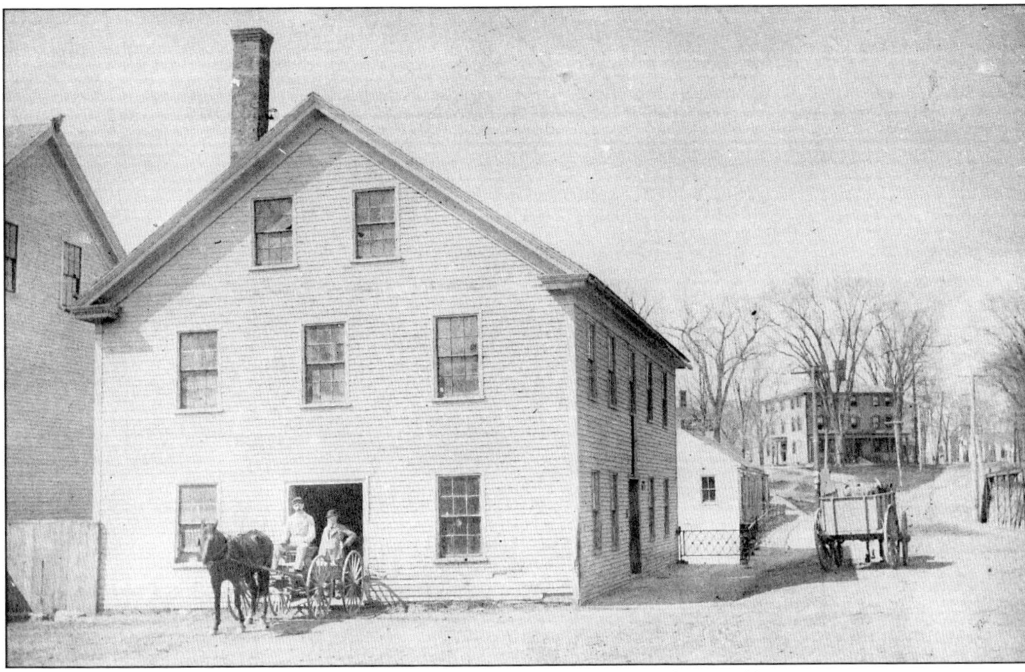

The Grist Mill, *c.* 1890. It was built in 1869 to replace an earlier mill.

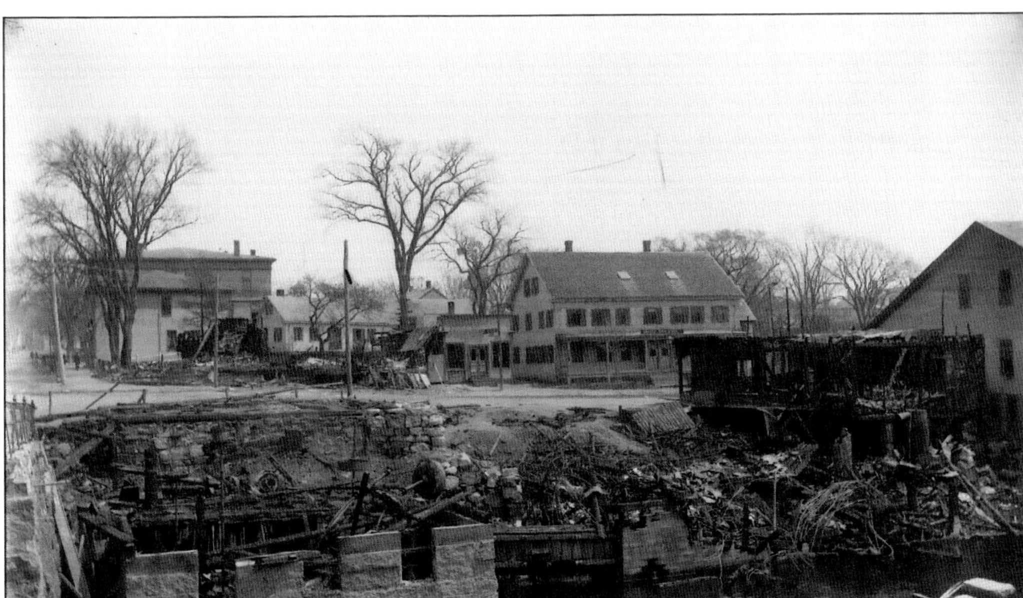

The destruction of the Grist Mill was complete. Twisted wreckage and its foundation are all that are left. On Water Street, Jennison's meat market and the Kennebunk House survived intact.

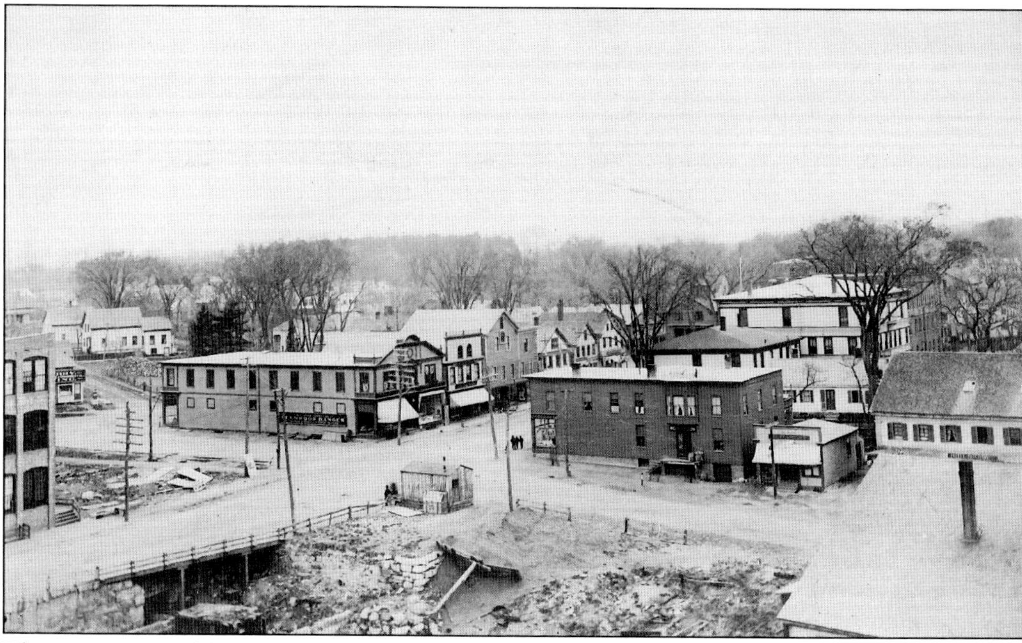

The reconstructed buildings on the corners of Main, Storer, and Water Streets, 1905. Damages from the fire eventually totaled over $80,000. Insurance coverage came to less than $30,000. The biggest loss was suffered by the town, who held no insurance on the Davis Mill; damages there were estimated at $35,000, including the electric light plant.

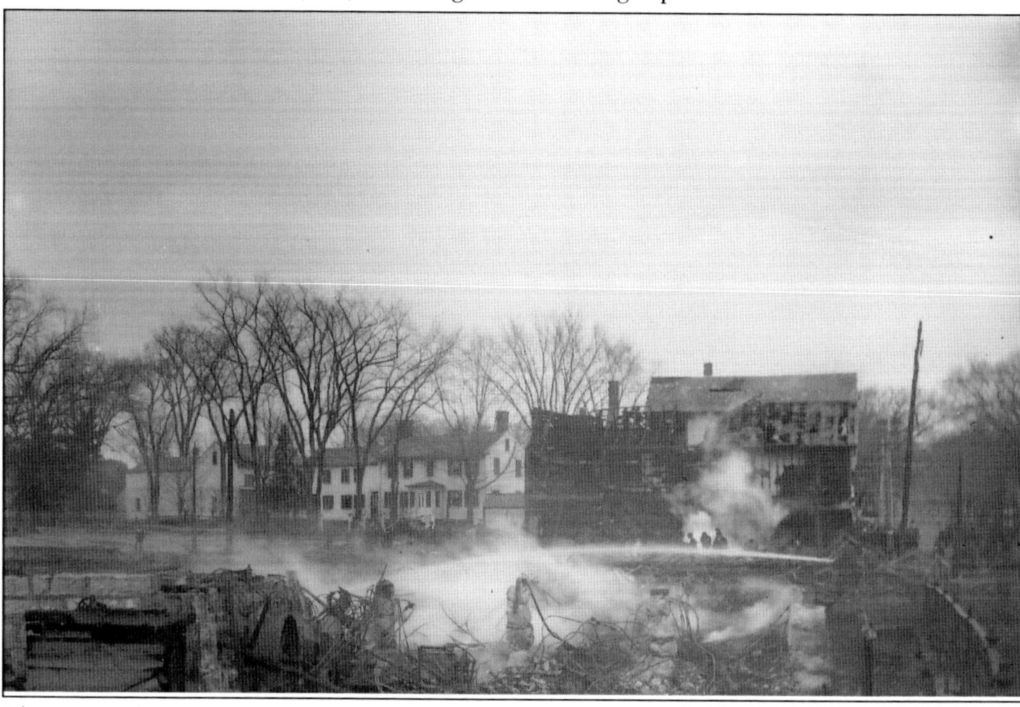

This 1903 photograph looks towards Garden Street, and shows the mill ruins. The house in the center is the Orrin Ross House, which was built in 1800 and razed in 1960. This is the only existing photograph of this house and barn.

Five

Tavern Hill

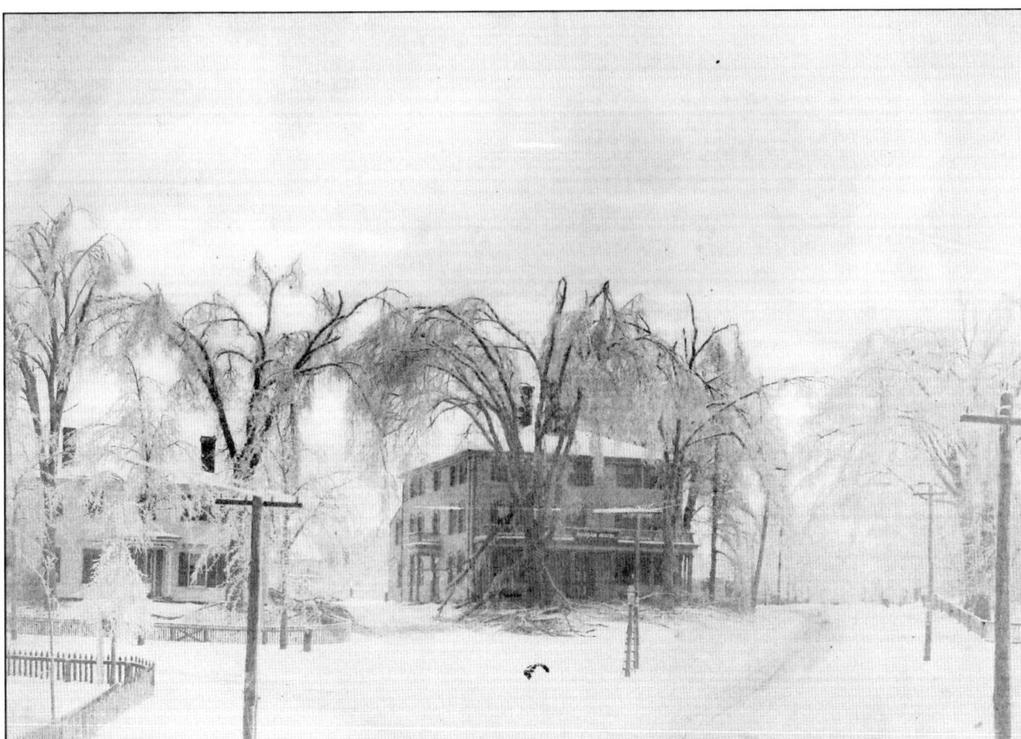

The Mousam House and the Jefferds House, after a winter storm in 1886. Today's Route One, York Street, runs through the site of the Mousam House. In this photograph, Brown Street is on the left and High Street—the original road between Wells and Kennebunk—is on the right. The fence on the right surrounds the Unitarian Parsonage. Notice the majestic elm trees lining the streets. The lane between the two buildings was a right of way that led to the Mousam Stables.

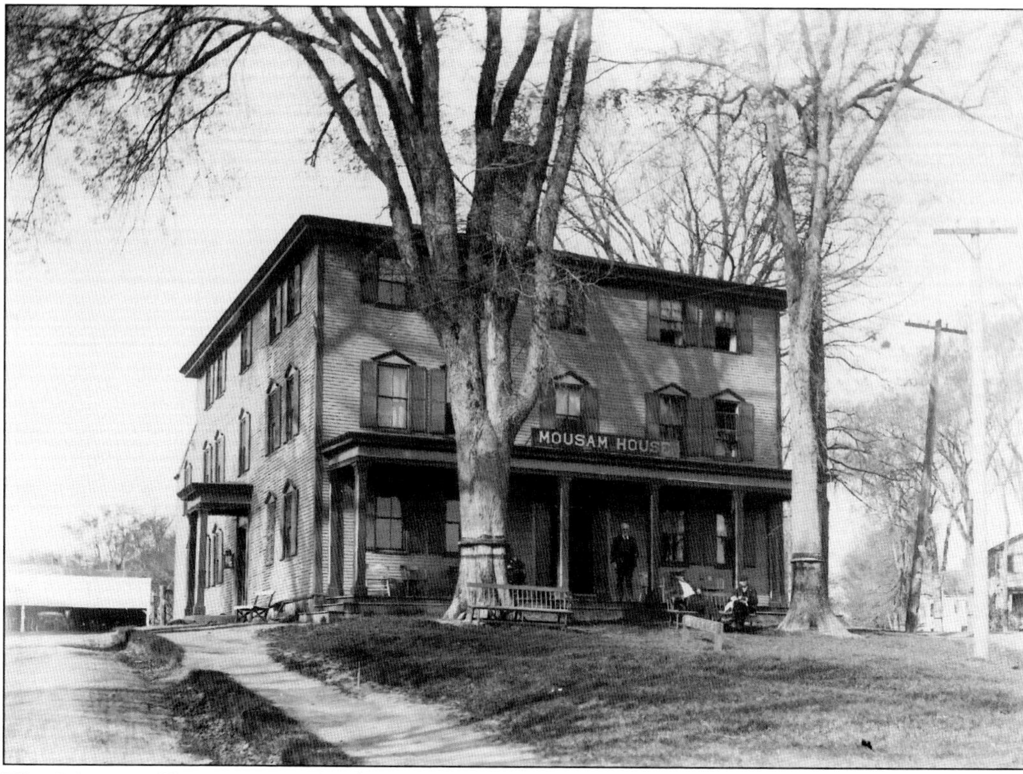

The Mousam House, c. 1915. The porch was added in 1870 and the plate glass windows in 1910. The demolition of the Mousam House in 1938 to make way for a service station is one of the greatest architectural and historical loss in Kennebunk's history. In 1784 Dominicus Lord purchased the lot from Hannah Storer, and soon after he constructed a small home there. In 1791 Lord sold his house to William Jefferds, who opened an inn. In 1814 Jefferds' son George took over the inn. It was probably at this time that the three-story addition to the front was constructed, which resembles the work of Thomas Eaton. William Jefferds died in 1820 and the inn was sold to Captain John Hovey of Boston. He leased it to Nathaniel Towel, who ran it for about ten years. The name was changed to the Towels Hotel, and it was here that General Lafayette dined on June 25, 1825. Lafayette was not the only famous person to dine at the inn. George Jefferds had the honor of hosting President Monroe in 1817. Hovey eventually took over the inn and changed its name back to Jefferds. When he died in 1856, William Lord, William Lord Jr., George Lord, and Ivory Lord bought the inn. In 1861 they leased the property to B.F. Goodwin, who brought his furnishings and sign up from the Old Brick where he had operated a boarding house. From that time, the inn was called the Mousam House. Lorenzo and Abby Parsons became the next owners in 1870, and they then sold it to John L. Baker. Baker's daughter inherited the inn when he died, and she leased the inn out to various managers. She eventually sold the inn to Charles and Nellie Tibbets in 1889, who enlarged it from twenty-five rooms to fifty. After her husband's death Nellie operated the inn by herself until poor health forced her to close in 1936. For several the years the Colonial Beacon Oil Co. leased part of the inn from Nellie, and used it as a service station. After her death in 1937, the historic inn was sold to Marshall Weeman.

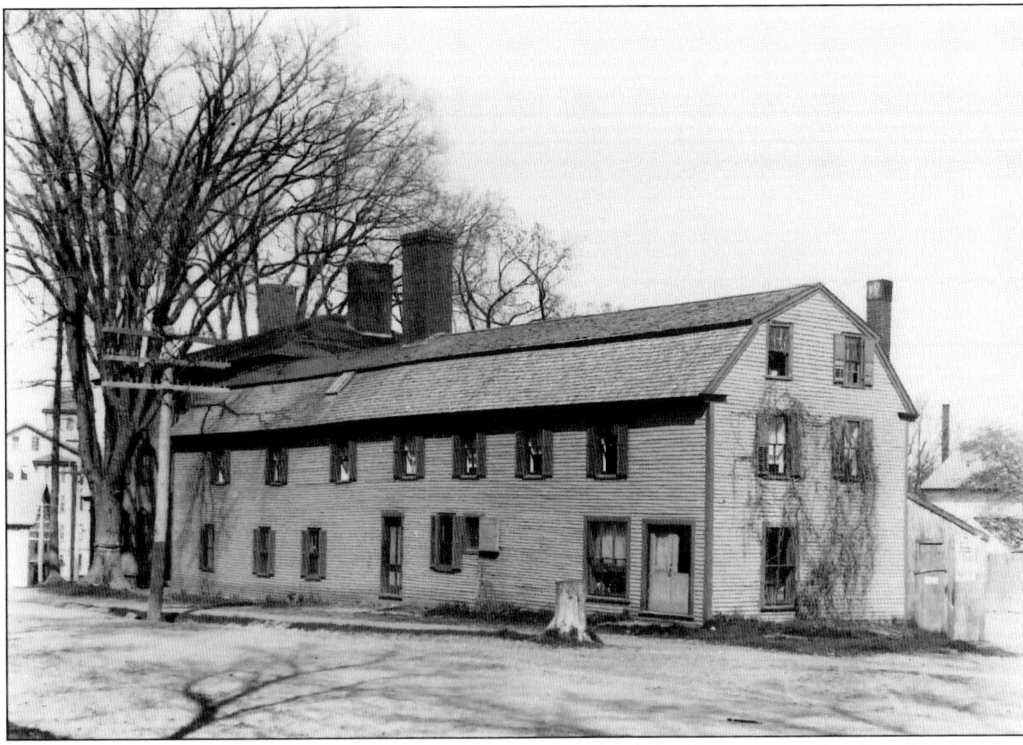

The back ell of the Mousam House, part of which was built by Dominicus Lord in 1784.

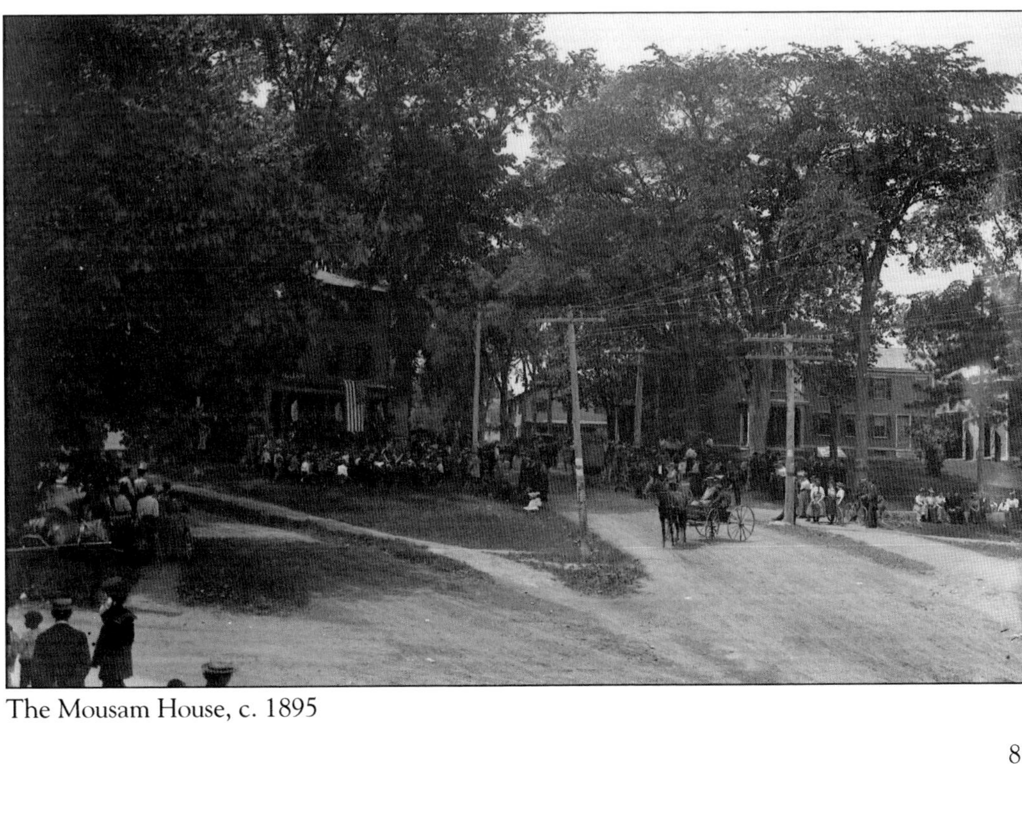

The Mousam House, c. 1895

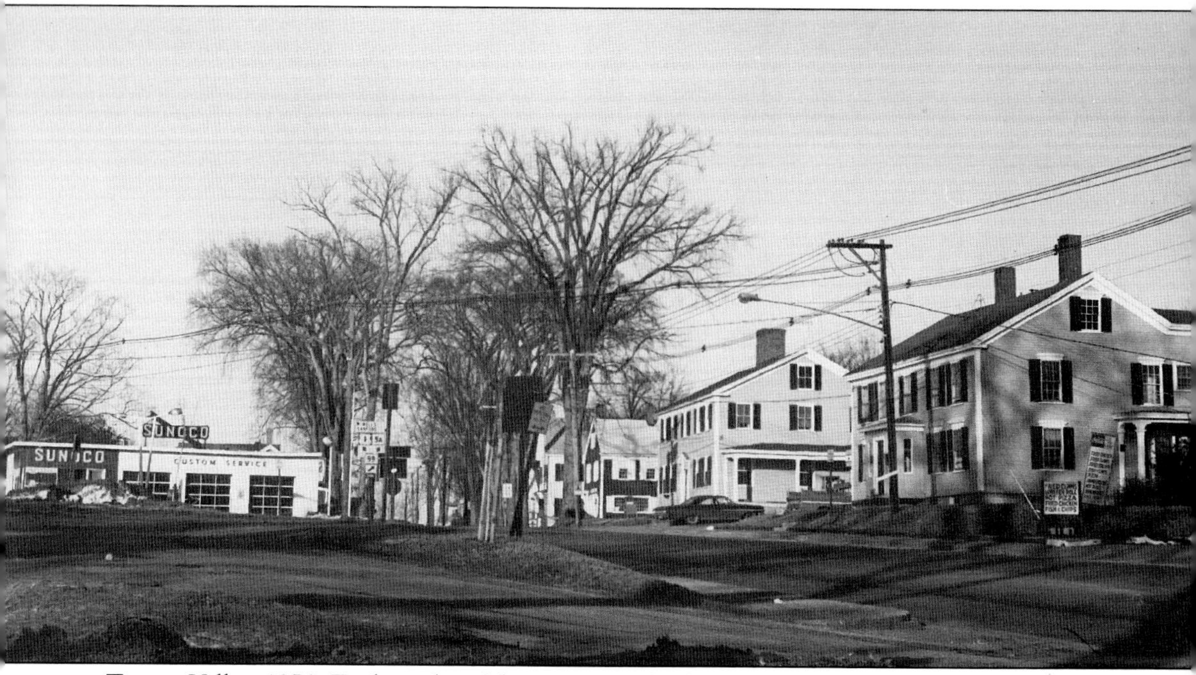

Tavern Hill in 1970. To the right of the picture is the former Unitarian Parsonage, built in 1797 by Captain John Low. Just beyond it is the house built by Dimond Gilpatrick in 1802. The parsonage was moved several feet up High Street in 1962 to make room for the Dairy Queen. In 1964 the *York County Coast Star* purchased both properties and moved from Garden Street to this new location. The *Star* constructed a building connecting the two homes to house their presses. Today that building houses Paul's Superette. Paul Bedard bought the property in 1979 when the *Star* moved to a new building on York Street. Despite the protests of many residents, both historic homes were razed for a parking lot. The loss of these two homes, along with the loss of the Mousam and Jefferds Houses and the reconstruction of Route One, have forever altered this important and historic section of Kennebunk.

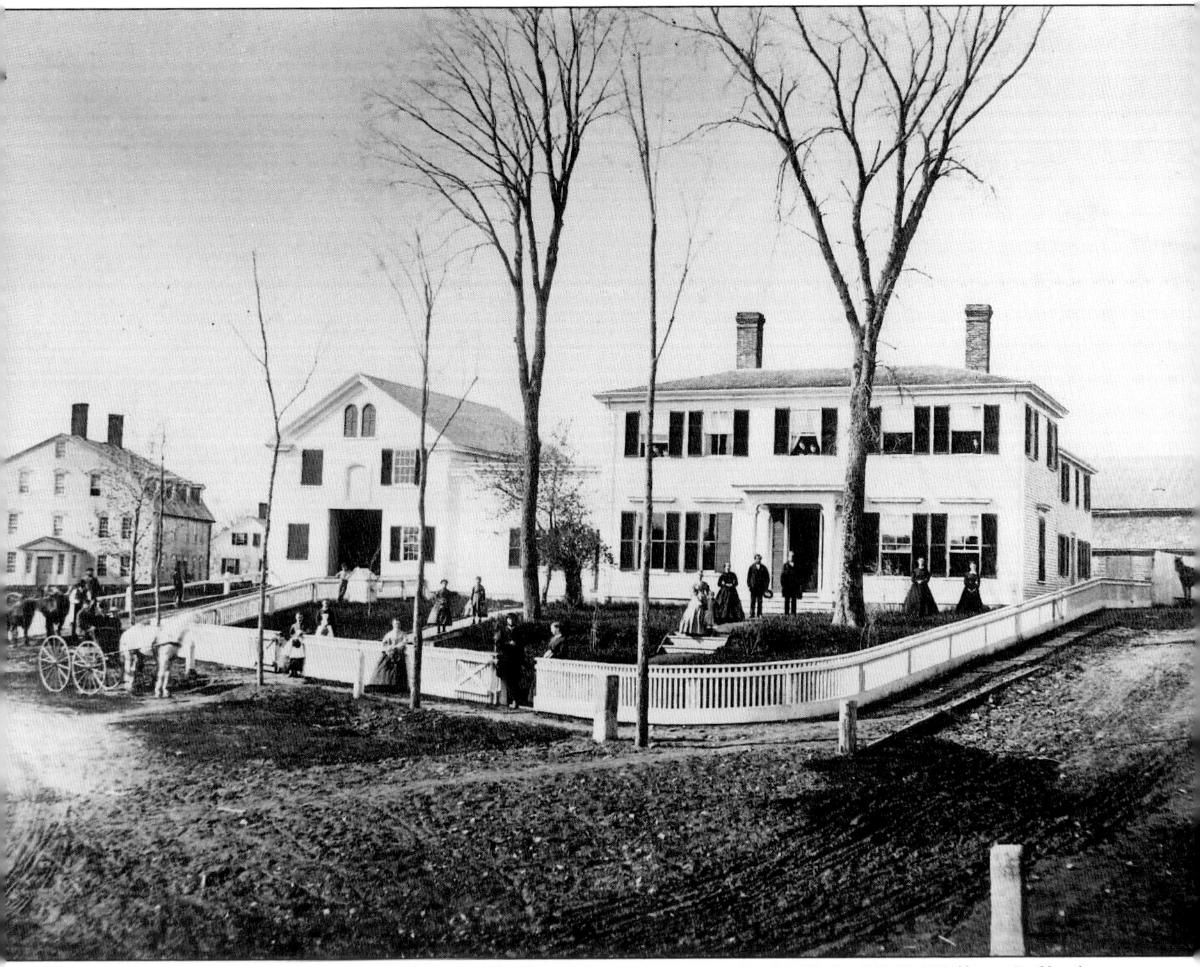

Members of the Jefferds family gather on the lawn for a photograph, 1865. In 1777, William Jefferds and Richard Gilpatrick purchased a tract of land along the Mousam River and began clearing it. William Jefferds built his house soon after and later sold it to his son Nathaniel Jefferds in 1804. The front section of this house appears to have been added to the early house built by William Jefferds. Nathaniel was a clothier and owned a store near the Mousam River Bridge. Nathaniel sold the house in 1866 to Samuel Clark, who converted the house into a duplex. When Clark died he left the home to his two sons. The large gambrel roof building to the left of the picture was constructed in the 1790s and was the home of the Gilpatrick family. Despite its size, it was moved back several feet to allow Brown Street to be laid out. By 1884, when it burned, it was being used as a boarding house for mill workers.

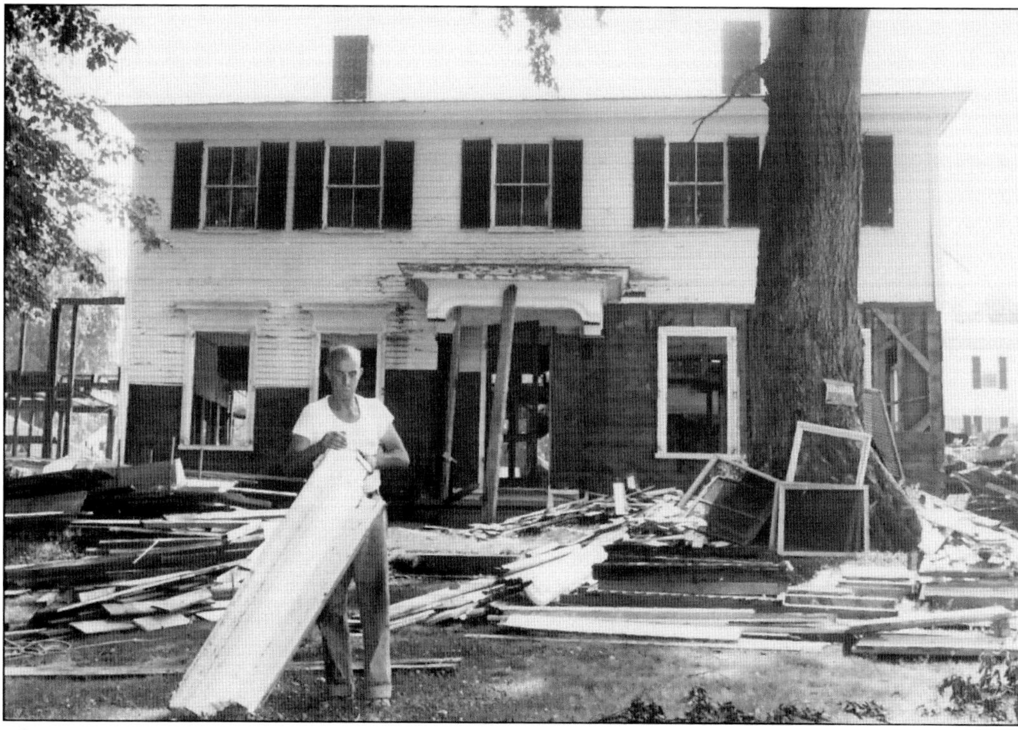

The N.T. Fox Lumber Company purchased the property from the Clark heirs in the 1940s. In 1963 the Jefferds House was razed to allow the lumber yard to expand.

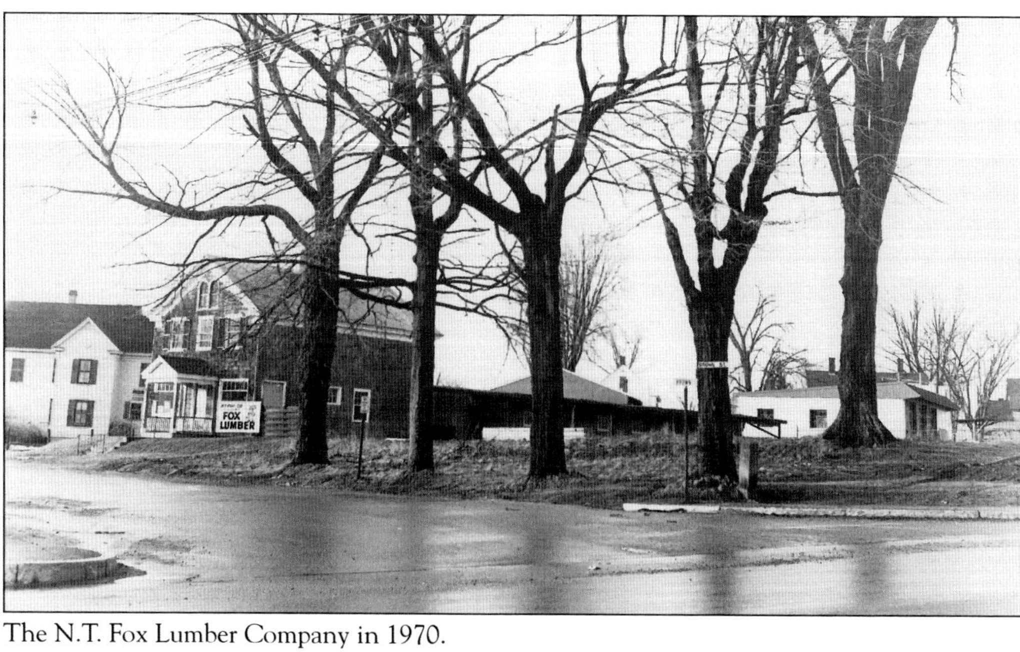

The N.T. Fox Lumber Company in 1970.

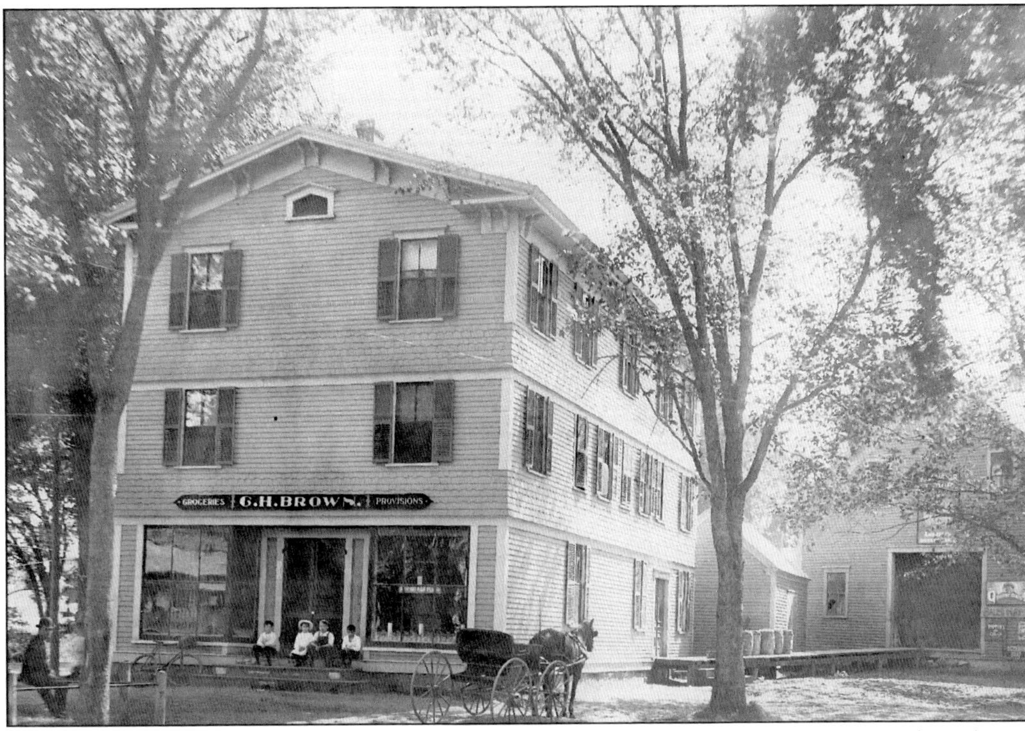

A *c.* 1910 photograph of G.H. Brown's grocery, located on the point between High and York Streets. Dimond Gilpatrick operated a blacksmith shop on this site for many years. That shop was razed in the late 1880s when this store was built. In 1945 the building was moved across the street next to Weeman's store, where it still stands.

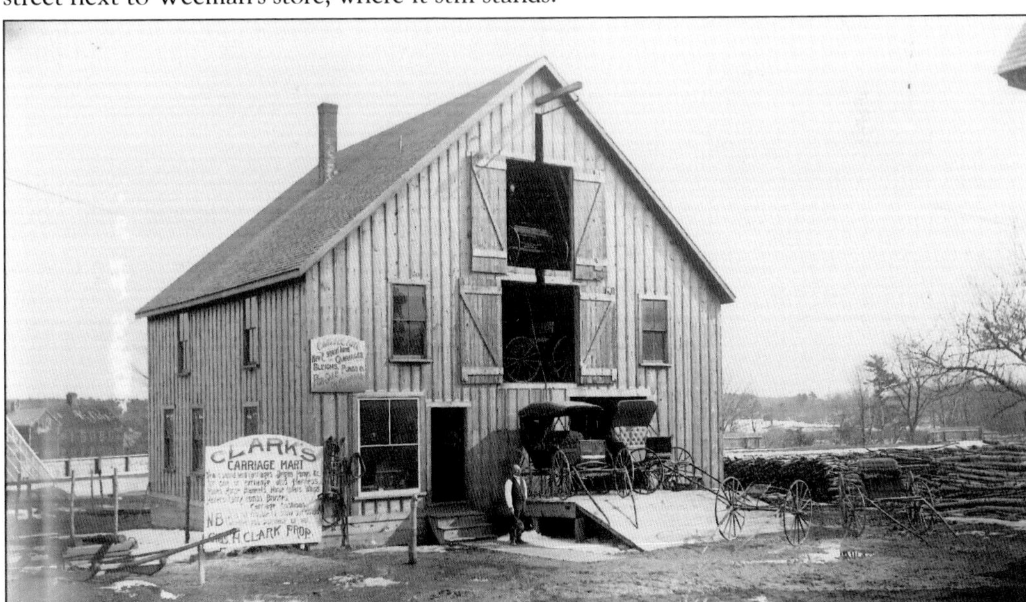

Clark's carriage shop on Brown Street, *c.* 1885. Charles H. Clark owned and operated this shop, which stood just past the current site of Brown Street Florist. Clark sold the business to his nephew John Lord in 1910.

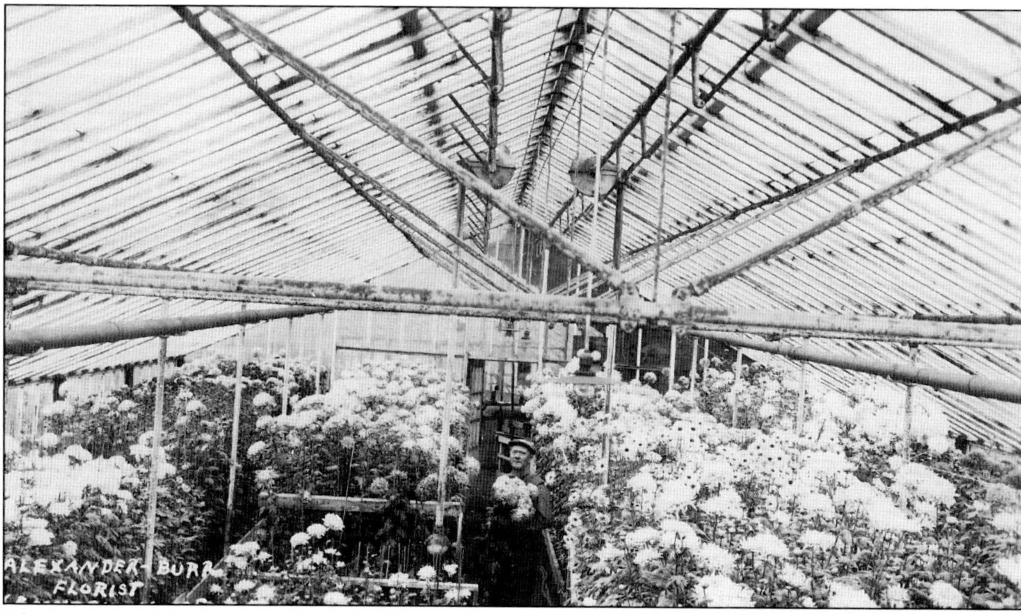

The interior of the former J.O. Elwell greenhouses on Brown Street, *c.* 1940. Alexander Burr Jr., the author's grandfather, along with the author's father, leased the greenhouses for many years. In the late 1940s the Elwell family sold the property to the Emmons family, who continue to operate the business today.

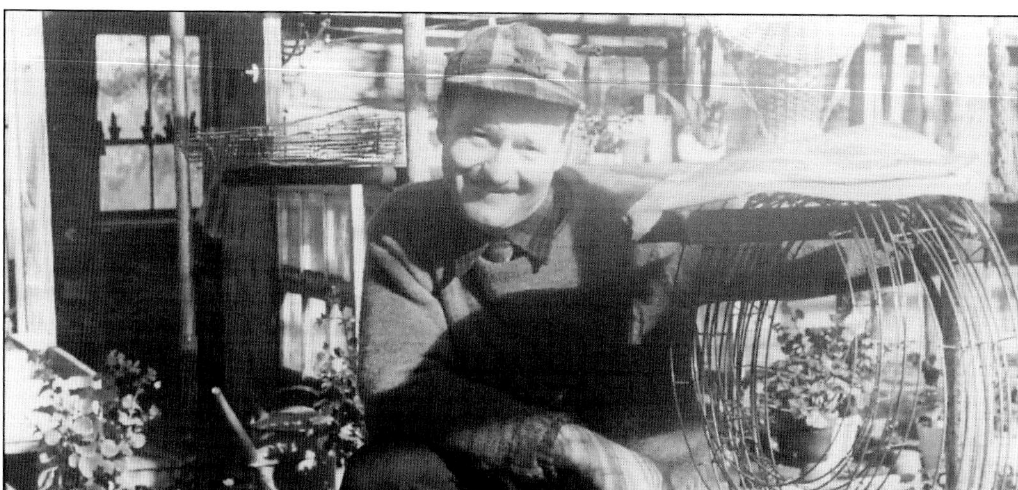

Alexander Burr Jr. at the Brown Street greenhouses. After the property was sold, he opened his own greenhouse and florist shop on Portland Street. (Photograph from the author's collection.)

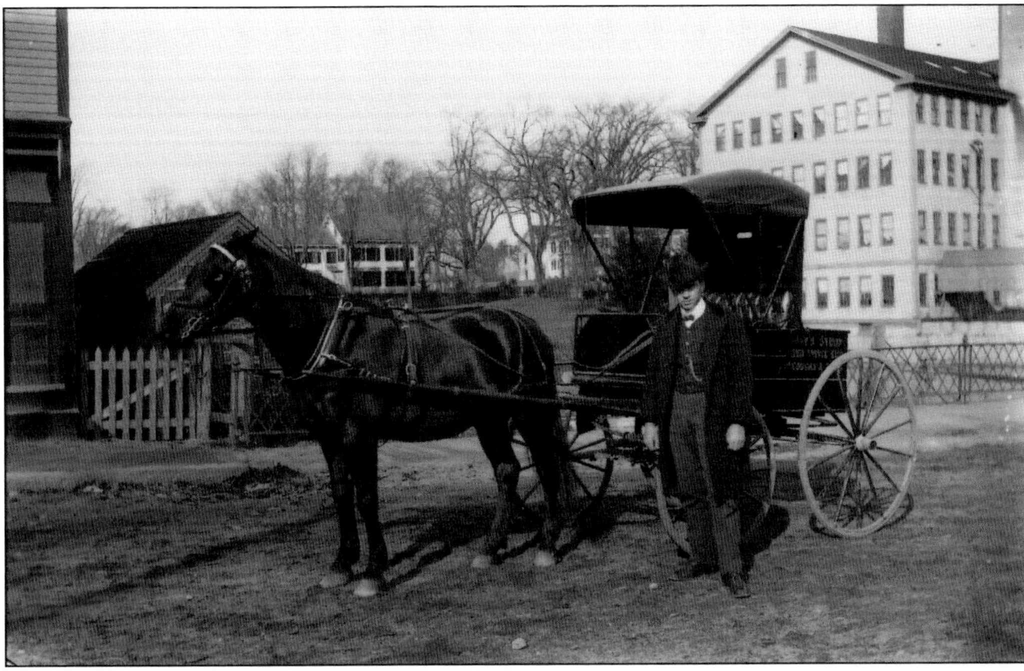

This photograph was taken *c.* 1895. The man is a traveling salesman for Ray's Syrup. He is standing in front of the Sawyer Store (later Tomlinson's) on the bridge. The Davis Shoe Factory is behind him.

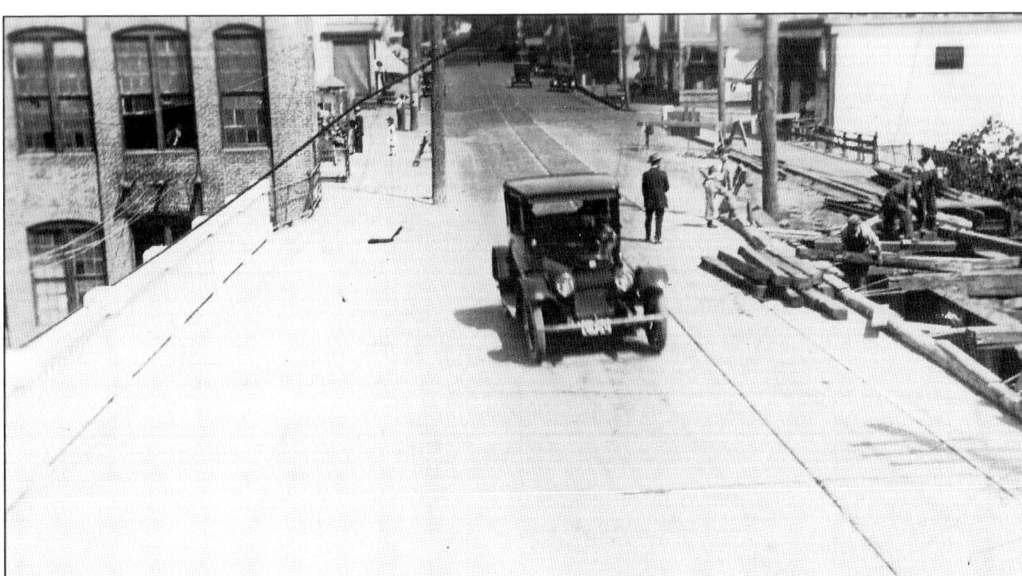

The new concrete bridge under construction in 1921. The present bridge was constructed in the late 1960s.

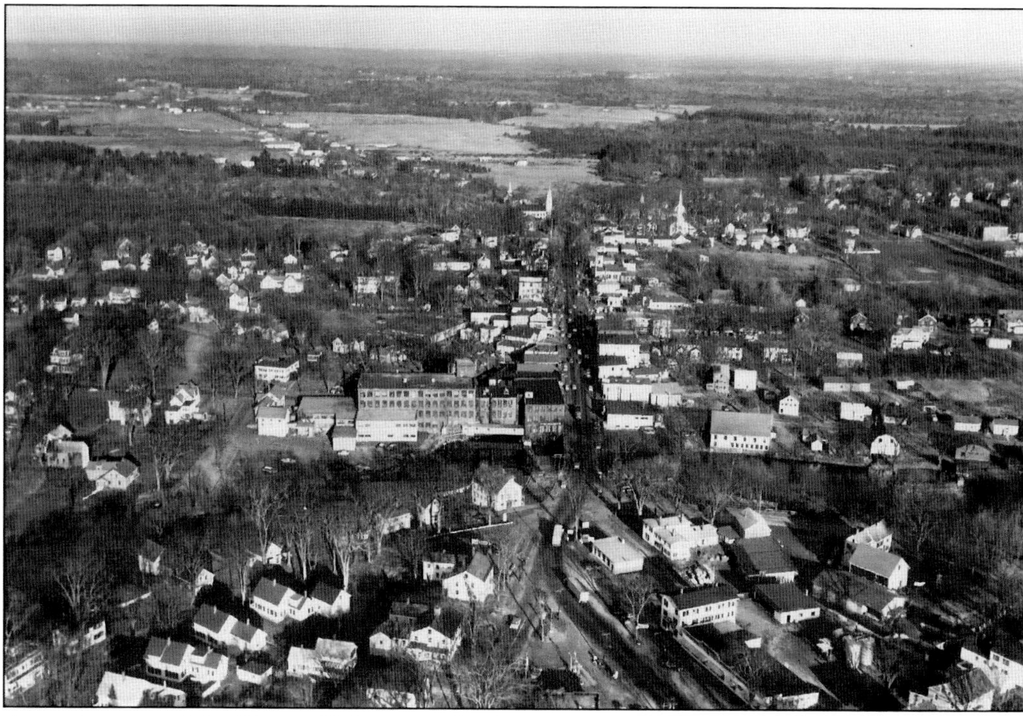

An aerial view of the Tavern Hill area, *c.* 1960.

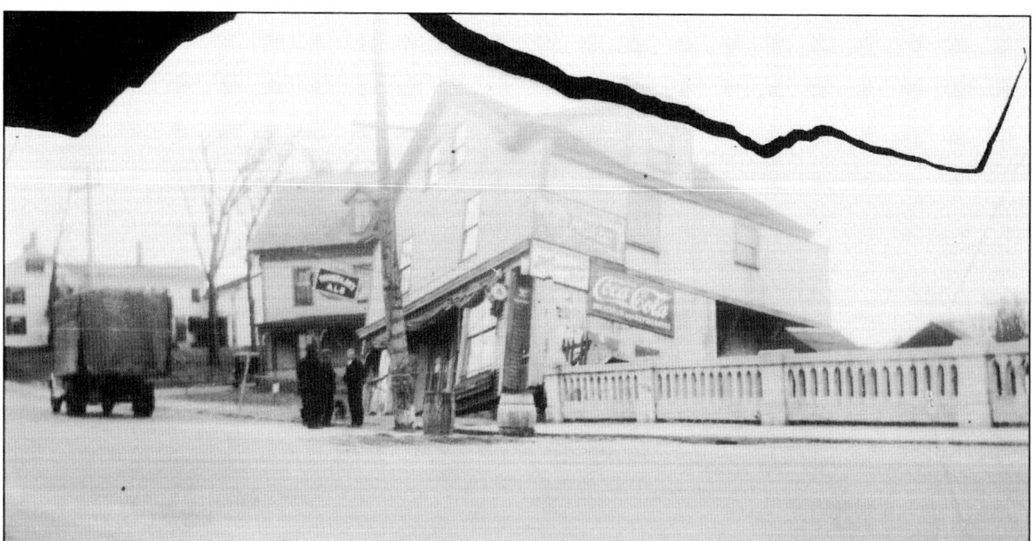

The Tomlinson store after falling into the river during the 1936 flood. It was built in 1869 by Captain N.L. Thompson, and was used to enclose the head gates of the big flume. Later it was used as a store, barber shop, and apartment building. After it fell into the river it was razed. Just beyond it Pleasant Street can be seen.

Six

Grove Street to Dane Street

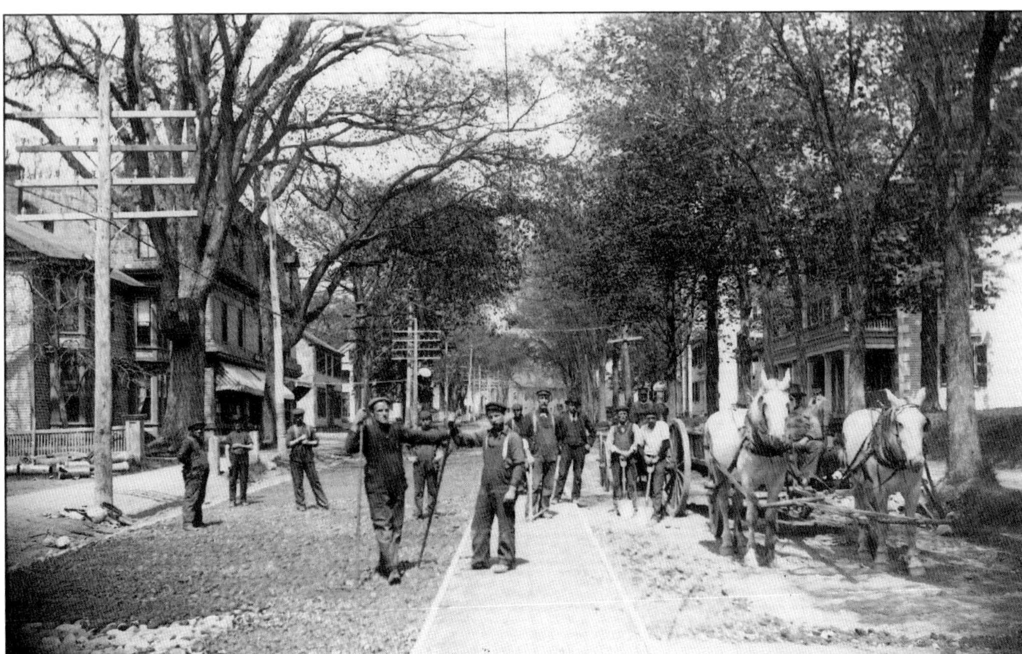

Main Street, 1904. These men have stopped work to pose for the photograph. They have been laying the track for the trolley cars which will soon travel down Main Street. On the right is the Brown House; on the left is the Pythian Block.

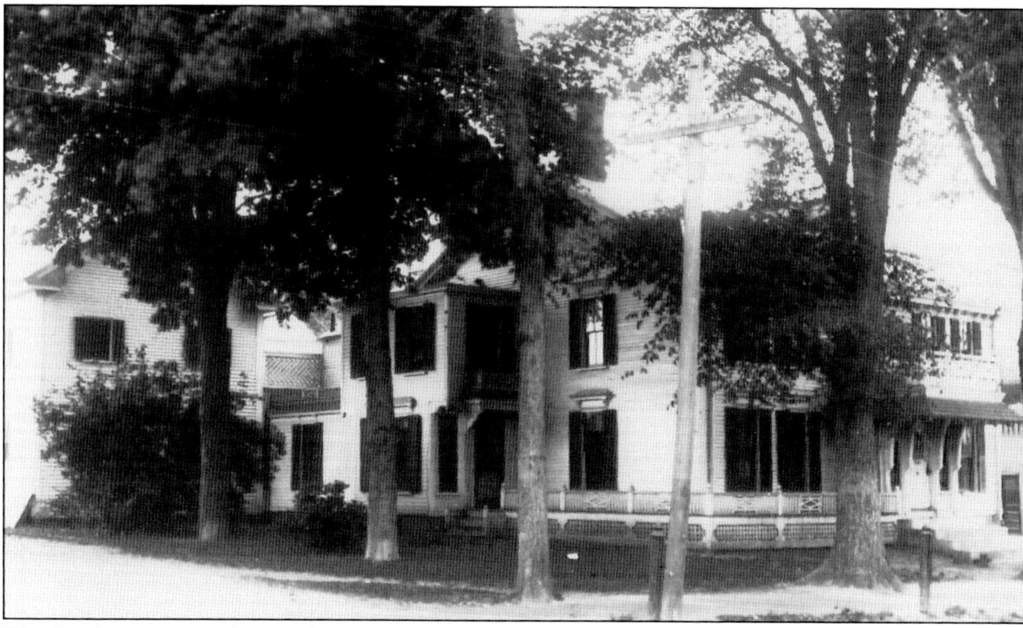

The Dr. Ross House (Kennebunk Inn), *c.* 1885. Today, the Kennebunk Inn's dining room and bar are located on this side. The inn was built in 1799 as a private home by Phineas Cole. Cole soon sold the building to Benjamin Smith, whose family lived there until 1875. In 1876 Dr. Orrin Ross bought the home and when his son, Dr. Frank Ross, married in 1880 he gave the property to him. Dr. Frank Ross specialized in obstetrics and was proud of the fact that he never lost a mother, altogether he delivered 1,000 babies during his long career. Dr. Ross died in 1926 and the property was then sold to Mr. and Mrs. George Baitler, who opened the Kennebunk Tavern in 1928.

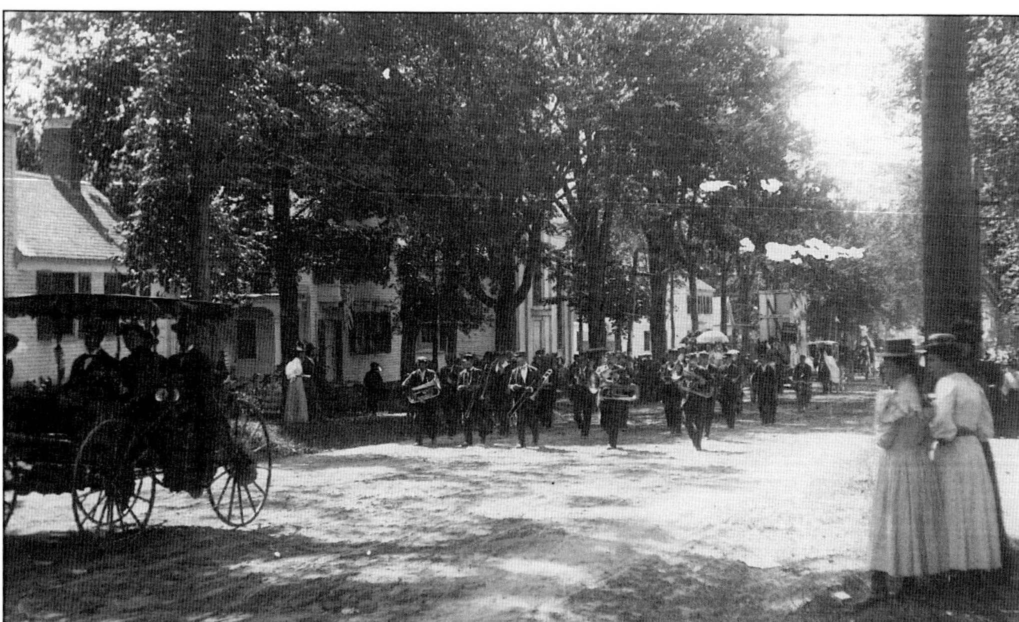

A photograph of the 1897 Labor Day Parade.

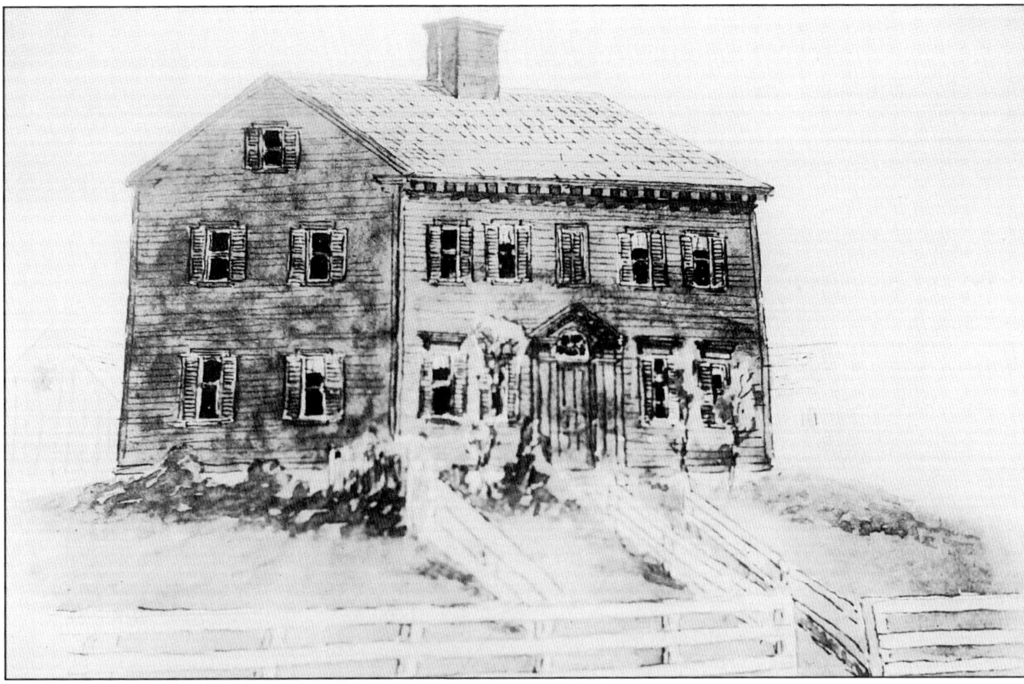

The Pomfret Howard House, built *c.* 1788. Howard, a hat maker, operated an inn here until competition forced him to close. This drawing shows the high ridge on which the house sat. Stephen Thatcher, the next owner, ran a private school here. The property was sold in 1934 to the Mobil Oil Co., who moved the house back and graded the lot for a service station. Some time later the house was torn down to make way for a parking lot.

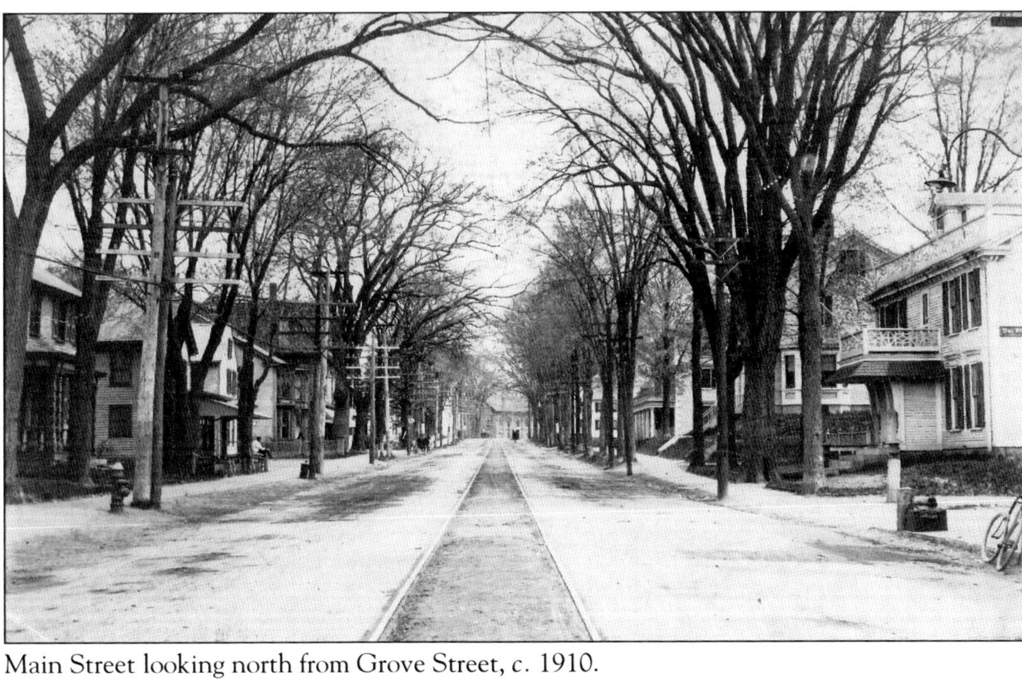

Main Street looking north from Grove Street, *c.* 1910.

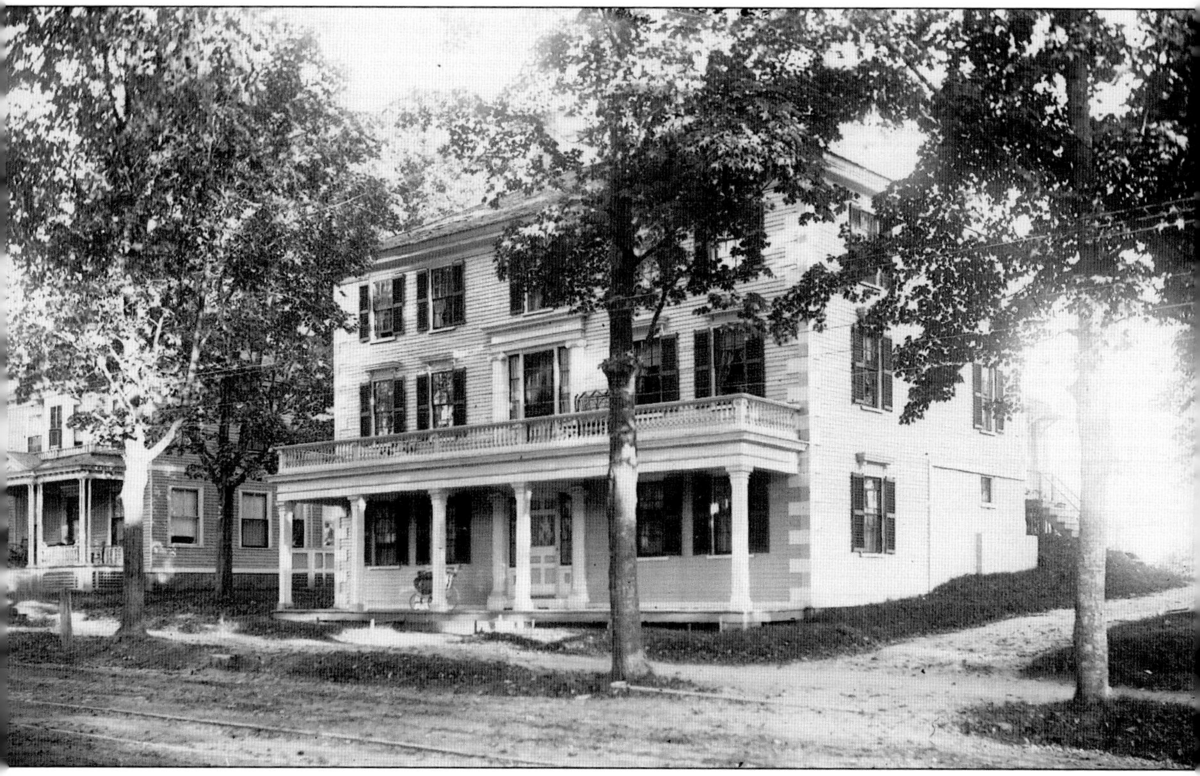

The Benjamin Brown House, c. 1905. Brown built the house as a store in 1784, with living quarters above. Dr. Jacob Fisher, who married Brown's daughter, bought the house in 1796 for rental income. Upon Fisher's death in 1840, the house was sold to Oliver Littlefield, who removed the ridge in front of the house. He then had two large rooms and a hall added on to the lower level, which were used as store fronts. The building was sold in 1939 to E.C. Snowden, and was razed for a filling station.

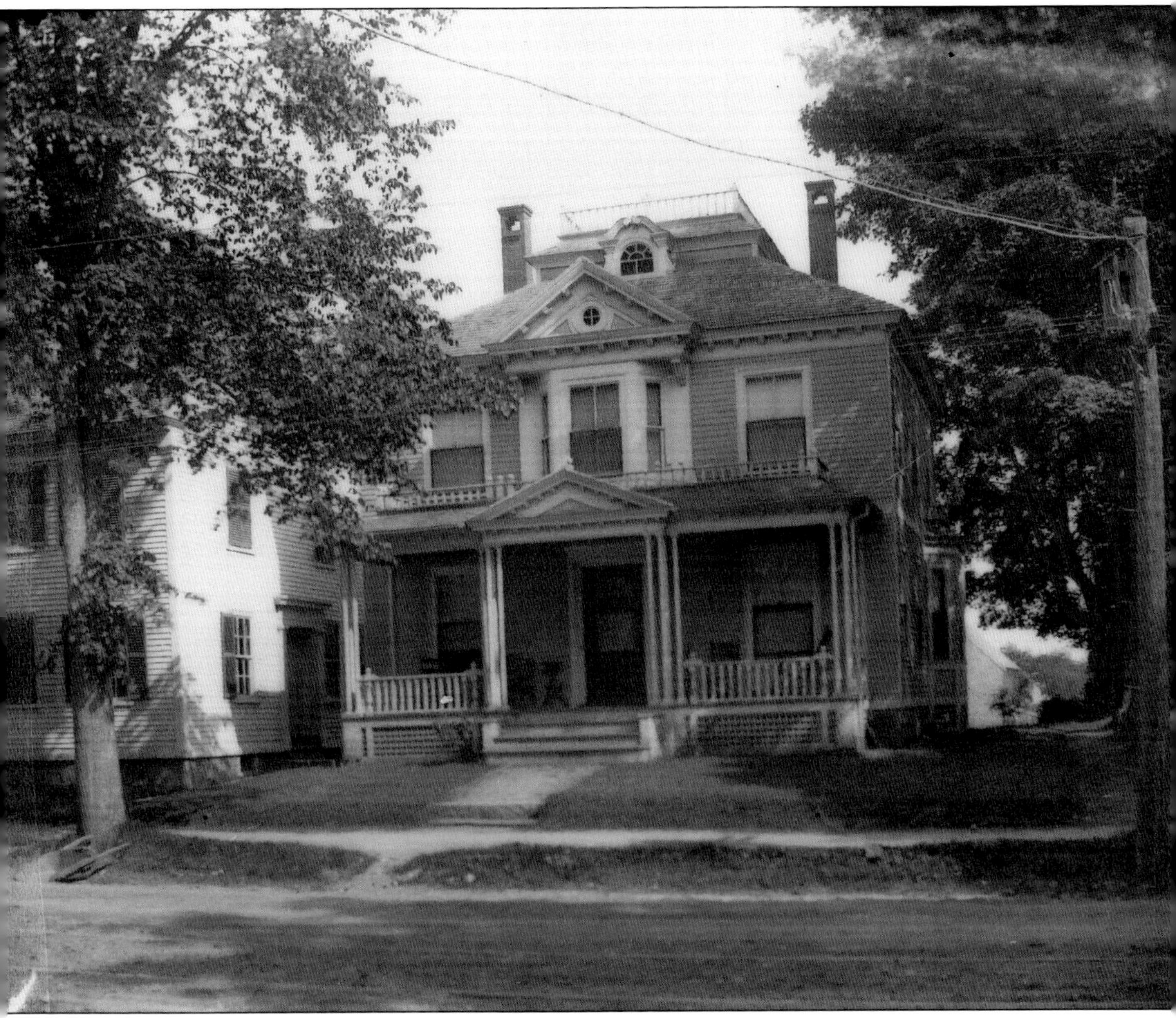

The Dr. Crediford House, built in 1898. It was possibly designed by local architect and historian William Barry, as it resembles his work. It was razed in 1969 when the Gulf Station (now the Texaco Station) situated adjacent to it was expanded.

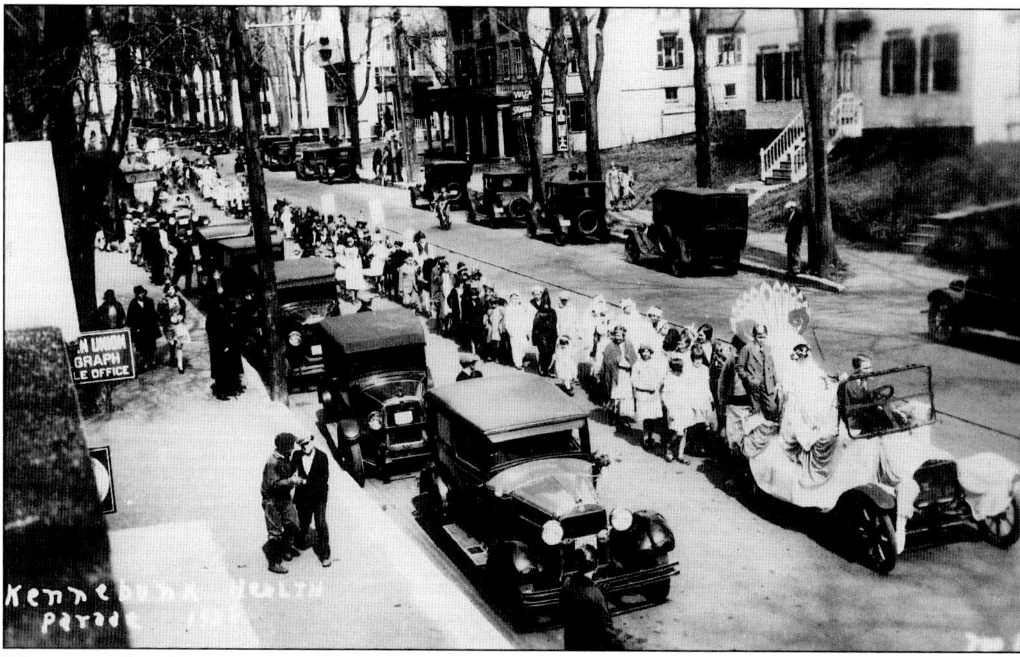

The Kennebunk Health Parade makes its way down Main Street in 1928. In the background is the Howard House; to the left of the photograph is the Crediford House, and to the right is the Brown House.

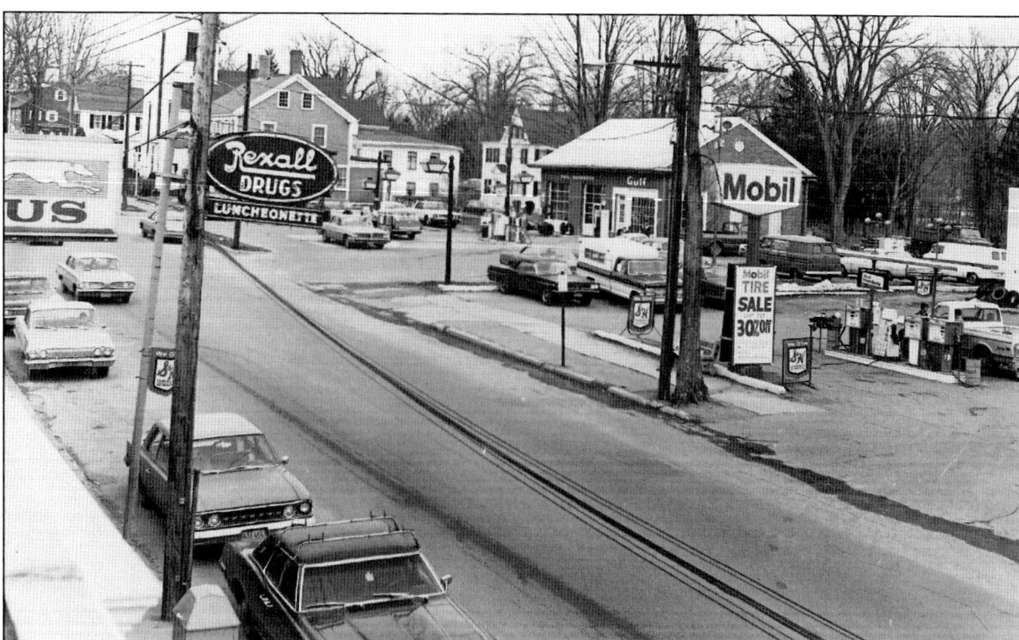

A 1970 photograph of Main Street.

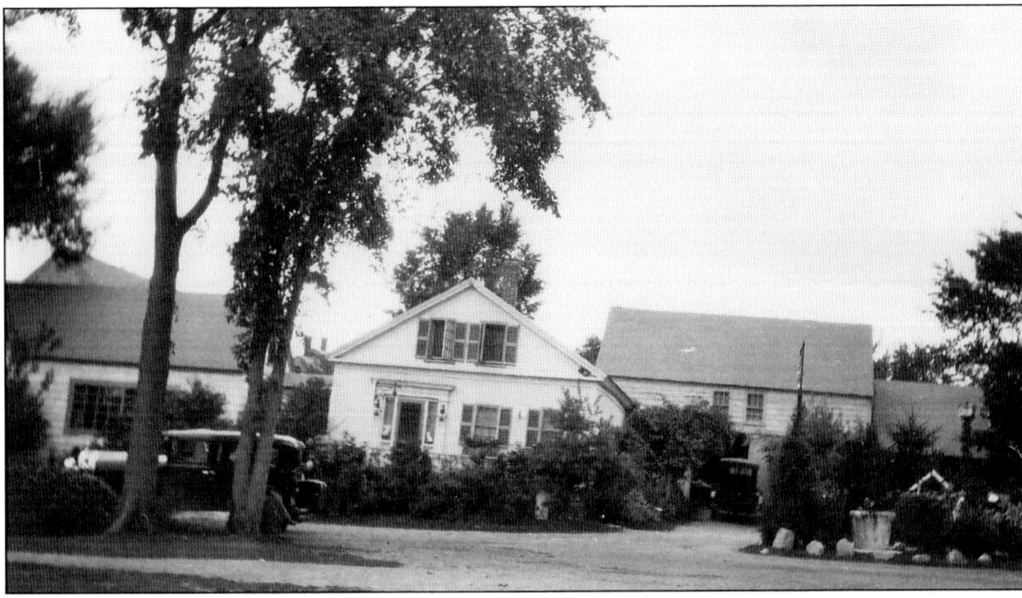

The Blue Wave Gift Shop, *c.* 1935. This was a popular store for tourists, and locals too. It was located in a small house which originally stood on Main Street. Dr. Crediford had the house relocated to its present site in 1897. Nason Court, where the shop was located, was originally called Fisher's Lane, after Dr. Jacob Fisher.

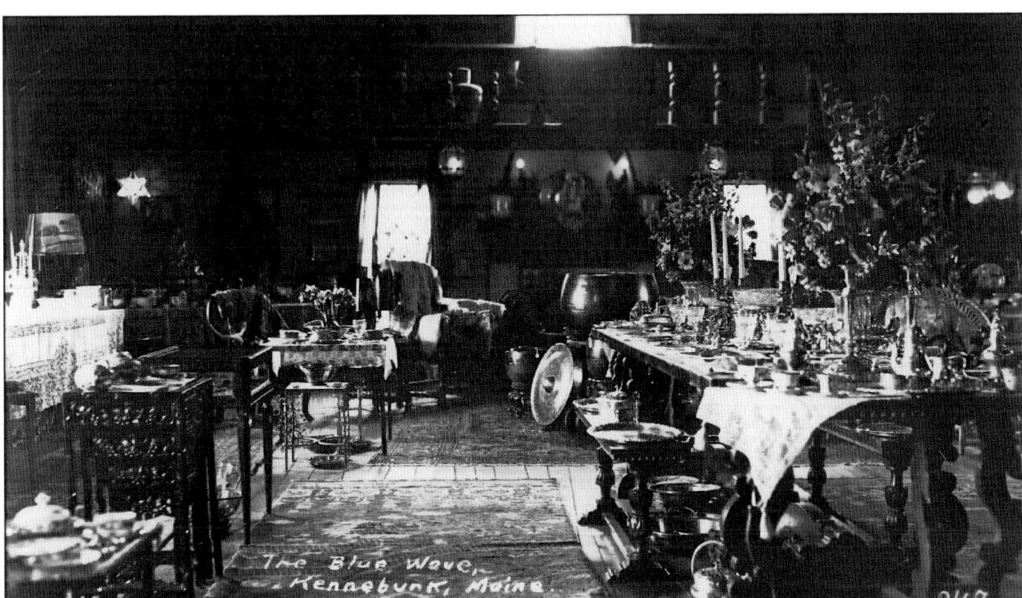

An interior view of the shop. Mr. & Mrs. Norman Wiggin bought the business in 1943 from Mrs. L. Irving, who started the business with her husband in 1921. (Photograph from the author's collection.)

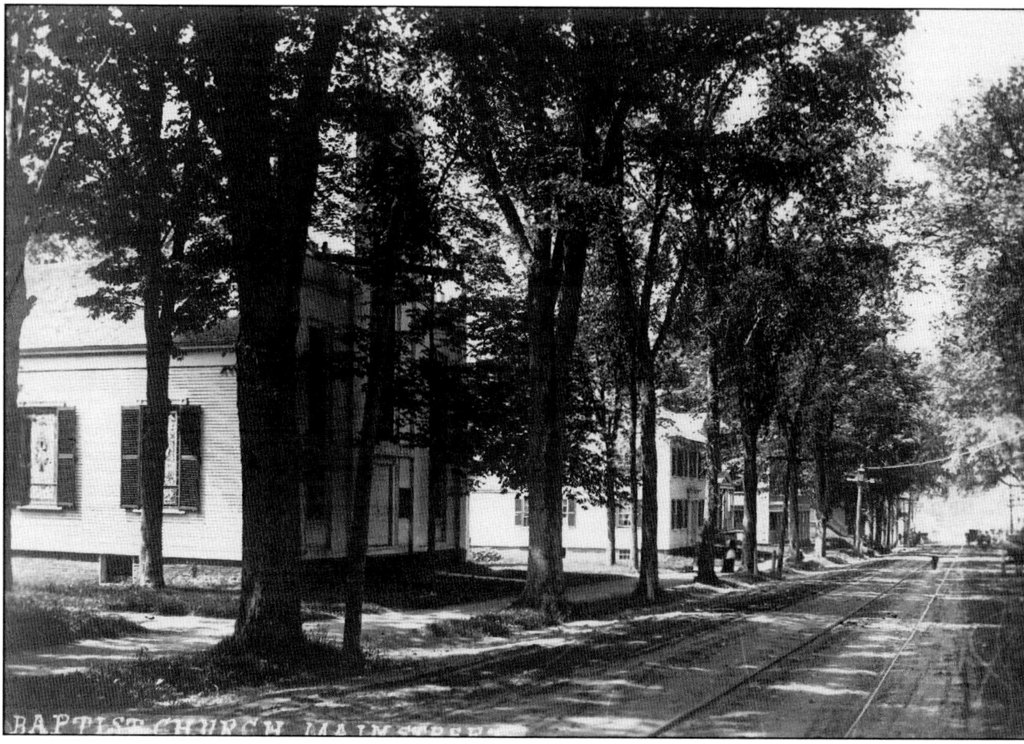

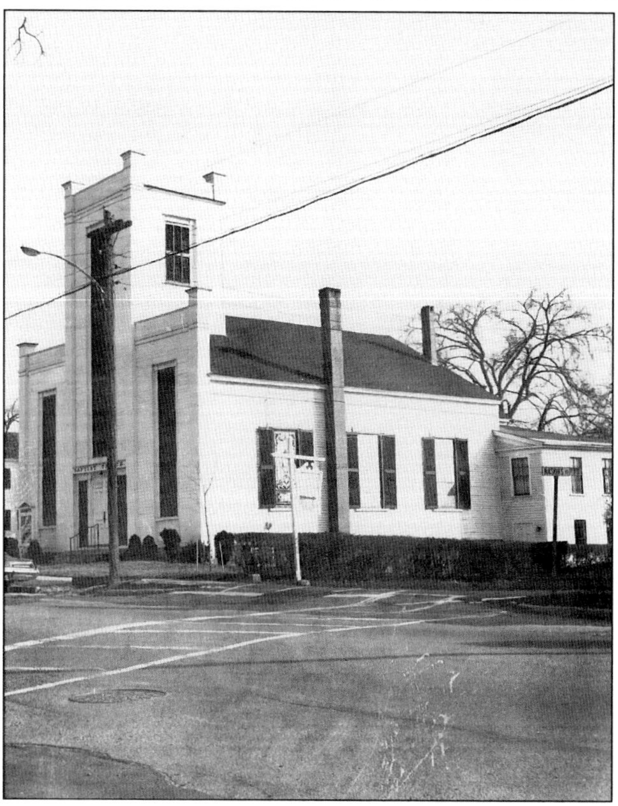

Looking south towards the river, 1906. The Baptist church is to the left in this photograph. The Richard Littlefield House, built *c.* 1840, to the right. It was modernized in 1971 when the Downing Agency—which is still located there—bought it.

The Baptist church, *c.* 1970.

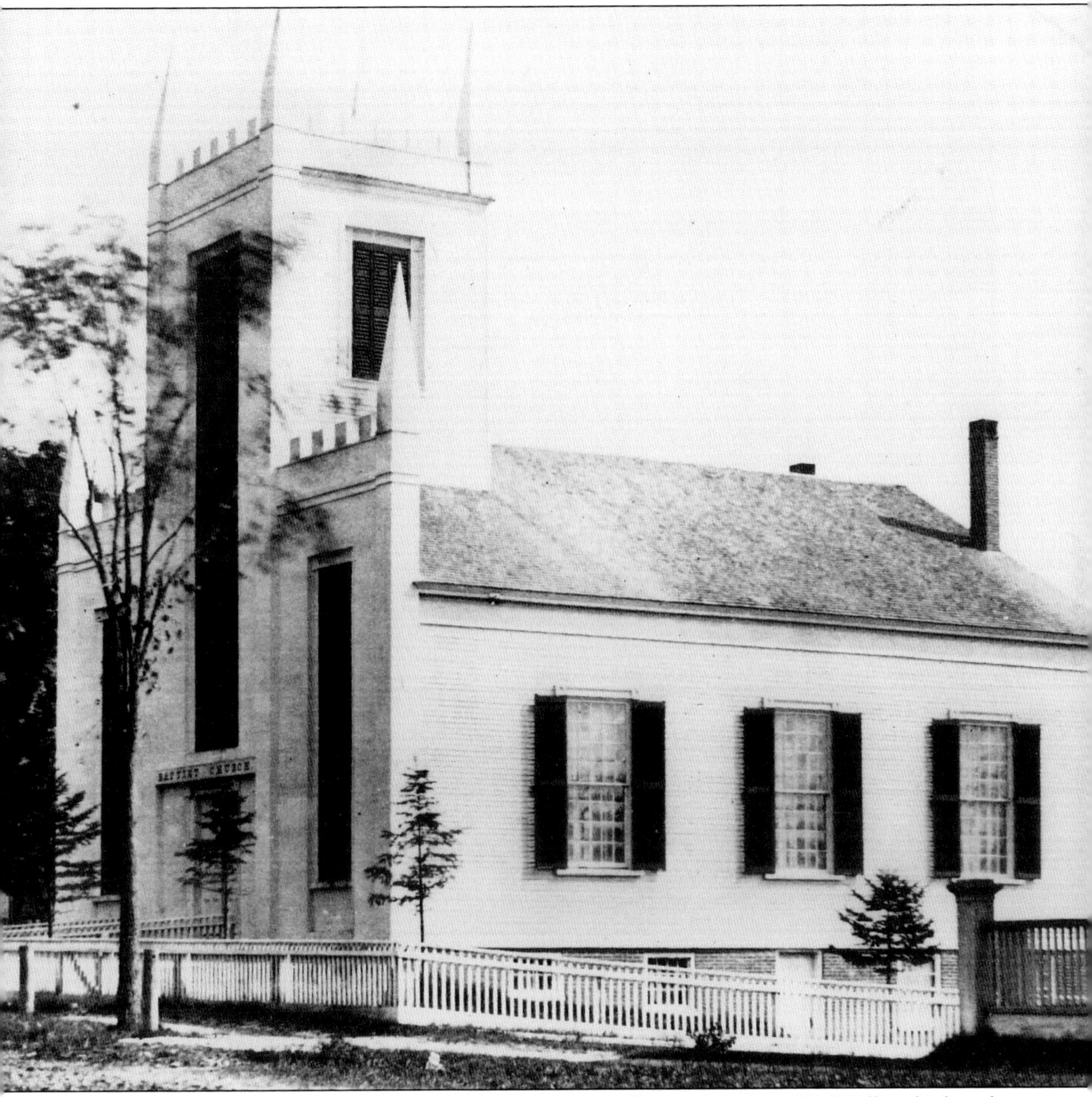

The Baptist church, 1895. On this site stood the law offices of George W. Wallingford and another house, later moved to Bourne Street. Wallingford's office was moved to Water Street after 1825. The Calvinist Baptist Church was founded on July 16, 1834. The first minister, Thomas O. Lincoln, was ordained on December 10, 1834. The corner stone of the Tudor-style Village Baptist Church was laid on May 27, 1840, and cost $4,000 to build. In July 1890 it became incorporated as the Village Baptist Church. In 1926 the name was changed to the Kennebunk Baptist Church. In 1894 William Barry was hired to remodel the interior, which included adding 12 feet to the back. The singing gallery was removed and the center entrance built, closing the two side doors; a baptistry was built in the upper level, with space for the church choir and the organ. Stairways were built leading to a room used by baptism candidates. In 1902 electric lights were added, and in 1908 an organ was given to the church by Nellie Parsons Perkins. New classrooms were built in 1937.

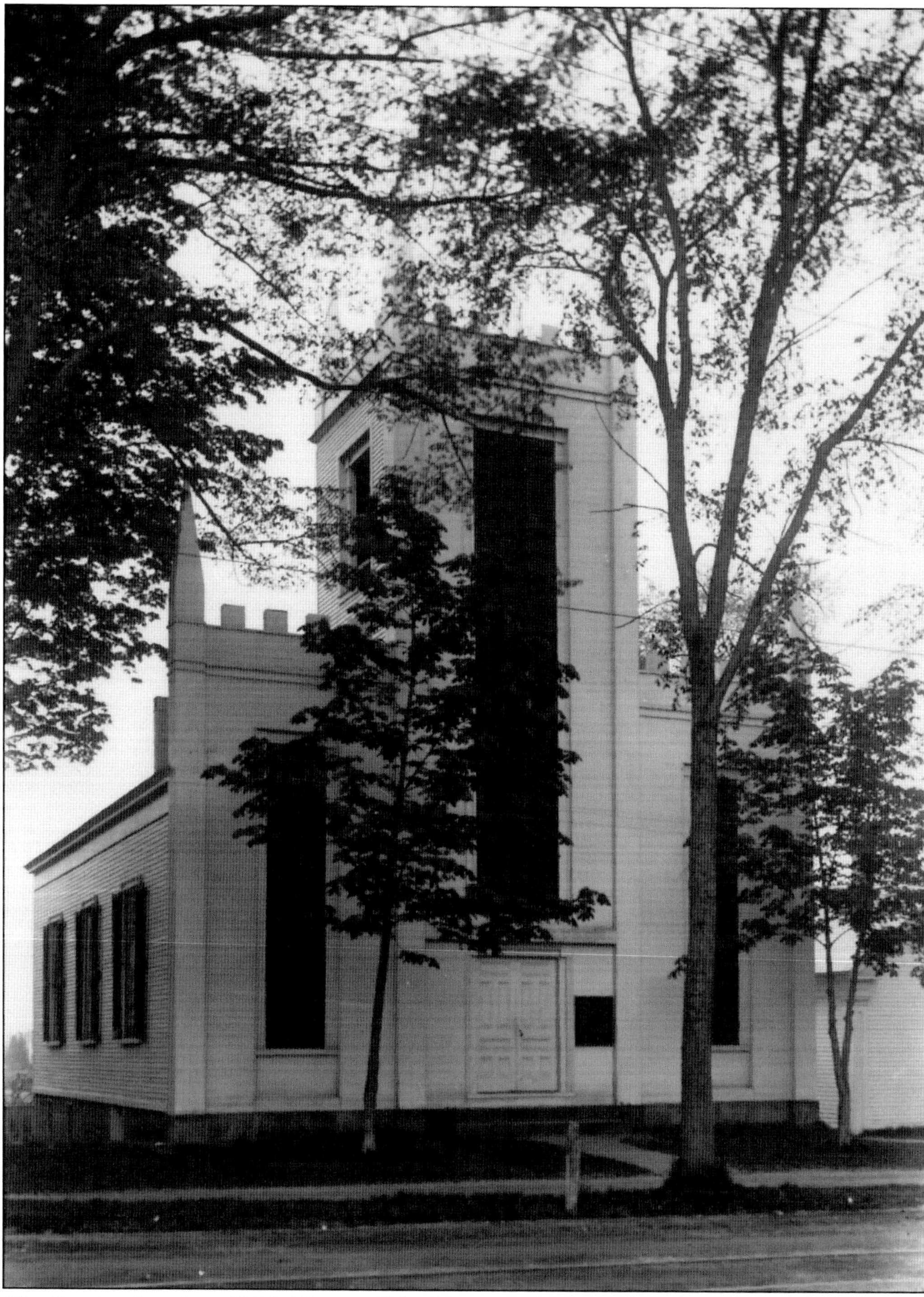

The Baptist church *c.* 1905. The small building on the far right was a vestry constructed in 1873. The wonderful Tudor Revival details were hung on the church's front like a stage set. Notice the plain side walls. All of these original details were later removed or covered when vinyl siding was added.

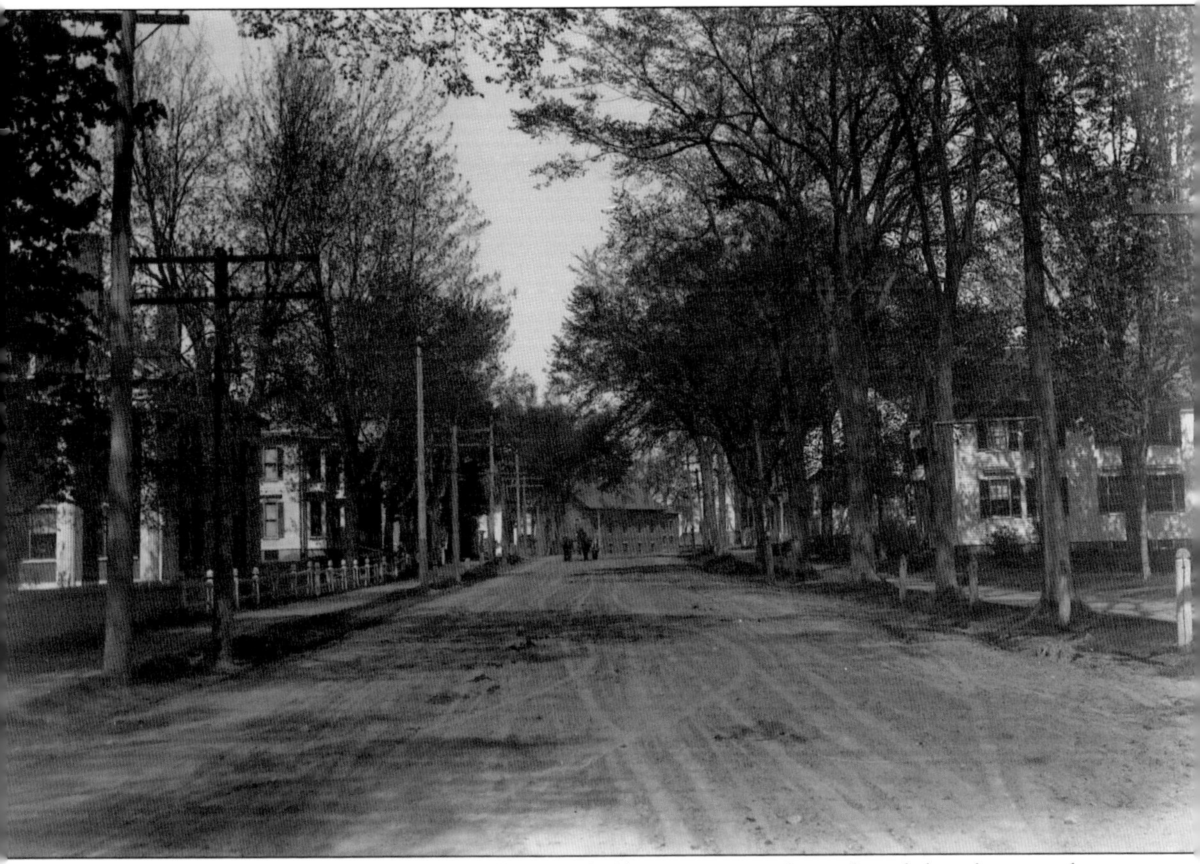

Main Street, looking north, c. 1895. The Mitchell House is to the right of the photograph. Samuel Mitchell purchased the land and buildings from Oliver Littlefield in 1838. The Mitchell House may have originally been a store built by Dr. Fisher for rental income. The exact date of its construction is unknown. Mitchell was the first station agent of the Portland, Saco, and Portsmouth Railroad. In 1866, his house was sold to the Second Congregational Church (Christ Church) who used it as a parsonage. Today it is the offices of the Cole Agency.

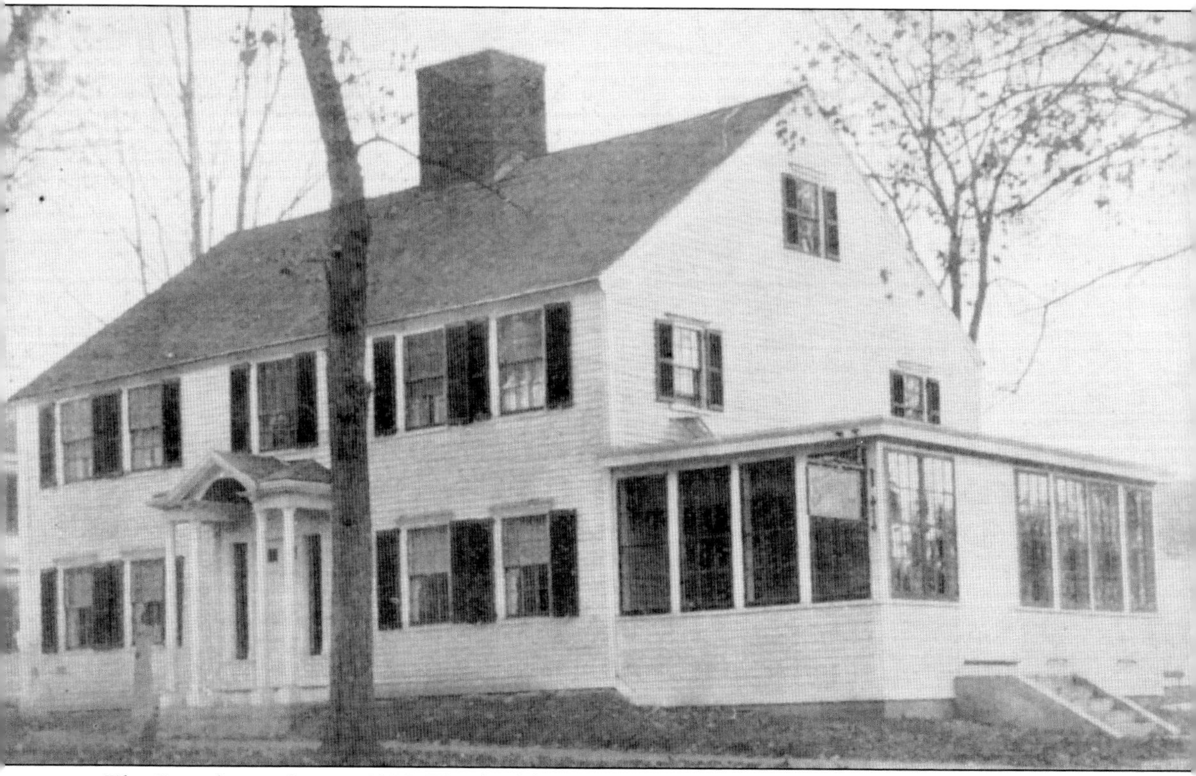

The Snapdragon Inn, *c.* 1920. This building was built as a two-family home in 1788 by Benjamin Brown (who also built the Brown House). It was called the Long House because before 1867 it was connected to the Grant House next door by a one-and-a-half-story shop. Brown sold the house in 1793 to William Jefferds and Stephen Tucker. In 1799 Jefferds sold his half to Captain John Grant, who constructed a one-and-a-half-story addition to the left side of the building. His daughters Sally and Abigail used this space as a millinery shop and a school. When Abigail had her home built on the lot beside the Long House, it was built onto the addition. Grant and his son Edward operated a men's clothing and shoe store. They ran into financial trouble in 1806, owing $1,672.70 to their suppliers, Baylies and Howard of Boston. In a judgment against the Grants, Baylies and Howard were awarded the property and its contents. John's daughter Sally purchased the property back and used it as her home. The Grant addition was moved in 1867 by N.N. Wiggins to Barnards Lane for use as a home. In 1907 the Town of Kennebunk purchased both halves with the intention of building a new high school on the site, but this never happened, and the building was eventually sold at public auction to Blanche Potter. Potter ran a millinery shop downtown. In 1923 she opened the Snapdragon Inn and Tea Room, which she operated for many years. (Photograph from the author's collection.)

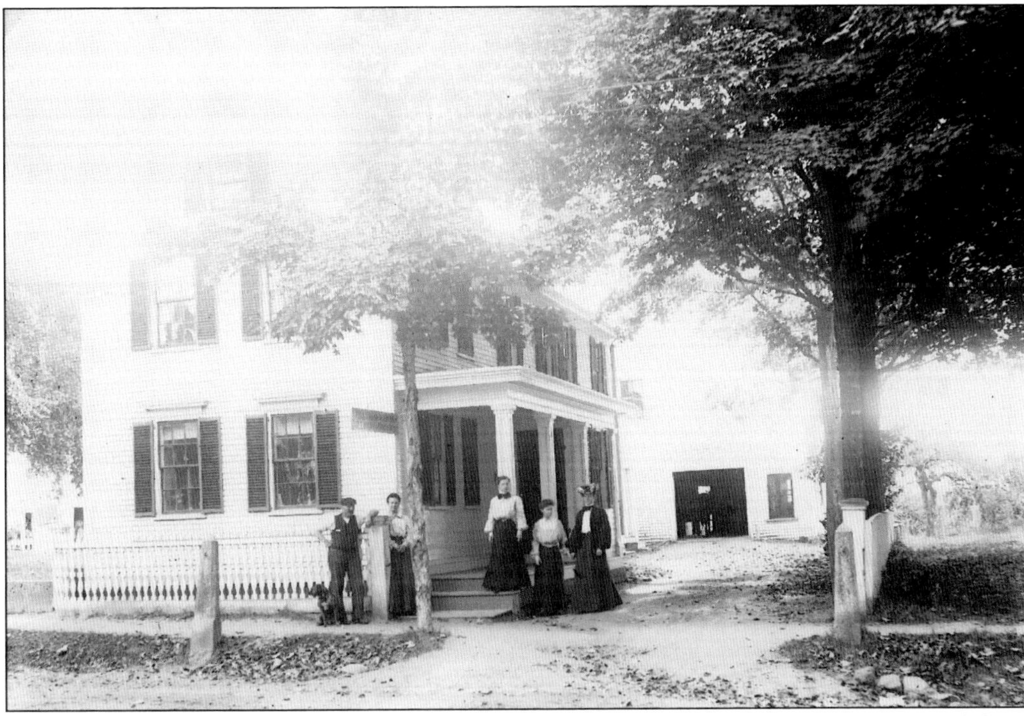

The Abigail Grant House, built c. 1828 at a cost of $2,350. Abigail, who never married, lived there until 1867. She died in Portland, Maine, in 1881, at the age of ninety-three. Abram Hill bought the property in 1867 and lived there until his death. He added windows to the right side of the house when the addition was removed from the house next door. This photograph was taken c. 1895, when Hattie Davis ran a millinery store in the front of the house.

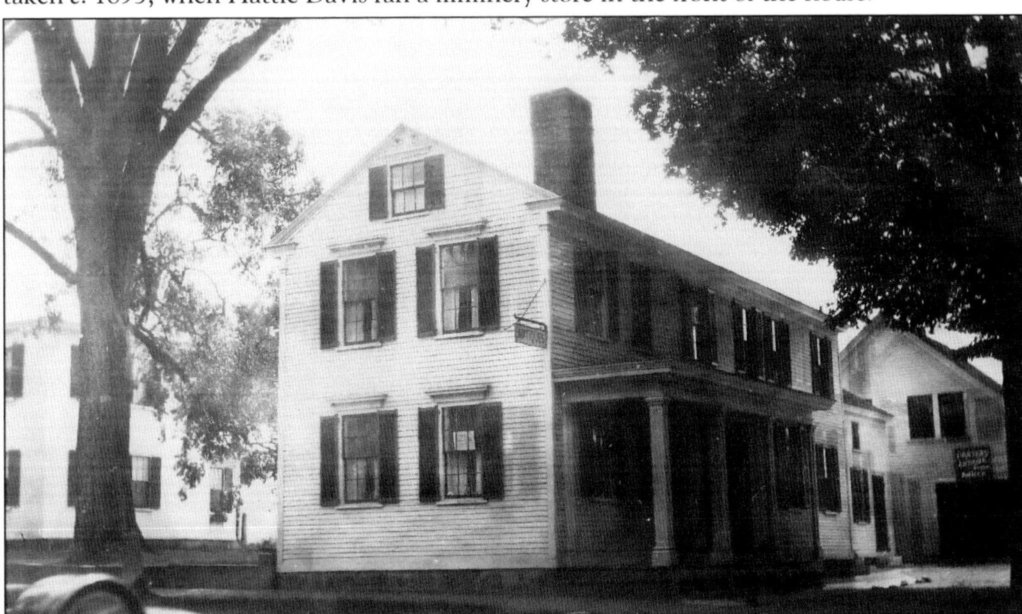

This photograph was taken c. 1930. Lotta McAlpine owned the house and ran an antique shop there.

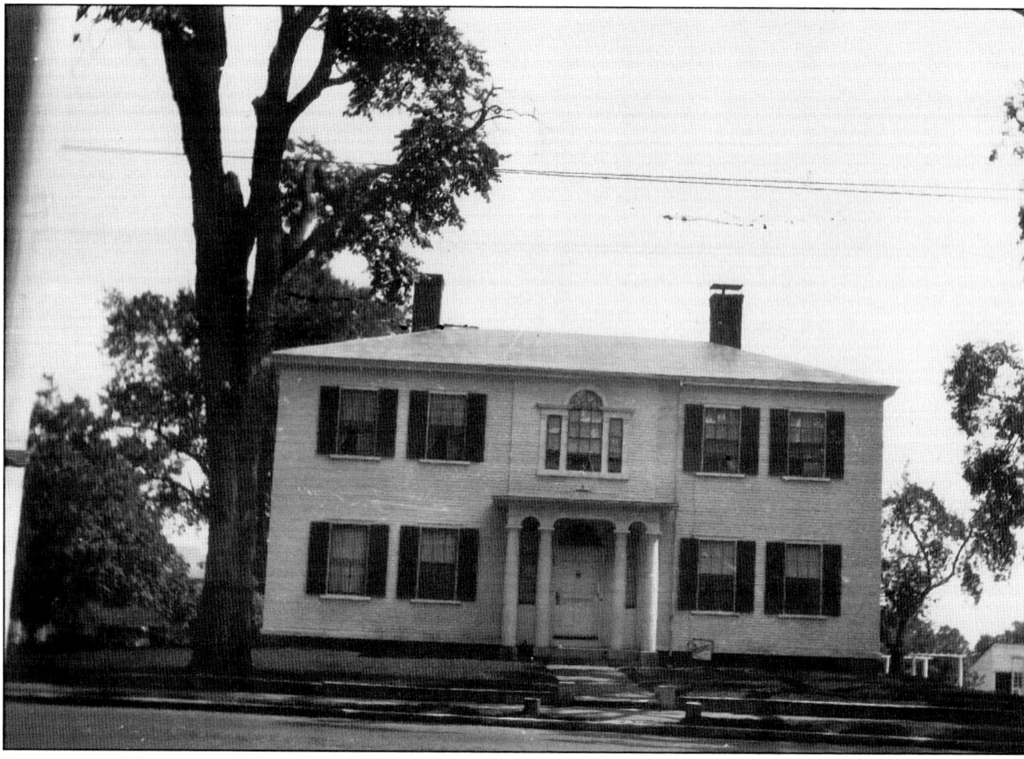

Lexington Elms, *c.* 1925. This building was designed by Thomas Eaton for Nathaniel Frost, a local merchant, in 1799. Today, the house looks much as it did when it was first built. The interior of the home is typical of Thomas Eaton's other work in the area. The Hillard House stood on this site before Lexington Elms was built (see p. 69). Frost opened his store in 1793, in the building that now houses Libby's Realty. The house was named for the elm trees which once graced its front lawn. They were reputedly planted by Theodore Lyman and a Mr. Kimball on April 19, 1775, as a memorial to the Battle at Lexington, Massachusetts. The house was framed by Moses Littlefield, a local carpenter, who may have framed many other local homes. The front porch was added by Captain Noah Nason in 1854, and was removed after 1936. The original roof balustrade was removed prior to 1900 by Nathan Dane Jr., a later owner. Charles Cutts, secretary of the U.S. Senate, lived here for a few years. In 1863 the home was sold to Dr. N.E. Smart and his son-in-law Captain William Symonds. On October 14, 1874, Captain Symonds and his wife and daughter were drowned in the English Channel when their ship, the *Kingsbridge*, went down.

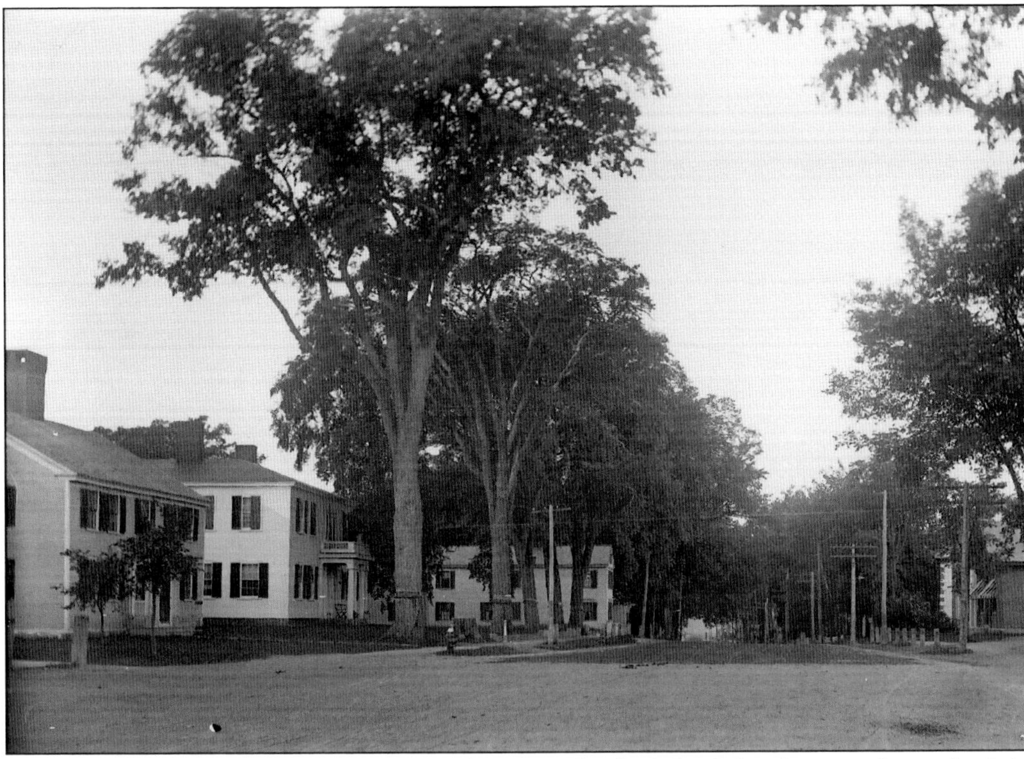

Main Street looking south, c. 1900. The house in the far left of the photograph was built by James Kimball Jr. in 1795. Kimball operated a blacksmith shop from behind his residence. He owned 12 acres of land, which included the property where the Park Street School now stands. Before Kimball sold the property, he sold a lot to Moses Savory, who built the store which now houses the Museum Shop. Kimball lived there until 1815, when Joseph Dane Sr. purchased the property. The Dane family lived there until 1872 when it was sold to Hartley Lord. Dane Street was not laid out until 1845, and was first called Union Street.

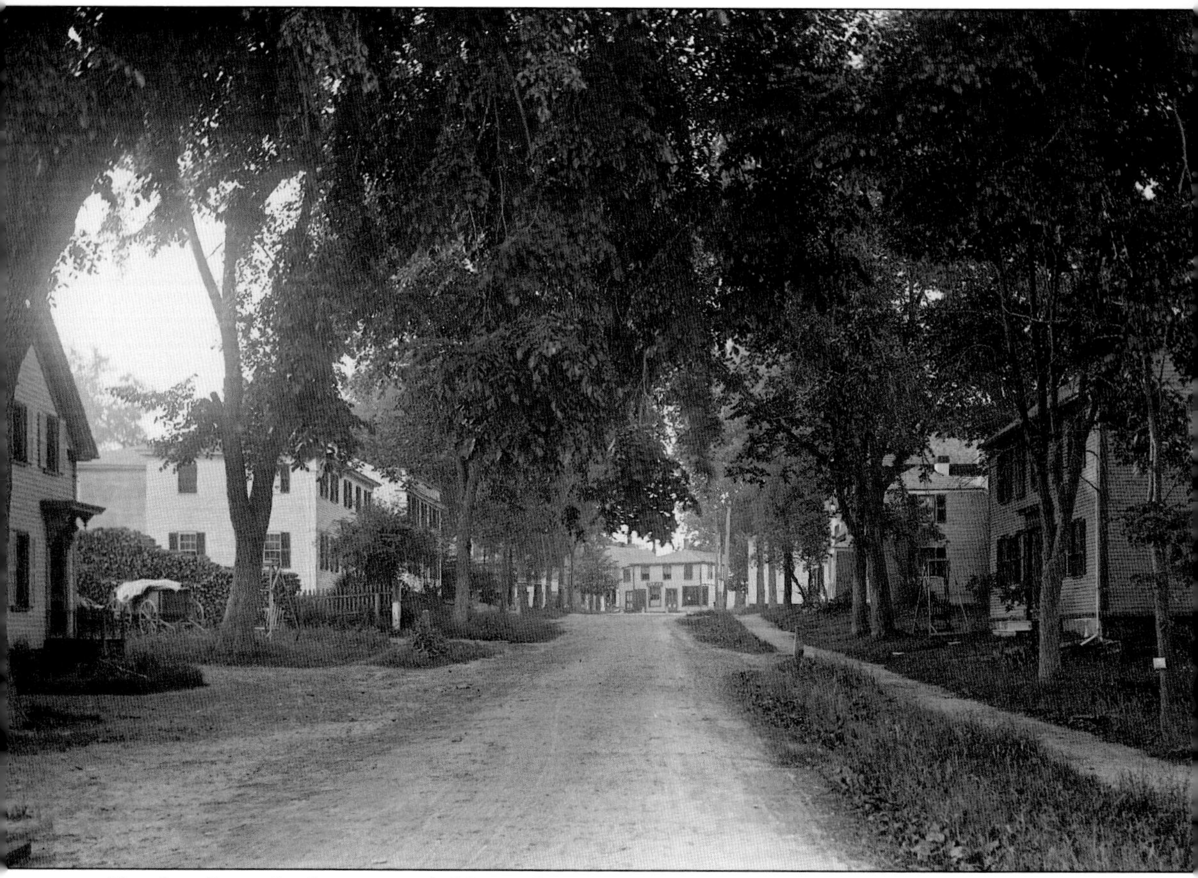

Fletcher Street looking towards Upper Square, *c*. 1880.

Seven

Kennebunk Celebrates

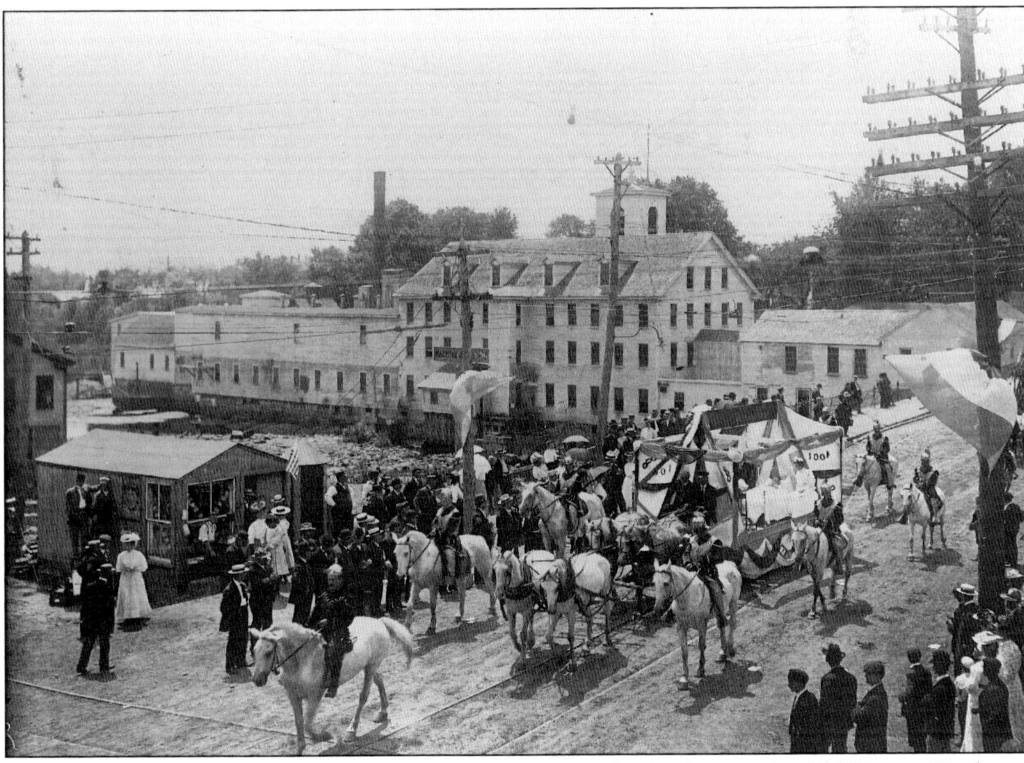

Kennebunk residents watch as the parade passes over the bridge, 1907. Old Home Week was a yearly celebration that recognized local businesses and people, especially those who had moved away. It was a time to return home, visit family and friends, and reaffirm your identity as a Kennebunker. Kennebunk today has fewer parades and celebrations of the sort that the community as a whole once enjoyed. The 1907 Old Home Week celebration was a huge event, because the new library was being dedicated—a gift from a local boy who left and prospered, but never forgot his roots.

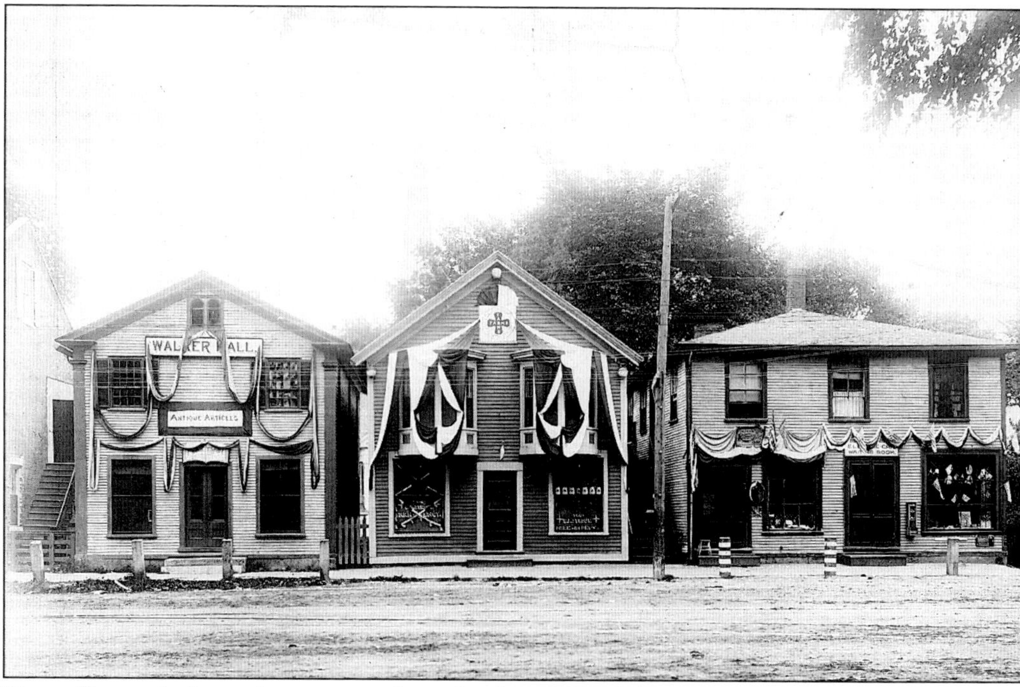

Upper Square is shown here trimmed out for the 1907 celebration.

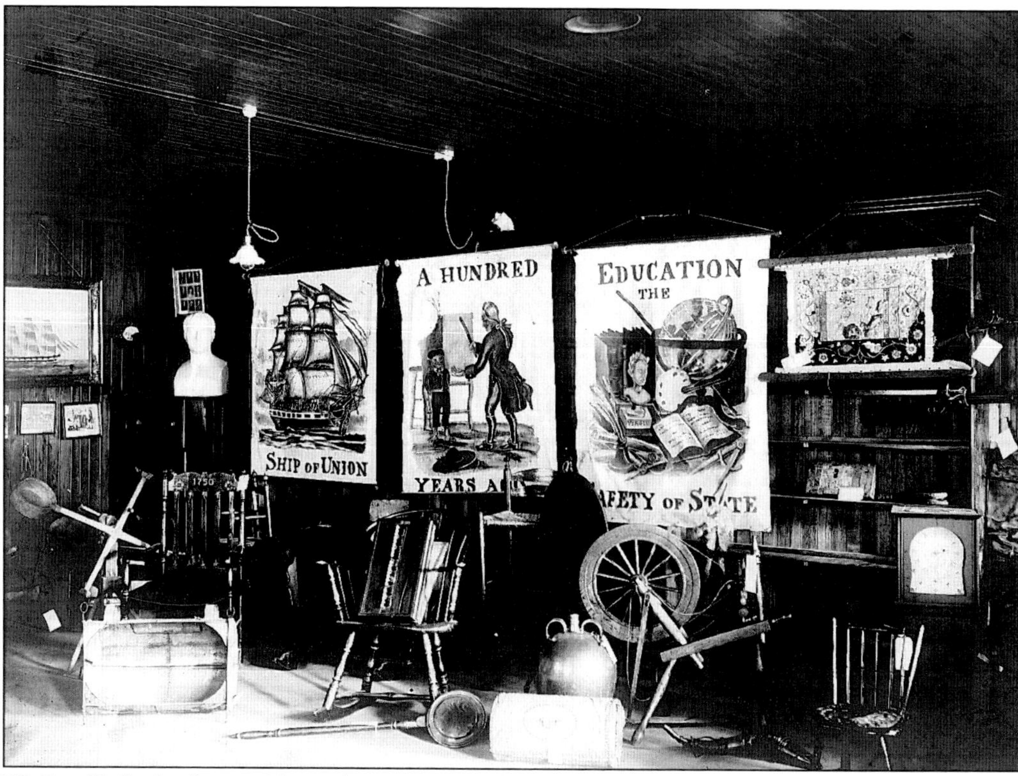

Walker Hall, the former library location, was the first museum in Kennebunk. Residents loaned family heirlooms for this display, which was protected by armed guards.

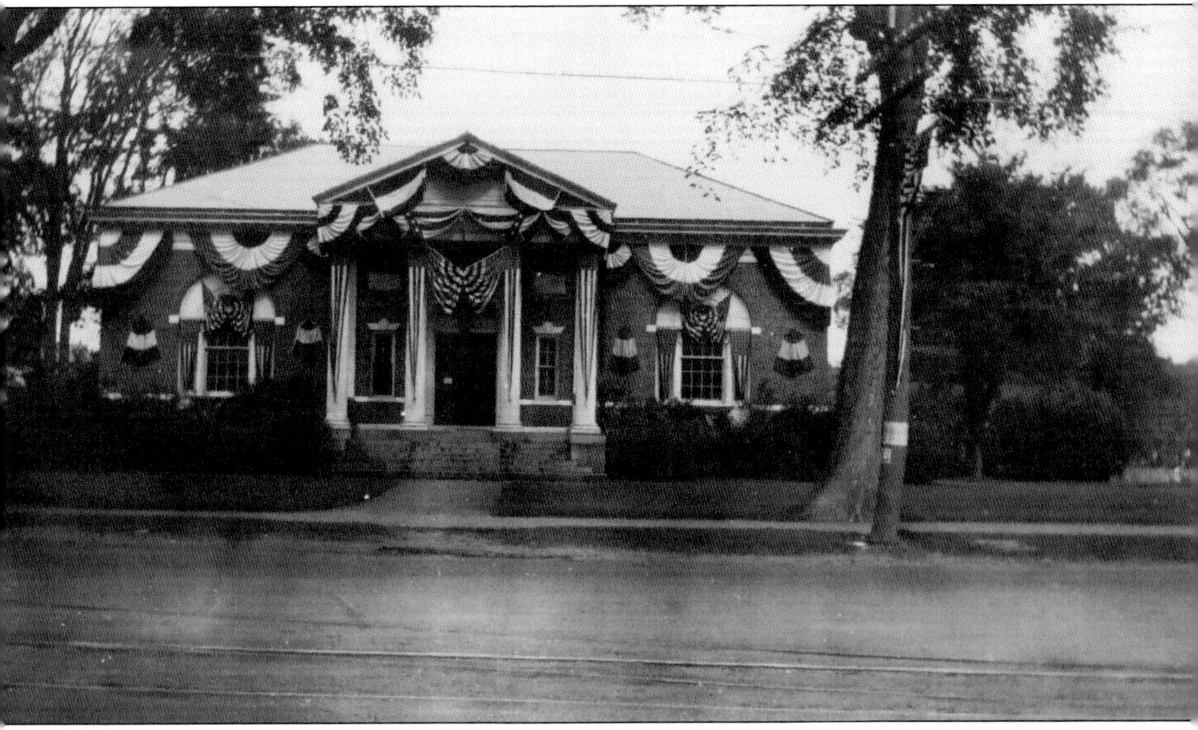

The new library was officially dedicated on August 2, 1907, during the Old Home Week celebration. The ceremony was held at the Mousam Opera House in the old town hall. The stage was banked in ferns and potted geraniums in colors of scarlet and white. Music was supplied by the Schubert Quartette of Portland. Walter L. Dane, president of the Free Library Association, gave the opening address, which included the history of the library. Reverend John Parsons officiated, and formally presented the keys to the building to Henry E. Andrews. The new library's interior was finished in oak trim with mahogany chairs upholstered in leather. Boston architect Frank Hutchins designed the Colonial Revival exterior to blend in with the other buildings on Main Street. Miss Ella A. Clark was the librarian, and the board trustees were Robert W. Lord, Henry F. Curtis, Frederick P. Hall, Herbert S. Brigham, Charles W. Goodnow, William E. Barry, Charles H. Cole, Eugene A. Fairfield, William Titcomb, Asa A. Richardson, and Henry E. Andrews.

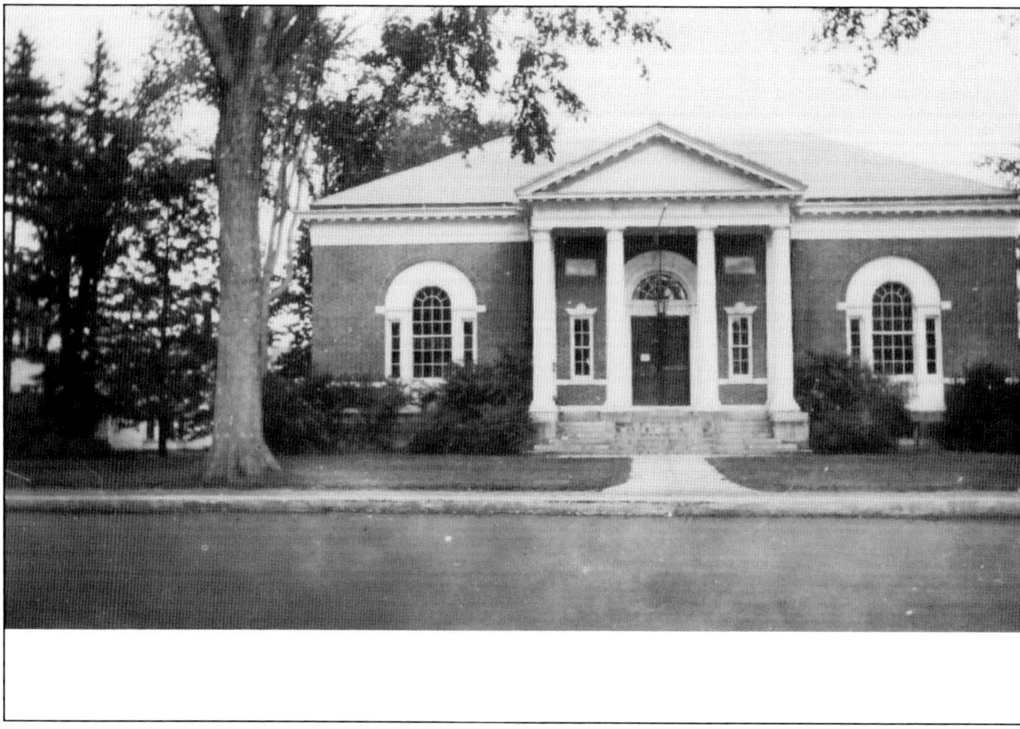

The 1907 Old Home Week Parade coming down Storer Street.

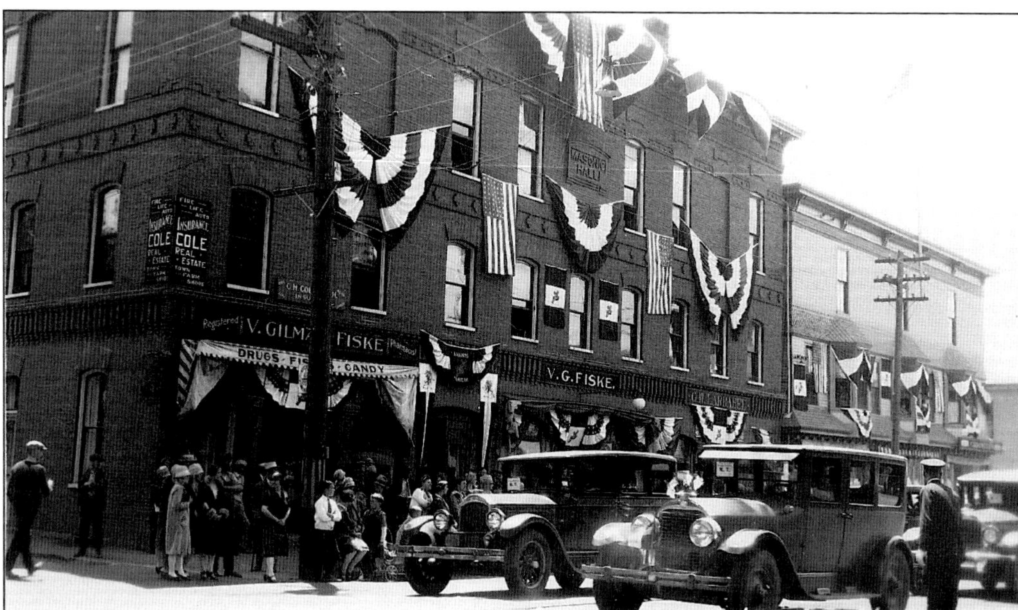

The Ross Block and the Odd Fellows Block, decorated for the 1920 centennial celebration.

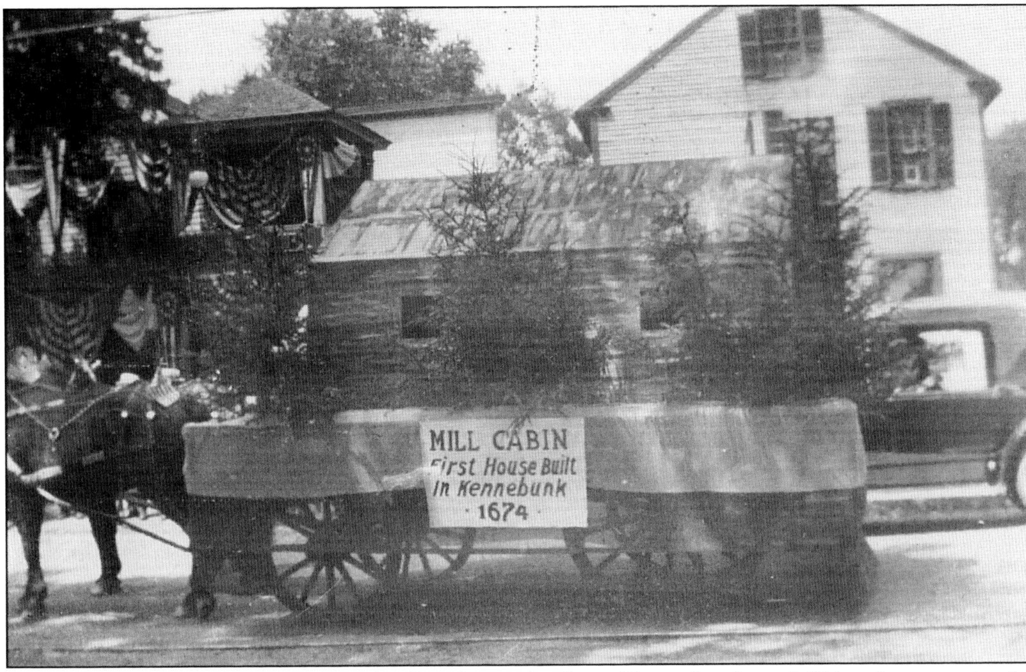

The Mill Cabin float, honoring the first house built in Kennebunk in 1674, takes part in the 1920 centennial parade. That structure, along with the mill, was burned by local Indians.

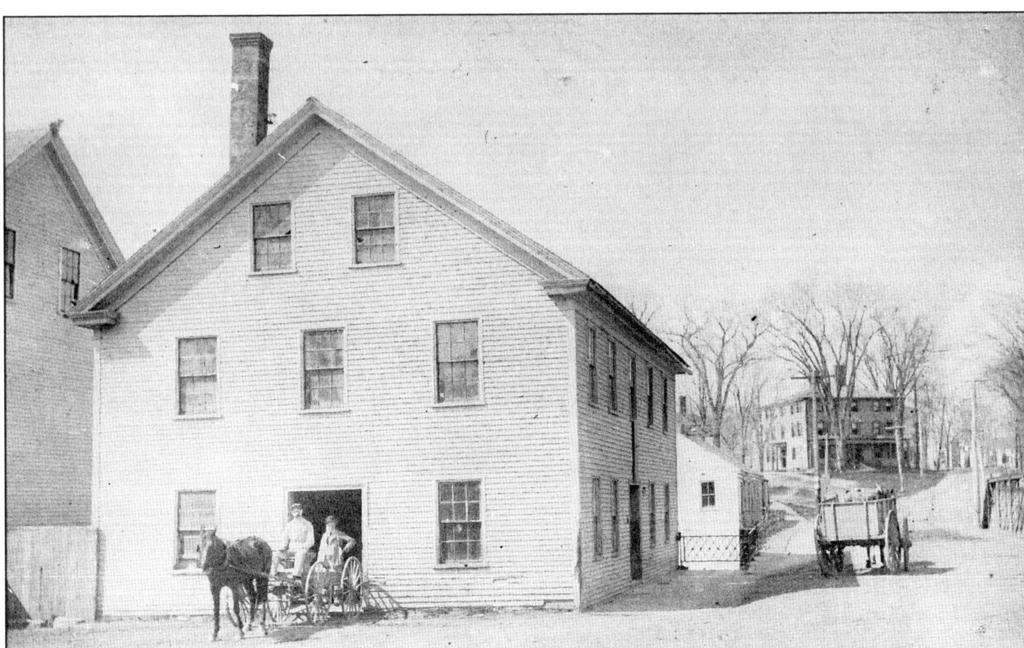
The Garrison House float.

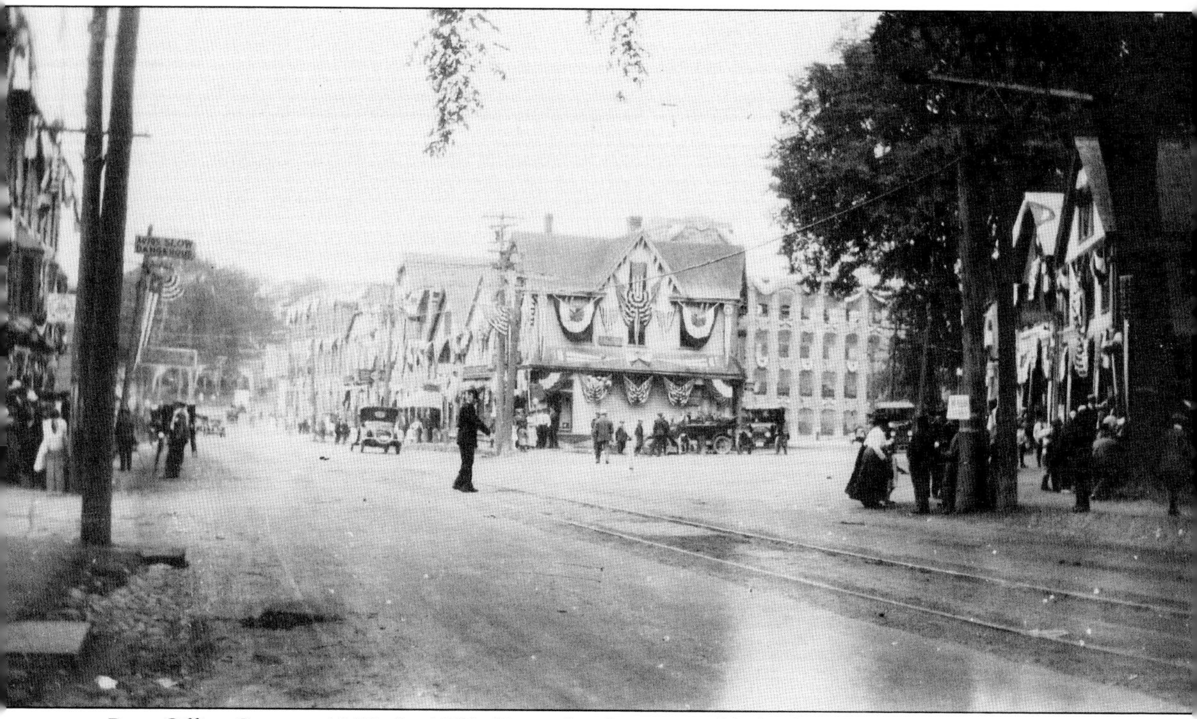

Post Office Square, 1920. In 1750, Kennebunk was established as the Second Parish of Wells and would remain a part of Wells until 1820. The subject of separation was approached for the first time in 1799. On that occasion, town officers discouraged Kennebunk residents from seceding from Wells. They chose Wells loyalist John Storer, who opposed separation, as the only representative of the Second Parish. In the past there had always been at least two or more representatives from Kennebunk. Other residents of the Second Parish refused to accept defeat, and brought a petition before the General Court of Massachusetts. A group of oppositionists called for a special town meeting on November 4, 1799, in a successful attempt to thwart separation. The General Court denied the petition. By 1814, Kennebunk had grown nearly threefold to 2,100 people, from 800 people in 1799. Again, Kennebunk sought separation from Wells. This time, Wells made it clear that it would not oppose the petition. At the town meeting, the petition was granted and a dividing line was established. However, at the request of certain individuals of the Second Parish, the division was postponed. They were concerned about the the costs of establishing a new town and the effects that the war against England was having on the economy. In 1820, Daniel Sewall began circulating a petition to see if the residents of Kennebunk were in favor of separating from Wells. At the town meeting on April 3, 1820, the petition was considered, and a committee selected to determine the town boundaries. On May 1, at an adjourned meeting, the committee made its report. The town voted unanimously to instruct its representatives to petition the state legislature for separation from Wells. It was passed by both houses and Governor William King signed it on June 24, 1820. The act took effect on July 31, 1820. At Kennebunk's first independent town meeting, on August 14, George W. Wallingford was elected the first town moderator and Timothy Frost was elected town clerk. Timothy Frost, James Dorrance, and Benjamin Titcomb Jr., were elected selectman, assessor, and overseer of the poor. Joseph Moody was elected town treasurer.

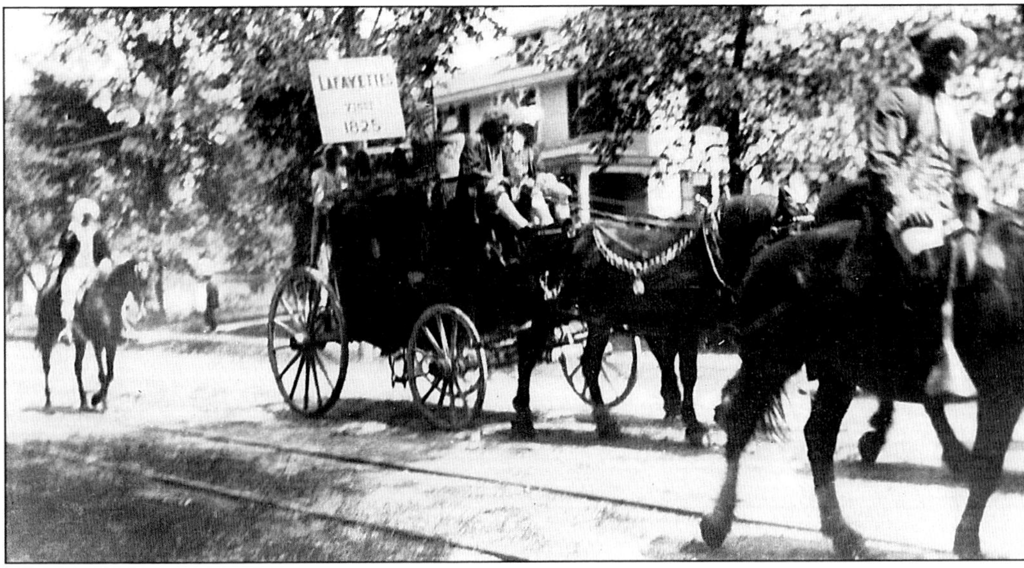

The Lafayette float commemorating Lafayette's visit to Kennebunk in 1825.

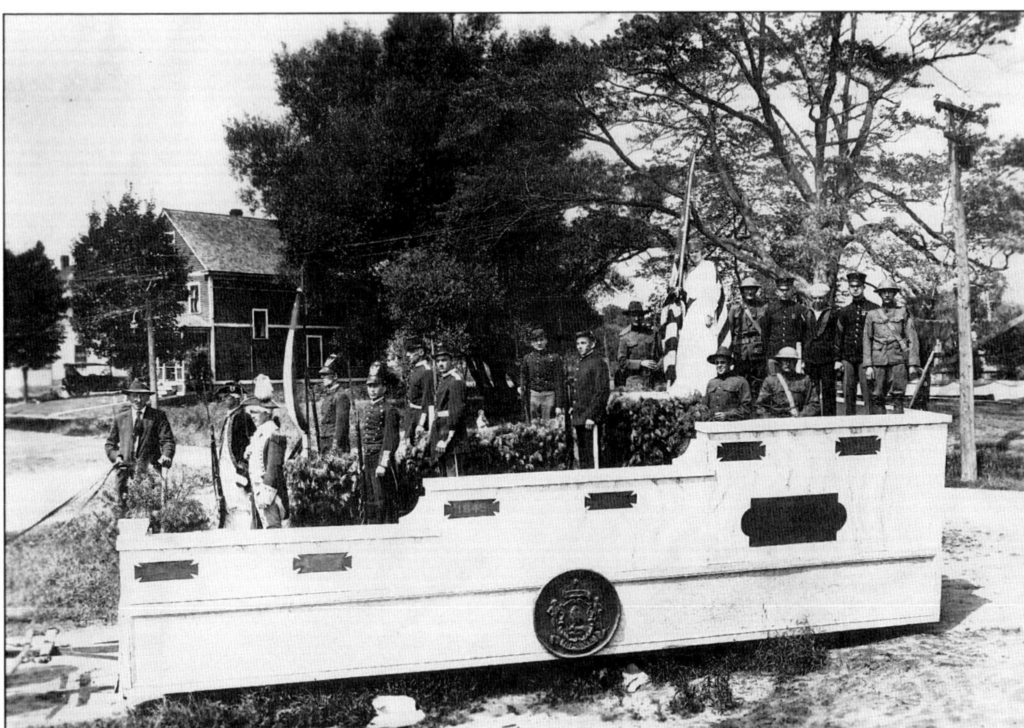

The State of Maine float in 1920.

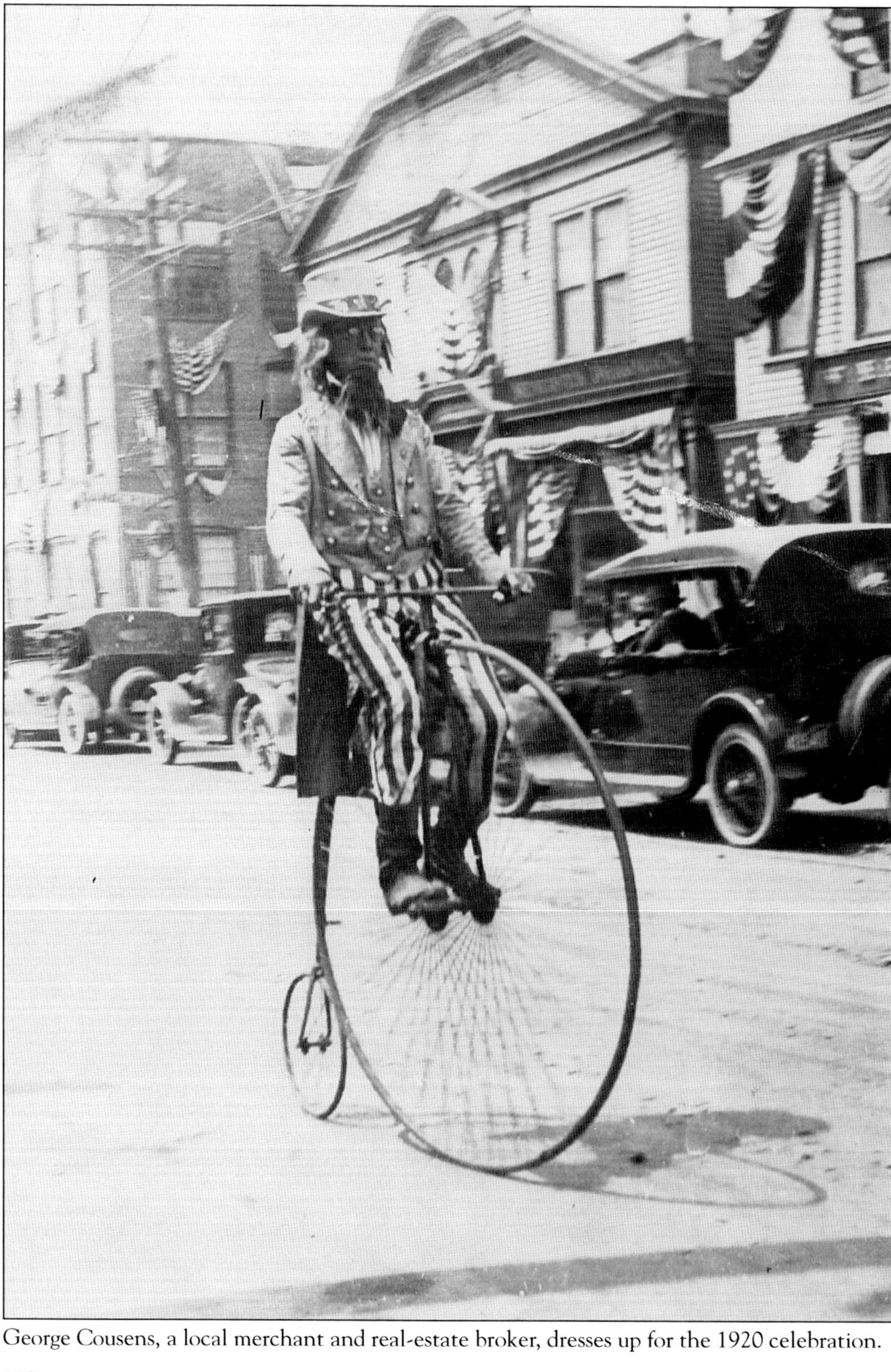

George Cousens, a local merchant and real-estate broker, dresses up for the 1920 celebration.

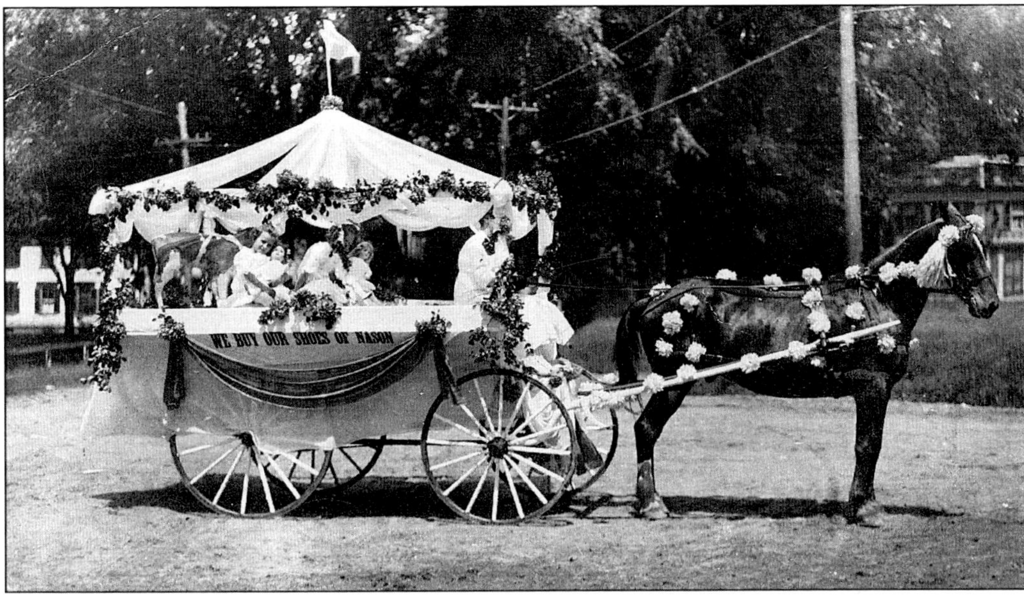

The Nason Shoe Factory float, 1920.

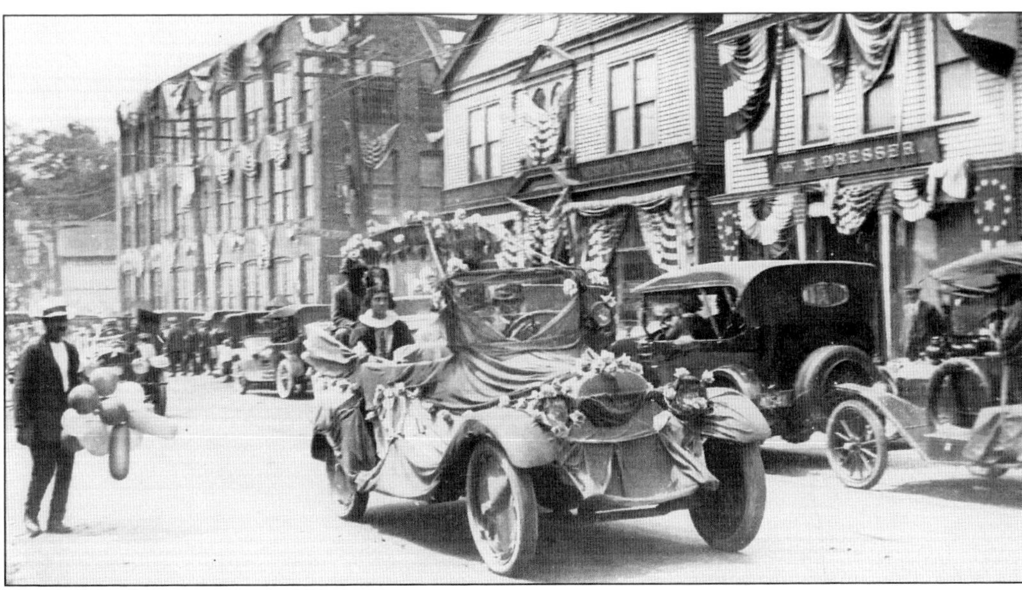

The parade comes up Main Street, 1920.

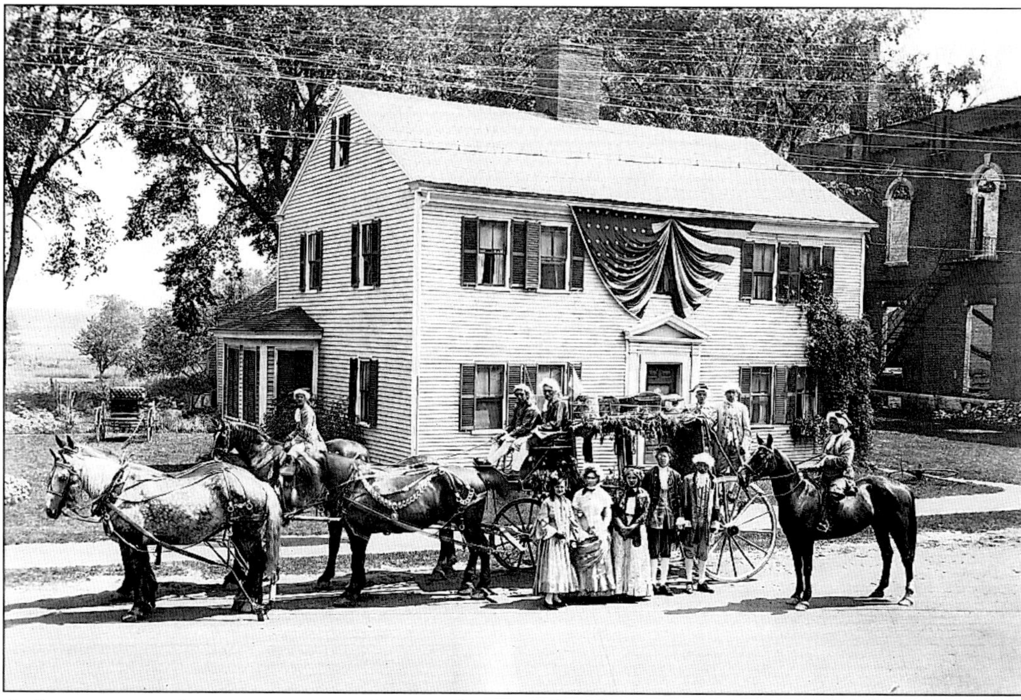

A float stops to have its picture taken in front of the Ebenezer Rice House, built *c.* 1770. The burned ruins of the town hall are visible to the right.

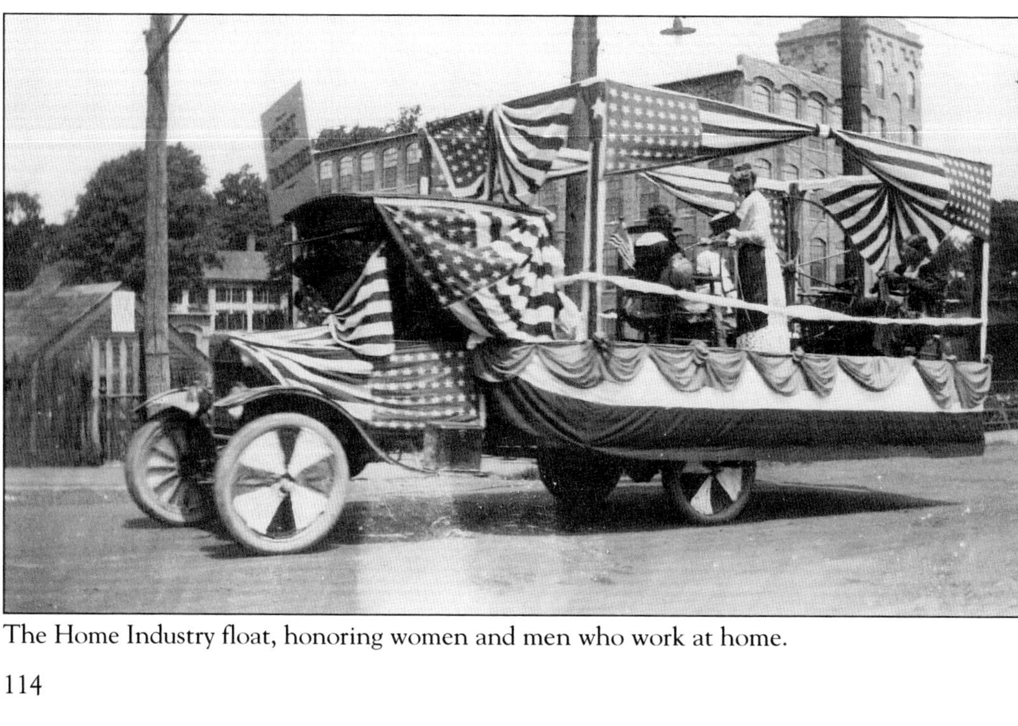

The Home Industry float, honoring women and men who work at home.

Eight

Upper Square

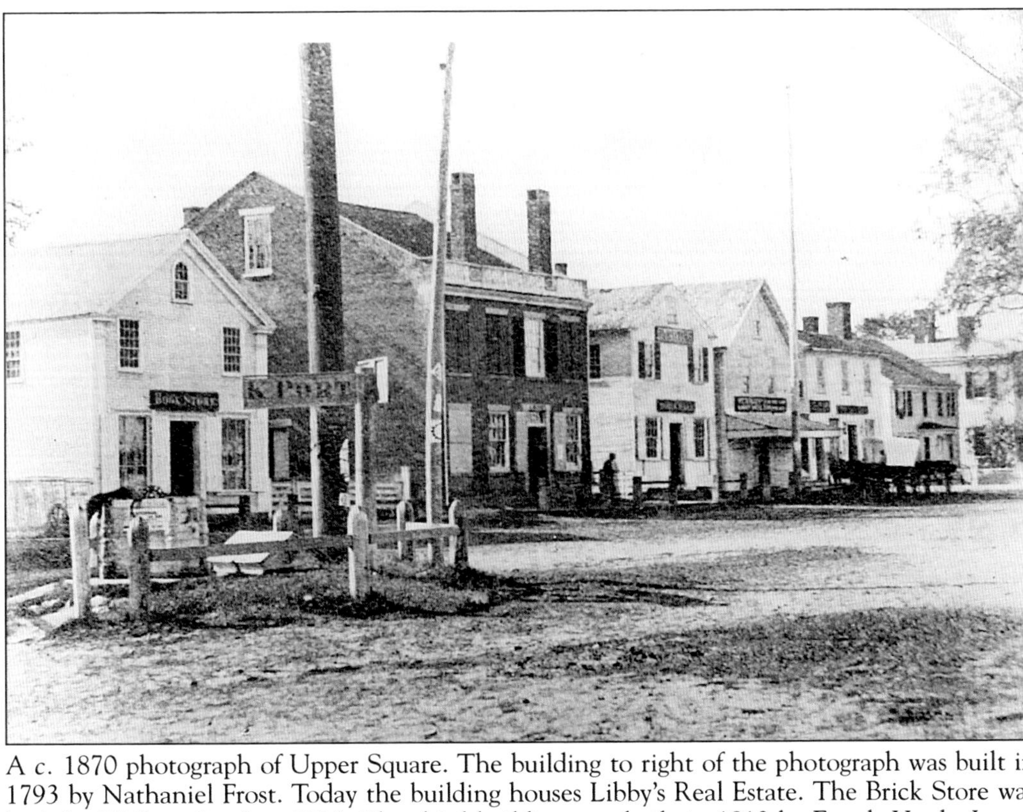

A c. 1870 photograph of Upper Square. The building to right of the photograph was built in 1793 by Nathaniel Frost. Today the building houses Libby's Real Estate. The Brick Store was built by William Lord in 1825. The third building was built in 1810 by Enoch Hardy. It was used as a country store and the second floor used as a tobacco factory. Andrew Walker had his furniture store here from 1857 to 1888. When he retired he gave the building to the Kennebunk Free Library Association. The fourth building was built by Samuel Clark in 1860. It was moved to this site in 1870 from the east corner of Water Street. The last store was built in 1814 by Moses Savary and was called "the white store" because it was painted white.

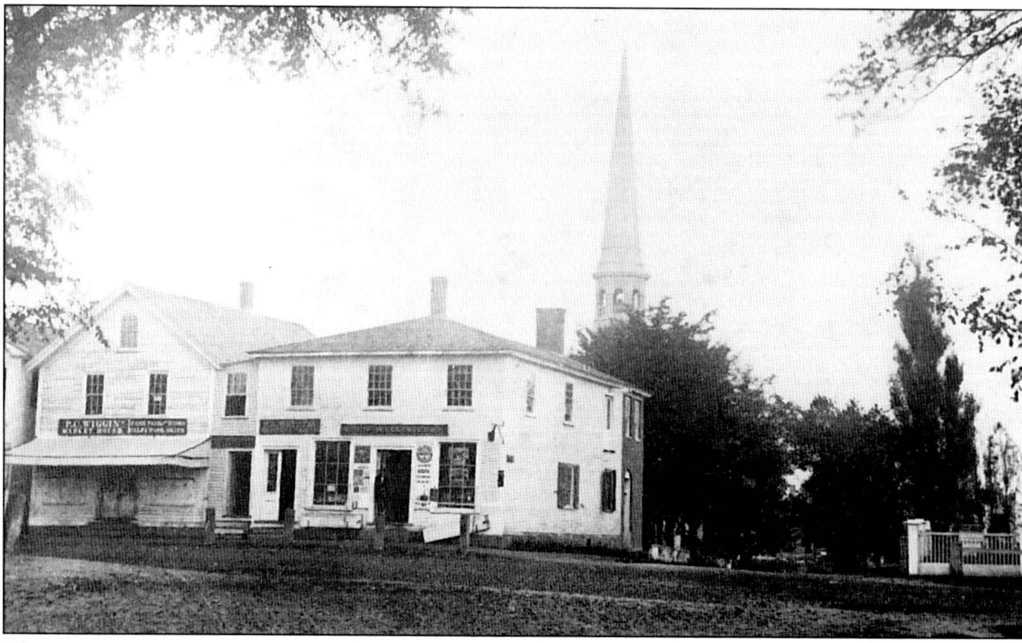

The Moses Savary store and the Clark store, *c.* 1870, with the spire of the Christ Church in the background. George Wallingford Jr. operated a drug store here before 1860. JohnW. Bowdoin later took the drug store over and relocated it to the Pythian Block in 1895. D. McKenny made harnesses in the upper floor of the building, and I.G.A. Grocery was located here until it moved to Green Street in the early 1960s. Today, the Brick Store Museum has a shop here.

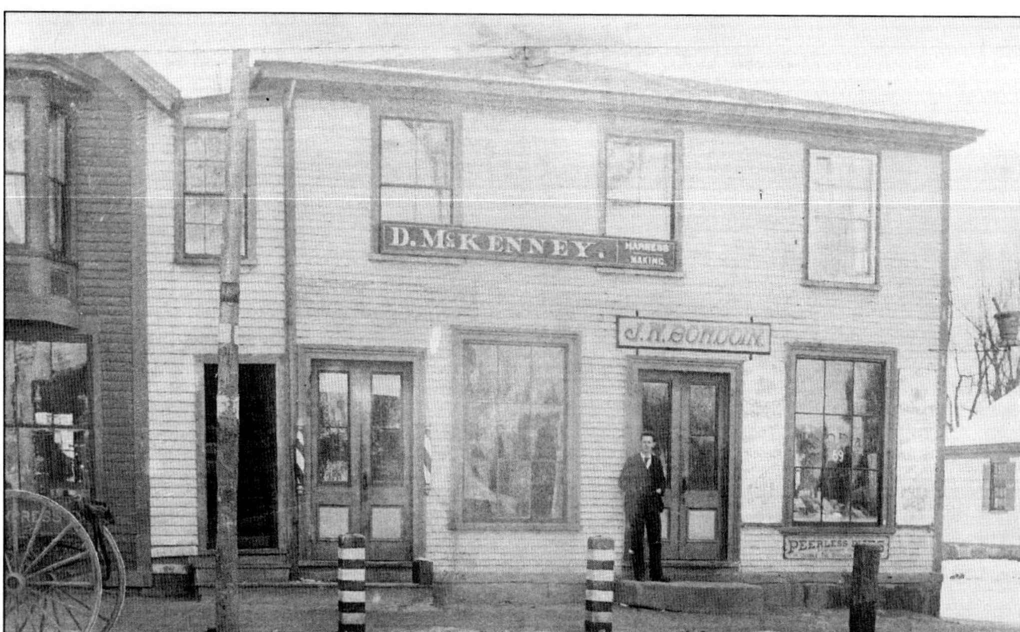

The same store in 1890. John Bowdoin is standing in front.

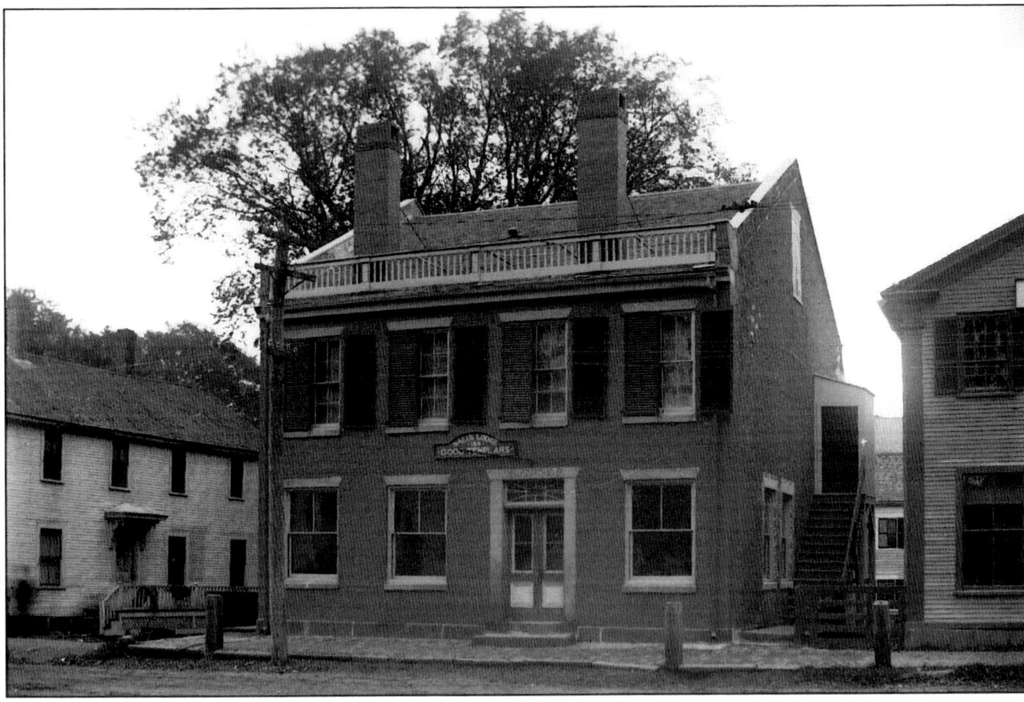

The Federal-style Brick Store, *c.* 1900. On the second floor, Increase G. Kimball had his law office and the rest of the space was used for public assemblies. In this photograph the Salus Lodge of Good Templars occupied the space. The Good Templars were formed in 1866, and were devoted to temperance reform.

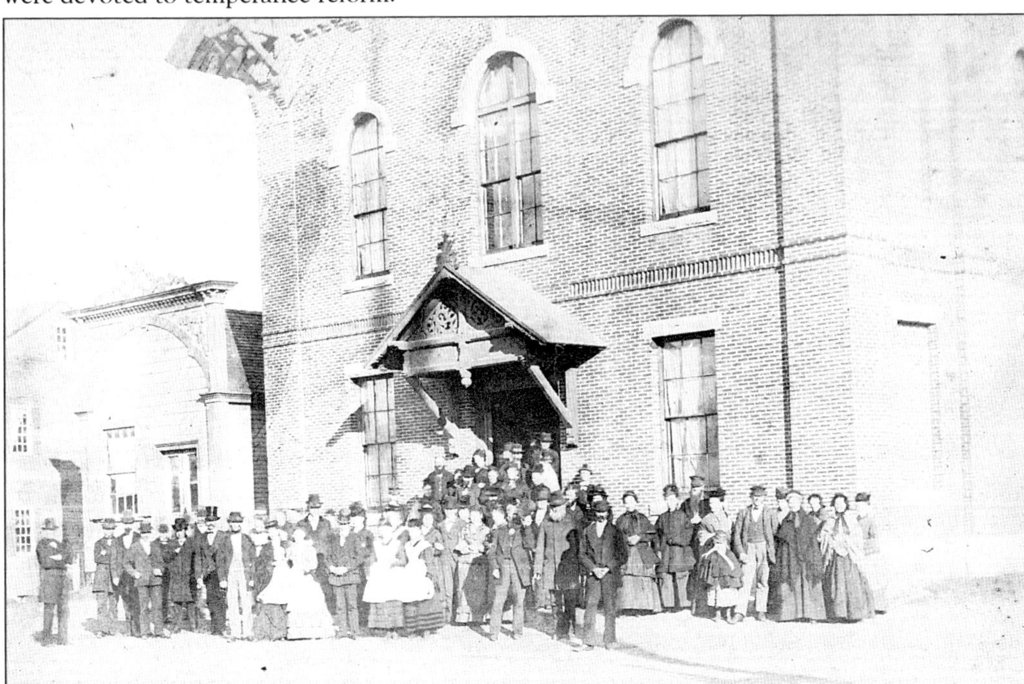

The Good Templars gather in front of the old town hall, *c.* 1880.

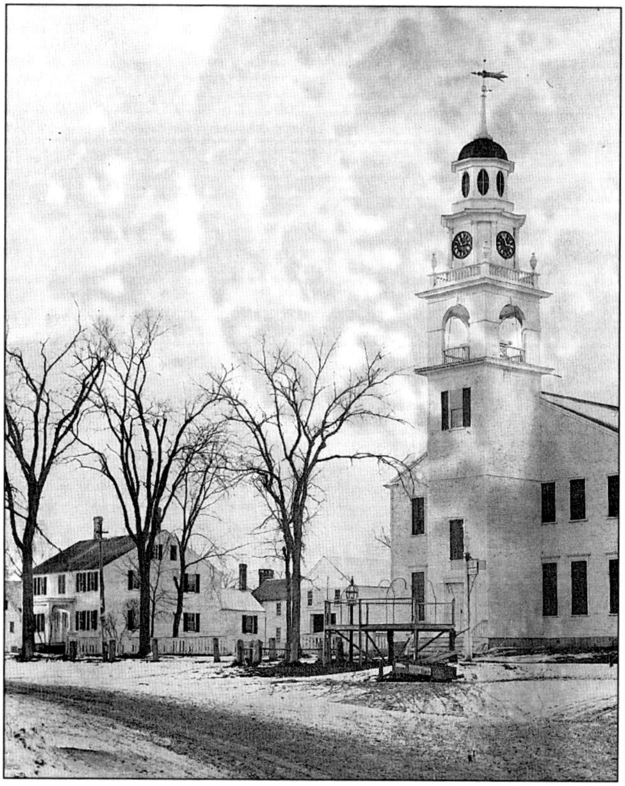

The First Parish Church, *c.* 1890.

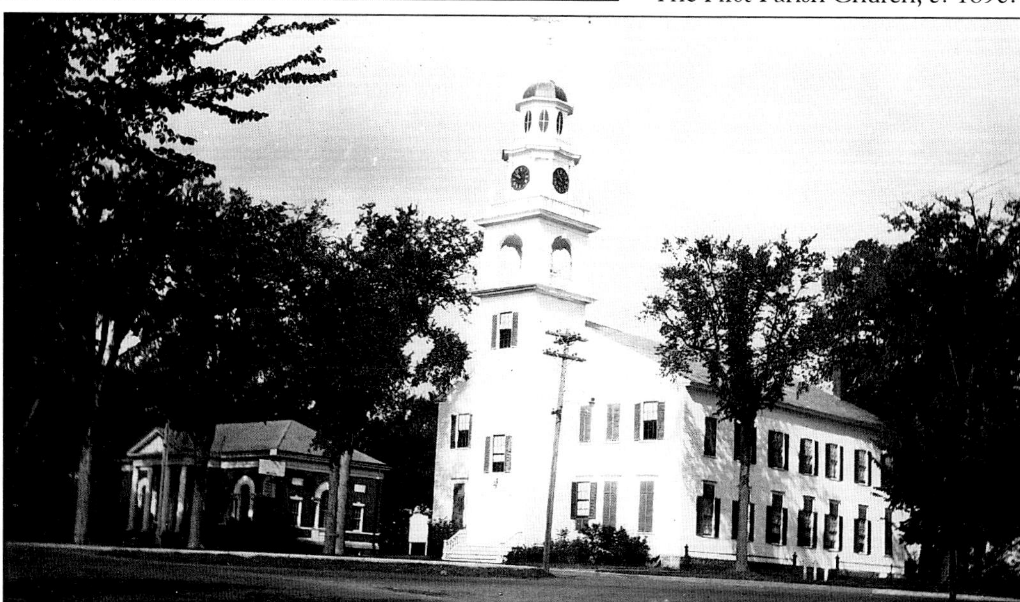

The church and library, *c.* 1915. The first meeting house in Kennebunk was built at the Landing, next to Durrells Bridge Road, in 1750. In 1775 a new meeting house was built on the site of the present First Parish Church. Upon its completion, the old meeting house was razed. In 1803 the new meeting house was expanded and redesigned by Thomas Eaton, who was influenced by the work of Asher Benjamin and Charles Bullfinch, of Boston.

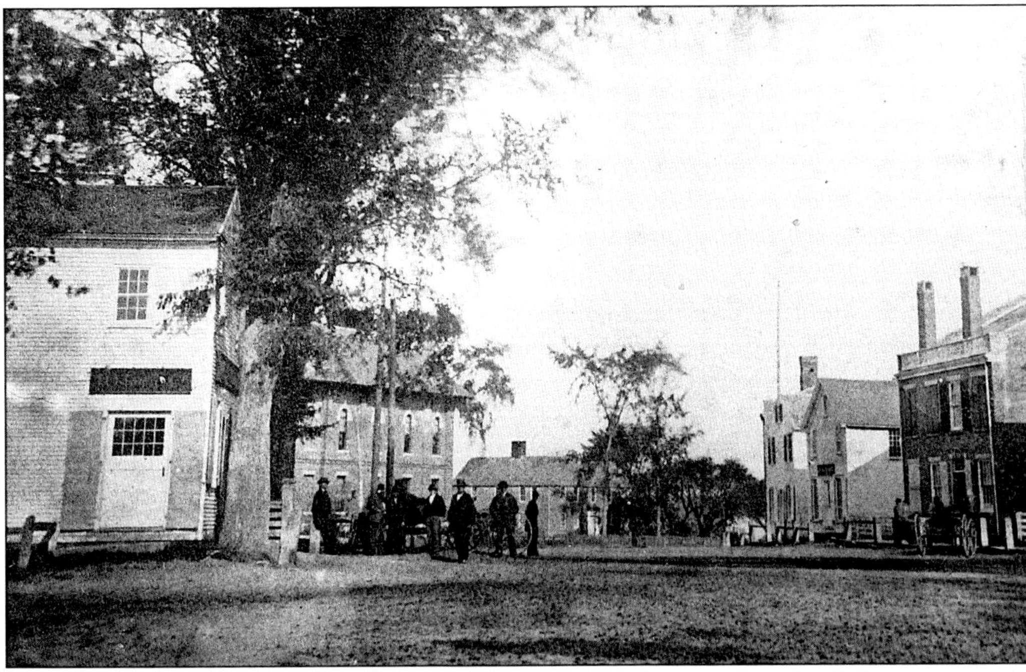

Upper Square, *c*. 1875. The building to the left in the photograph is the Osborn store at its original location, beside Fletcher Street. The second building to the left of the Brick Store was constructed by Palmer Walker in 1818. It was used as a saddler's shop. Just one hundred years later, the building would be used by Don Chamberlain as an auto show room.

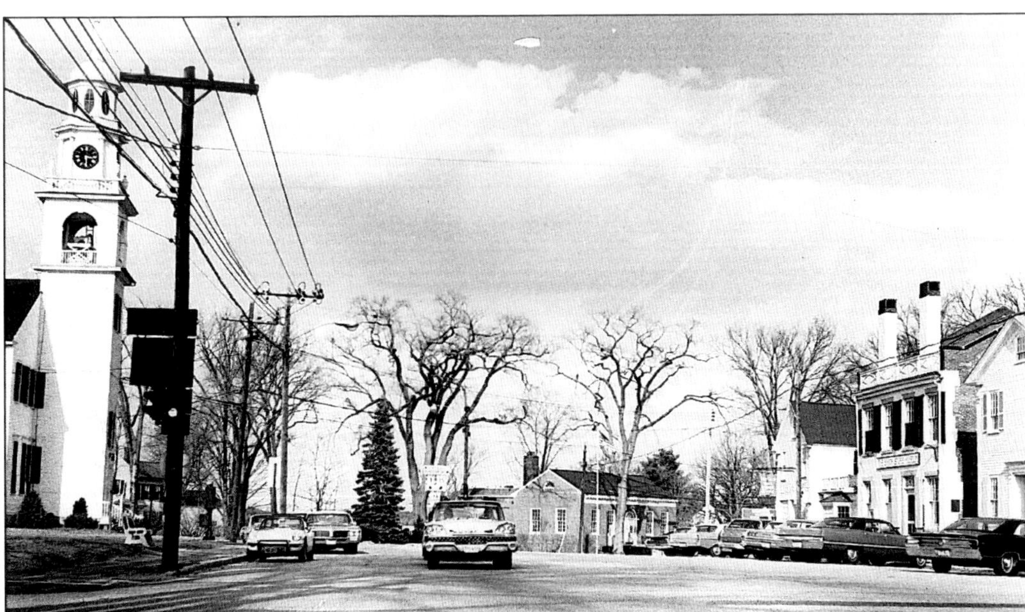

Upper Square, as it looked in 1970.

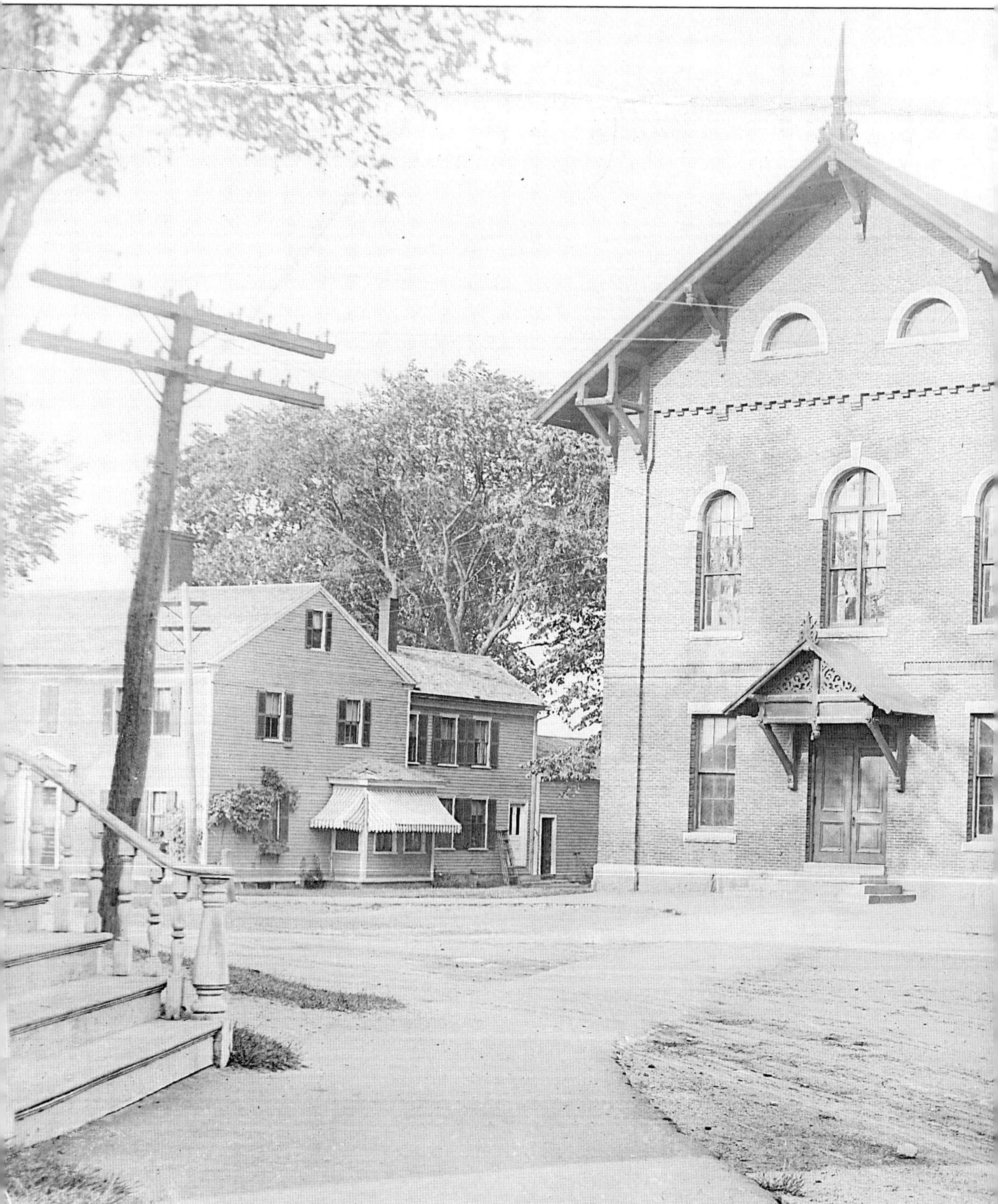

Old and new meet at the intersection of Summer Street and Portland Road, c. 1905. An automobile pauses at the intersection while a horse drinks from the water trough—representative of things to come and things about to go. Beyond the town hall, to the right of the photograph,

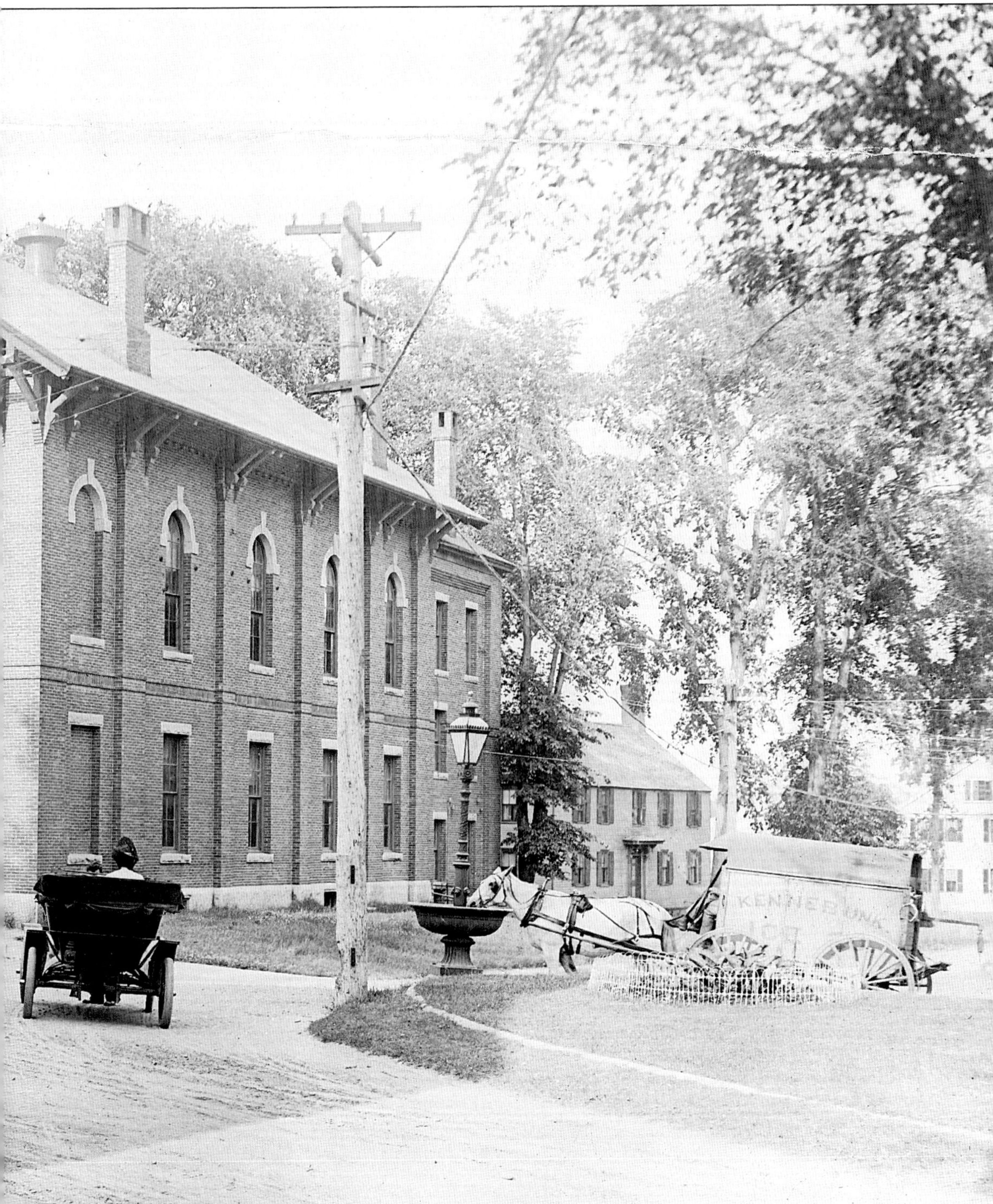

is the Kimball-Crediford House, and the Dr. Jacob Fisher House is just visible. The Fisher House was originally further up Summer Street and was moved to this location in 1840.

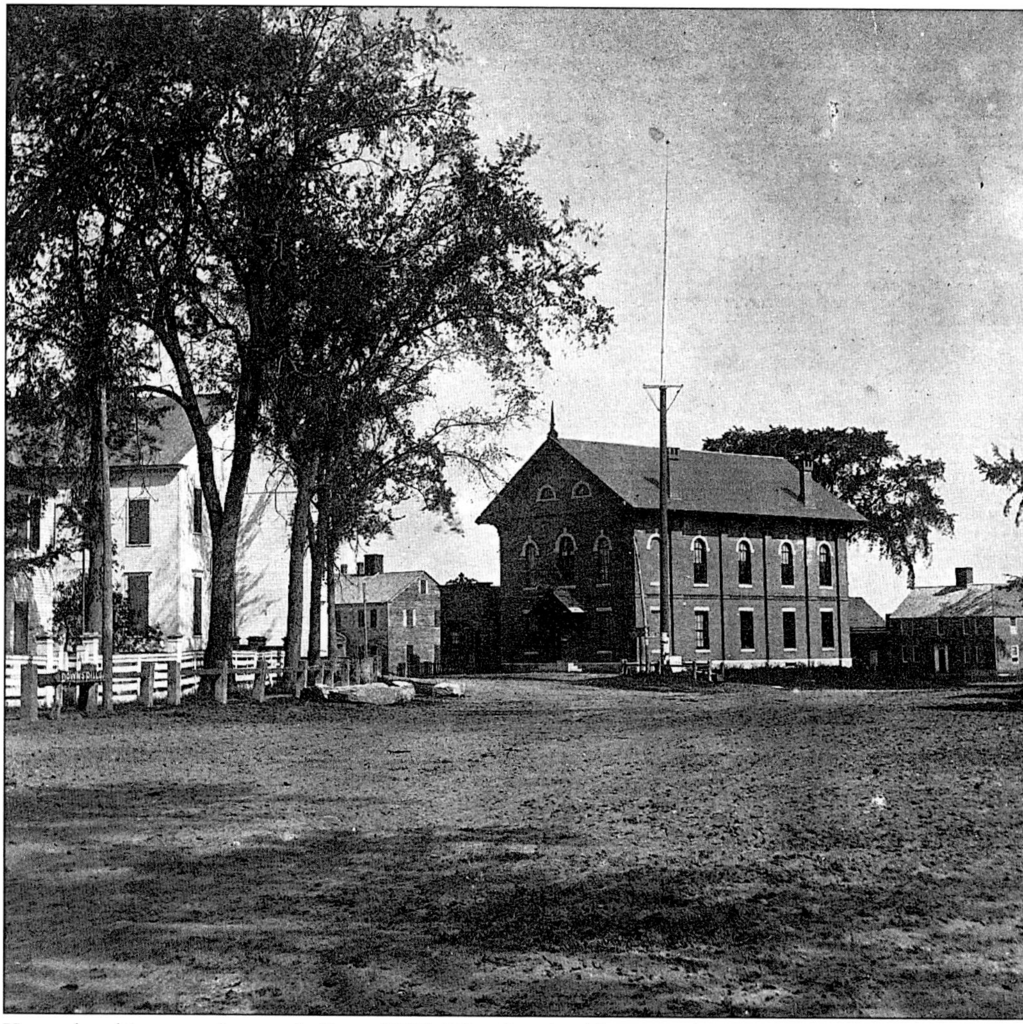

Kennebunk's second town hall, c. 1885. The first building on this site was called Washington Hall, and was built in 1812. This large building was 63 feet long and followed the curve of the road. A large multi-paned window was fitted into the curve, providing light for the business located there. This building contained the selectmen's offices and on the second floor there was a large assembly room for public events. Washington Hall burned on November 26, 1866, taking with it many valuable town documents. The town hall was built the following year and included space on the first floor for town business; on the second floor there was an opera house called Mousam Hall. The building cost $14,200 and was Kennebunk's most up-to-date building at that time.

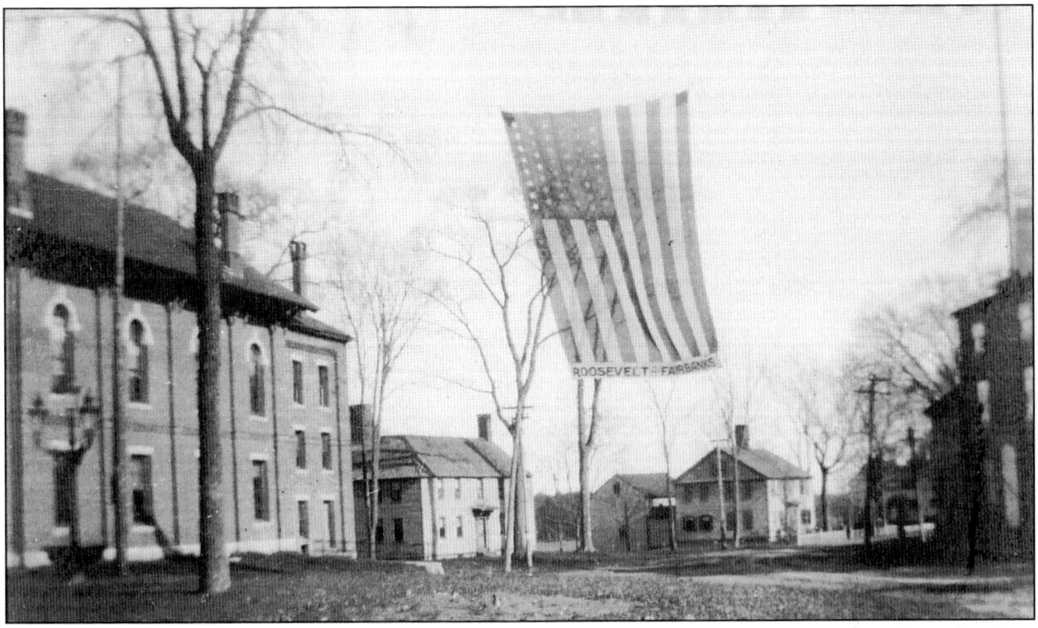

Upper Square looking toward Summer Street, *c.* 1901. The flag says "Roosevelt and Fairbanks." The early brick Warren–Kelly Building is on the far right.

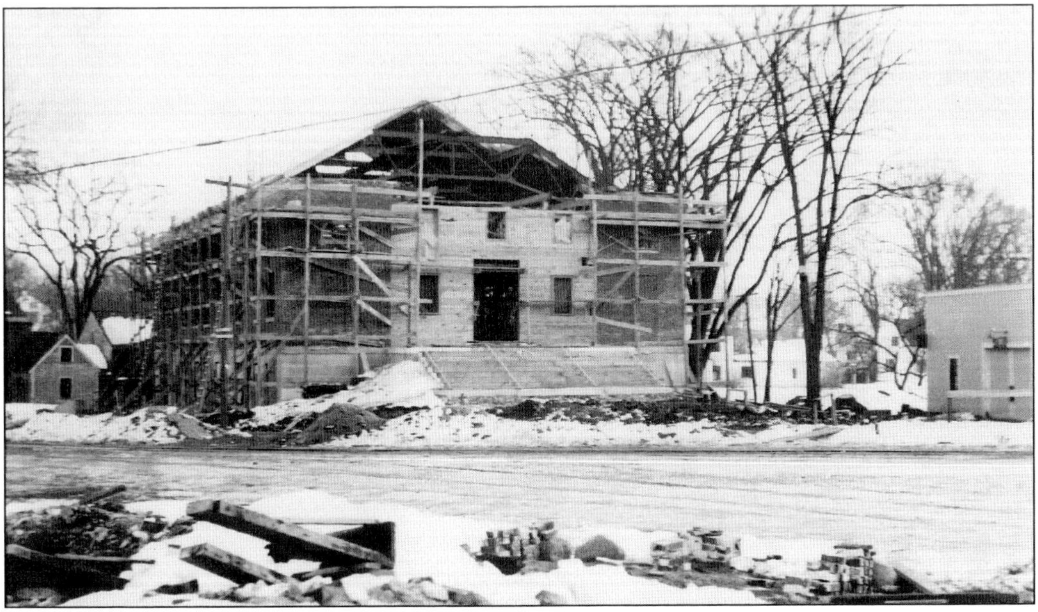
The new town hall under construction, 1921.

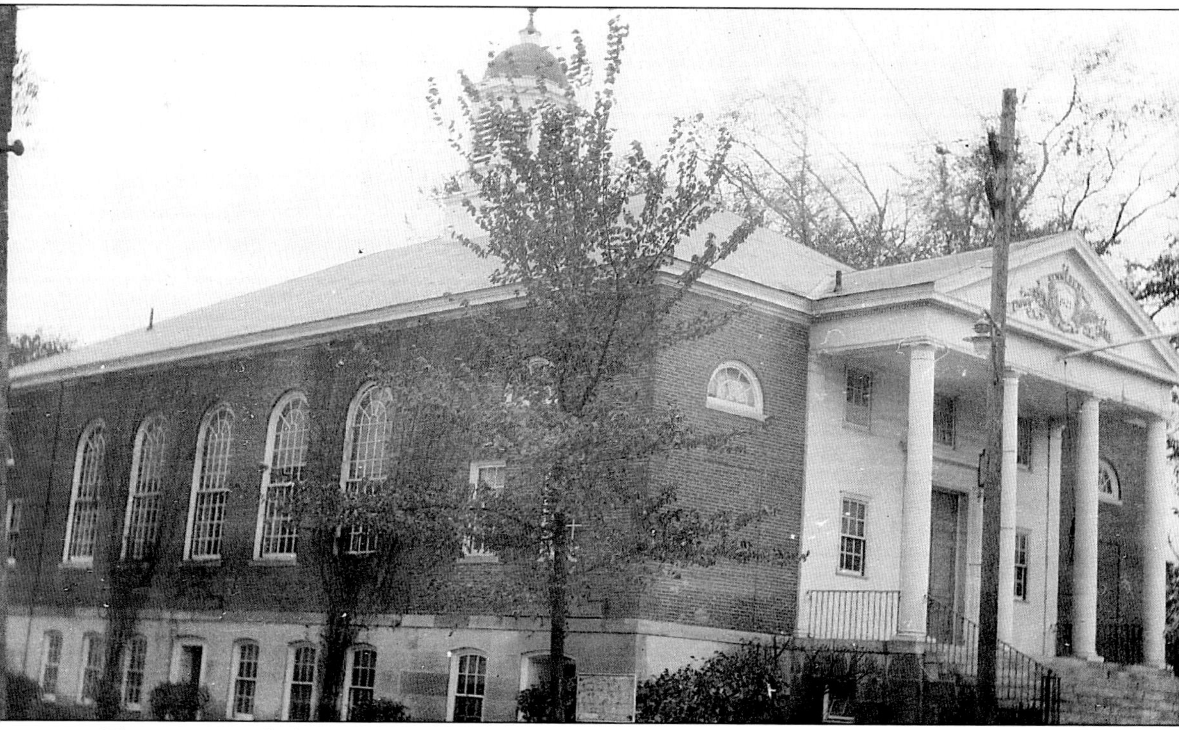

The new town hall, *c.* 1925. Henry Parsons purchased the land, had all the buildings removed, and then gave the land to the town as a site for the new town hall. The three-story brick Warren-Kelly Building was relocated across Green Street, making it the first and only brick building to be moved in Kennebunk. After a fire in 1960, the top two floors of the Warren-Kelly Building were removed. The remaining section was razed in 1987 to provide parking for the town hall. The present town hall was constructed in 1921 and was designed by Michael Dyer of J.D. Leland and Co. of Boston. J.M. Doiling was the contractor. In 1952 a rear addition was made to the building to house the fire station; this was removed in 1987 when a new three-story addition was built.

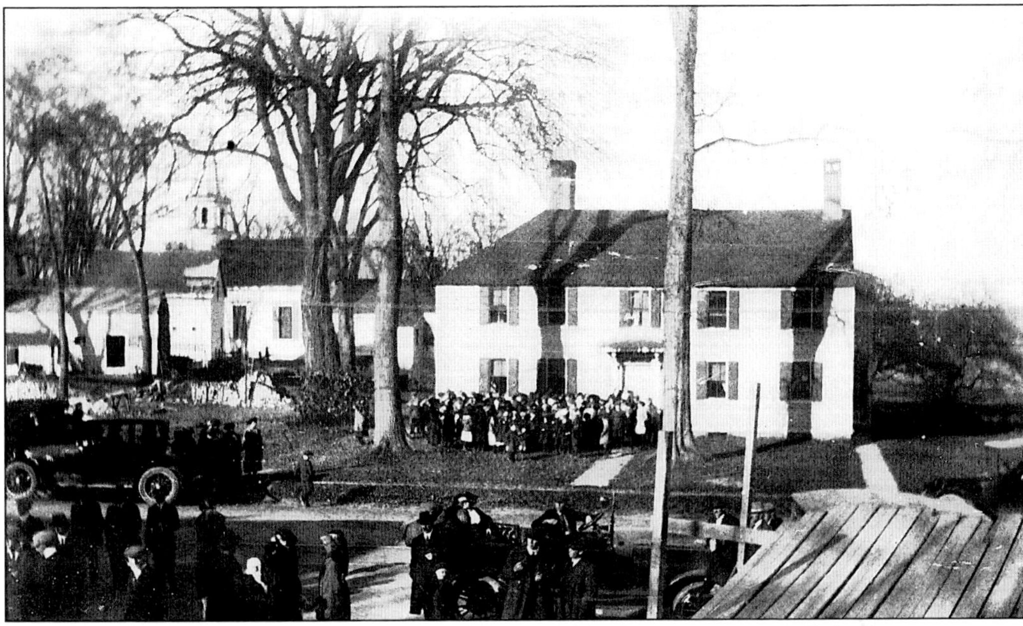

School children gather in front of the Kimball-Crediford House to sing while the corner stone for the new town hall is laid.

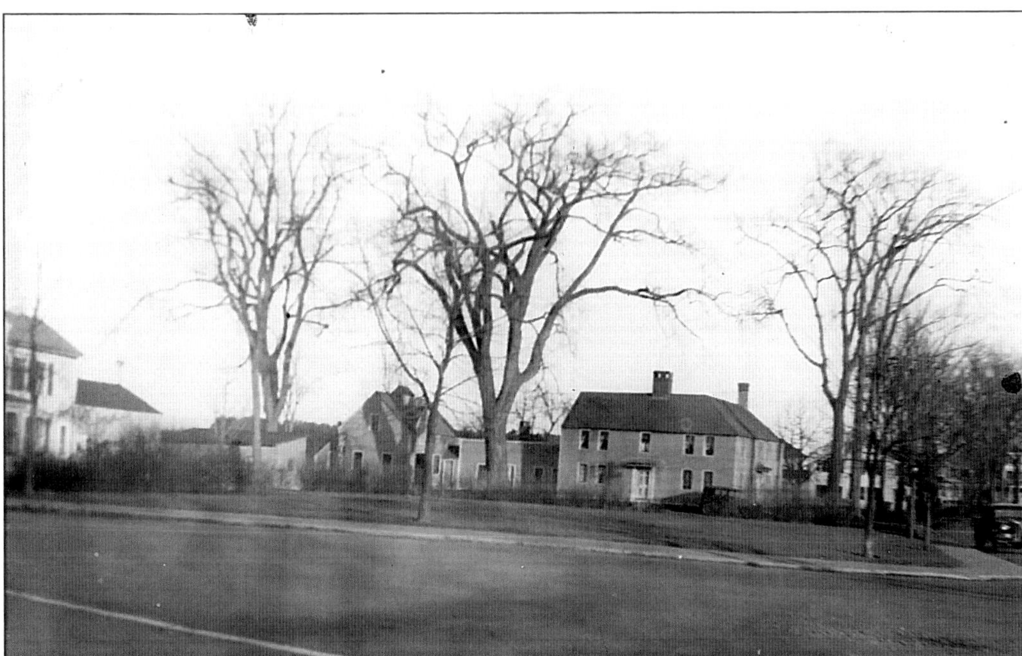

Looking towards Summer Street, *c*. 1920. The Kimball-Crediford House is on the left.

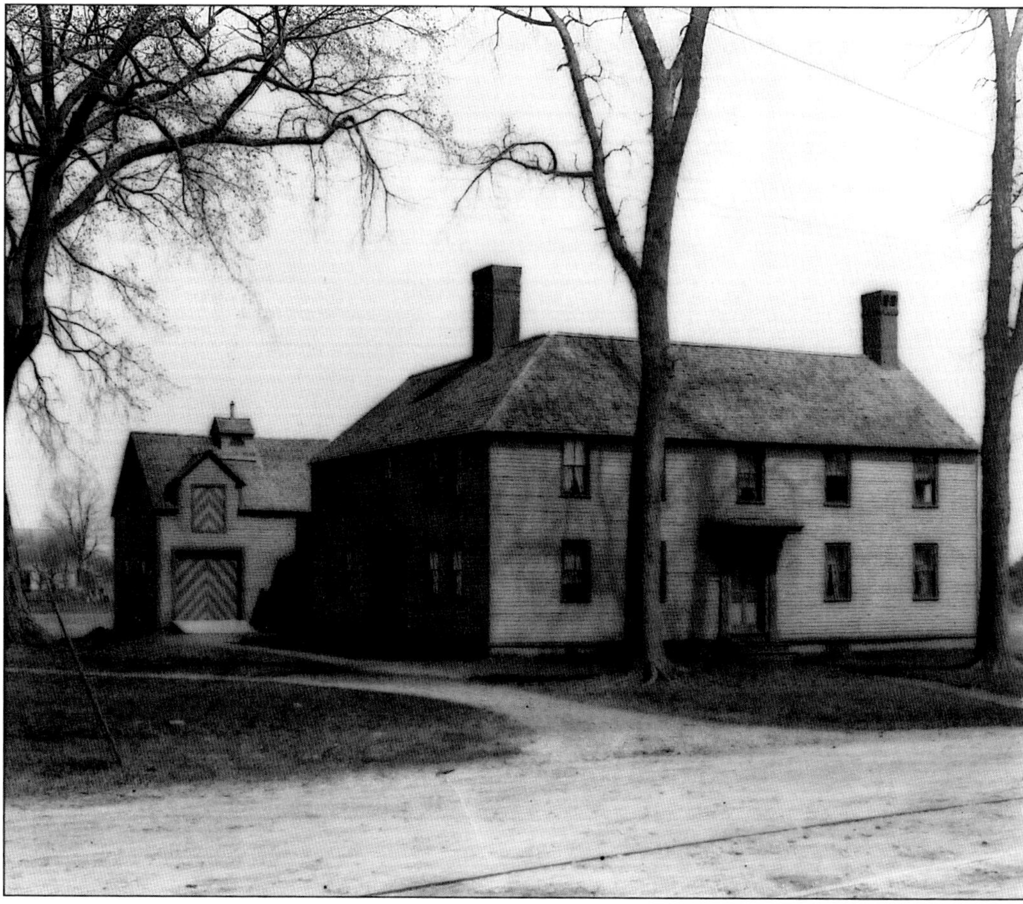

The Kimball-Crediford House, c. 1885. Annie Joyce Crediford sold the home, built in 1768, to the Federal Government in 1937 for $6,312 (that was a large sum of money in those days). It was razed and the post office was built in its place. James Kimball, who was a blacksmith, purchased the land in 1767 and built his house soon after. His grandson, John Clement Lord, eventually inherited the house, and when he died in the 1880s, he left it to the inhabitants of Kennebunk. There are few homes existing in Kennebunk today from this period, and none of them have the fine wood paneling and Georgian-detailing that this home had.

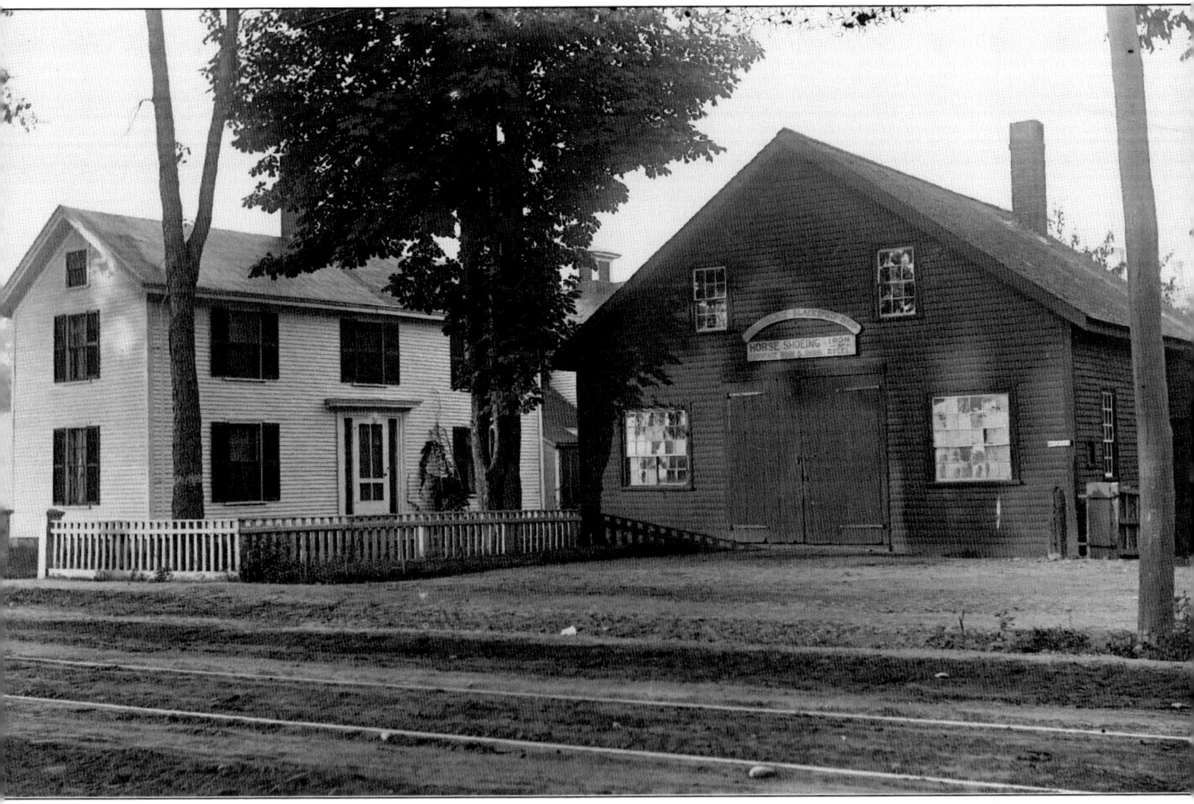

Kennebunk's last blacksmith shop, *c.* 1910. It stood where today's town hall annex is now located.

Acknowledgments

I would like to thank Greg Hubbard for his help in completing this book. His editing and suggestions made writing this much easier. A special thanks to the staff and directors of the Kennebunk Free Library Association, for their permission to do this book and for their continuing support. Penny Savage was invaluable with her suggestions, advice, and patience. My deep appreciation to the staff of The Brick Store Museum for their ongoing support and encouragement, as well as for all the "On The Job Training." And a special thanks to Joyce Butler and Katherine Hussy. I'm so glad that I had the good fortune to work with both of them. Joyce Butler's immeasurable encouragement and advice over the last two years have helped me in the writing of this book. Last, and certainly not least, thanks to my parents for always believing in me; and to all my friends for never giving up on me; and to my children, James and Kerri, for their unconditional love, and for just being themselves.